ANTHONY TROLLOPE

SOUTH AFRICA

VOLUME II

ALAN SUTTON · Gloucester
HIPPOCRENE BOOKS, INC. · New York
1987

First published 1877

Copyright © in this edition 1987
Alan Sutton Publishing Limited

This edition first published in Great Britain 1987
  Alan Sutton Publishing Limited
  30 Brunswick Road
  Gloucester GL1 1JJ

British Library Cataloguing in Publication Data

Trollope, Anthony
  South Africa.
  1. South Africa—Description and
  travel—1801–1900
  I. Title
  916.8′044   DT756

  ISBN 0–86299–357–1

This edition first published in the U.S.A. 1987
  Hippocrene Books, Inc.
  171 Madison Avenue
  New York, N.Y. 10016

ISBN 0–87052–434–8

Cover picture: detail from A Hottentot Kraal
on the Banks of the Gariep
*By courtesy of the South African Permanent Mutual
Building Society*

Typesetting and origination by
Alan Sutton Publishing Limited.
Photoset Bembo 9/10
Printed in Great Britain
by The Guernsey Press Company Limited,
Guernsey, Channel Islands.

CONTENTS

THE TRANSVAAL

GRIQUALAND WEST

THE ORANGE FREE STATE

CONTENTS

BIOGRAPHICAL NOTE

In his *Autobiography*, Trollope explains how he spent the early years of his life 'in a world altogether outside the world of my material life.' In this world nothing impossibly fantastic happened, but stories developed in a serial way over months and even years. Although nothing was written down, these imaginings obviously provided the foundation for Trollope's later prolific creativity.

The reasons for this mental need to escape from the real world are not difficult to find. For the first twenty-seven years of his life Trollope was unhappy and unsuccessful. He was born on 24th April 1815, the fourth of six children born to Thomas and Fanny Trollope. Thomas was a qualified barrister, but had the wrong personality to make a success of his profession. Consequently, he moved his family from Keppel Street in London out to a farm he owned in Harrow, but he did not know enough about farming to make the land pay, and finally was forced to let out the farm. He moved into a cottage in the grounds and dedicated the rest of his life to compiling an ecclesiastical dictionary which nobody wanted.

In an attempt to provide for her family, Fanny took all her children, except Anthony, to America, but her efforts to set up in business there were a failure, and it was only on her return, three years later, that she finally made some money, with the publication of her successful *Domestic Manners of the Americans*. In the meantime Anthony had been sent to school at Harrow and Winchester, and left very much to his own devices. William Gregory wrote of the young Anthony: 'He was not only slovenly in person and dress, but his work was equally dirty. He gave no signs of promise whatsoever, was always in the lowest part of the form and was regarded by masters and boys as an incorrigible dunce.' He left school in 1834 and through friends of his mother obtained a clerkship in the General Post Office in London. Since his mother had now moved to Bruges, he lived on his own in dreary lodgings in Marylebone. Within the next two years a brother and a sister died of consumption, and his father fell victim to mercury poisoning, because of his addiction to the drug Calomel.

Anthony must have felt further isolated by his mother's increased closeness to her eldest son, Tom, and his sister's marriage and removal to Cumberland. But his life, although to some extent lonely and poverty-stricken, was not without amusement. He enjoyed walking weekends in the country, and one feels that experiences such as those enjoyed by Charley Tudor in *The Three Clerks* were probably based on the activities of the clerks at the Post Office. Of his work, however, he writes: 'I hated the office. I hated my work. More than all I hated my idleness.' He finally found a release from the drudgery and boredom of clerical work in 1841, when he was accepted as a post office surveyor's clerk at Banagher, in King's County, Ireland.

'This', remarked Trollope of his Irish posting, 'was the first good fortune of my life.' He started to make a success of his job as inspector and investigator of the local postal service, in spite of, or perhaps because of, his brusque manner; he developed a taste for hunting and mixing with the Irish gentry; he married, and his English wife, Rose, bore him two sons. Most importantly, he started writing. The first four pieces of work published were not best-sellers, by any means, but two, *The Macdermots of Ballycloran* (1847) and *The Kellys and the O'Kellys* (1848), received some critical acclaim and showed the author's potential.

Trollope's first successful novel, *The Warden* (1855), was not finished until he was once again in Ireland, having completed an assignment in the South West of England reorganizing the postal system. It was while there, that he conceived the idea of Barsetshire. In 1857 *Barchester Towers* was published, and Trollope's reputation was further established with the appearance of *The Three Clerks* a year later. 1858 also saw the publication of *Doctor Thorne* and the completion of *The Bertrams* (published 1859). Thenceforth Trollope's output was considerable – two or three books appearing every year until 1883. He wrote well over forty novels, various collections of short stories, travel books, a translation of Caesar's Commentaries, a life of Cicero, an appreciation of Thackeray, and an autobiography.

Trollope's approach to his art was extremely disciplined. He would write a set number of pages before breakfast every day, no matter where he was. *Lady Anna* (1874), for example, was written on a voyage out to Australia. Of his technique he said he went to work 'just like a shoemaker on a shoe, only taking care to make honest stitches.' But another admission reveals that, in spite of his disciplined approach, he was totally involved in his characters: 'I have wandered alone among the woods and the rocks, crying at their grief, laughing at their absurdities and thoroughly enjoying their joy.'

The Post Office was indirectly responsible for Trollope's first travel book, because, after a successful mission to Egypt in 1858, he was sent to review the postal services of the Caribbean Islands and Central America. This voyage gave rise to *The West Indies and the Spanish Main*, an immediately successful travelogue. Trollope later wrote about the other continents he visited, producing *North America* in 1862, *Australia and New Zealand* in 1873, when he travelled out for the marriage of his farming son, and *South Africa* in 1878.

It was during the sixties that Trollope's most famous works appeared: *Framley Parsonage* (1861), *Orley Farm* (1862), *The Small House at Allington* (1864), *The Last Chronicle of Barset* (1867). After his trip to the Caribbean, he had been appointed Surveyor of the Eastern District of England, and he had bought a house in Waltham Cross. His new proximity to London allowed him to mix with the literati of England for the first time. He very soon became a popular member of the Garrick Club, the Athenaeum, and the Cosmopolitan, and he must have been stimulated by this new cultural environment. He admired and became friends with both Thackeray and George Eliot (at whose house he met many famous writers of the day including Turgenev). He was also a close friend of John Everett Millais, who illustrated *Framley Parsonage, Orley Farm*, and other novels. He visited his brother and mother in Italy several times, and there he met the Brownings and also a young American, Kate Field, whom he saw irregularly and with whom he corresponded until his death.

When he was fifty-two, in 1867, Trollope resigned from the Post Office and relied on his literary output for finance. He became editor of the new *St. Paul's Magazine*, but he did not enjoy the work and gave it up after three years. During that time he had political aspirations, as is reflected in the writing of the Palliser novels, but his attempt to stand as Parliamentary candidate for Beverley in 1868 was a failure.

Earlier in that same year, he had been in America, and had written *The Vicar of Bulhampton* while in New York. He thought that the story, which was about a prostitute, might be found distasteful, and therefore included an explanatory preface, but *The Times* commented: '. . . the general safeness of the story will make Bulhampton Vicarage welcome to all well-regulated families.' On the other hand, *Lady Anna*, written six years later caused considerable disturbance. The *Saturday Review* warned their readers against it, so that they 'may not be betrayed into reading what will probably leave a disagreeable impression'. Many people, however, did read the novel, and some wrote to Trollope expressing their objections. Apparently the idea of an Earl's daughter honourably marrying a tailor was too extreme a notion for the class-bound Victorian society.

In 1870 Trollope sold Waltham House and moved into London, to Montagu Square. He gave up hunting, but kept his horses and often rode in London. During the seventies he wrote prolifically and travelled widely. His fame was past its peak, but in 1873 he was featured in the popular weekly, *Vanity Fair*, with a cartoon and text, which included: '. . . He is a correct painter of the small things of our small modern English life . . . His manners are a little rough, as is his voice, but he is nevertheless extremely popular among his personal friends . . .' This character outline is complemented and extended by J.R. Lowell's description: '. . . Anthony Trollope; a big red-faced rather underbred Englishman of the bald-with-spectacles type . . . A good roaring fellow who deafened me'; and by G.A. Sala's: 'Crusty, quarrelsome, wrongheaded, prejudiced, obstinate, kind-hearted and thoroughly honest old Tony Trollope.'

All his life Trollope was subject to depression because of what Escott, his biographer, explains as an 'almost feminine sensibility to the opinions of others, a self-consciousness altogether abnormal in a sensible and practical man of the world, as well as a strong love of approbation, whether from stranger or friend.'

By the end of the decade, Trollope was a familiar figure at literary gatherings in London, and in the country. He was a guest both at Lord Carnarvon's home at Highclere, Hampshire, and at Waddesdon Manor, the home of Baron Rothschild. But his health was declining and in 1880 he moved from London to the more salubrious area of the South Downs. He bought The Grange at South Harting in Hampshire, and there he wrote his last novels. These reflected his pessimistic outlook, and two of them concentrated on problems of growing older: *Mr. Scarborough's Family* and *An Old Man's Love*, the first a study of eccentricity, and the second a story of an older man's love for a younger woman. In 1882 he started his final novel, *The Landleaguers*, which was, like his first novel, set in Ireland. He made two trips to Ireland during that year to collect material which probably contributed to a rapid deterioration in his health and in the October of that year he moved up to London for the Winter. He suffered a stroke in November, and died five weeks later on 6th December 1882. He was buried in Kensal Green Cemetery. 'He was removed in a lusty majority, and before decay had begun to cripple his indefatigable industry or dull the brightness of his versatile fancy' (from his obituary in *The Times*).

SHEILA MICHELL

THE TRANSVAAL

CHAPTER I

THE TRANSVAAL – NEWCASTLE TO PRETORIA

The distance from Newcastle to Pretoria is 207 miles. About 20 miles north from Newcastle we crossed the borders of what used to be the Transvaal Republic, but which since the 12th August last, – 1877, – forms a separate British Colony under the dominion of Her Majesty. The geographical configuration here is remarkable as at the point of contact between Natal and the Transvaal the boundary of the Orange Free State is not above two or three miles distant, and that of Zulu Land, which is at present but ill defined, not very far off; – so that in the event of the Transvaal being joined to Natal the combined Colonies would hang together by a very narrow neck of land.

Of all our dominions the Transvaal is probably the most remote. Its Capital is 400 miles from the sea, and that distance is not annihilated or even relieved by any railway. When I left home my main object perhaps was to visit this remote district, of which I had never heard much and in which I had been interested not at all, till six months before I started on my journey. Then the country had been a foreign Republic, not very stable as was supposed, and assimilated in my mind with some of the South African Republics which so often change their name and their condition and in which the staunchest lovers of the Republican form of Government hardly put much faith. Now I was in the country and was not only assured myself to its future security, – but was assured also of the assurance of all who were concerned. Whether Great Britain had done right or wrong to annex the Transvaal, every sod of its soil had instantly been made of double value to its proprietor by the deed which had been done.

Here I was in the Transvaal through which at a period long since that of my own birth lions used to roam at will, and the tribes of the Swazies and Matabeles used to work their will against each other, unconscious of the coming of the white man. Now there are no lions in the land, – and as far as I could see as I made my journey, very few Natives in the parts which had really been inhabited by the Dutch.

I cannot say that the hotels along the road were very good. By the ordinary travelling Englishman the accommodation would have been considered very bad; – but we did find places in which we could shelter ourselves, and beds of some kind were provided for us. A separate bedroom had become a luxury dear to the imagination and perpetuated by memory. We were a week on the road from Newcastle and pulled off our clothes but once, – when we were under the hospitable roof of Mrs. Swickhard, who keeps a store about half way at a place called Standers Drift. At one or two places there were little Inns, always called hotels, and at others we were taken in by farmers or storekeepers. Sometimes the spot on which we were invited to lie down was so uninviting as to require the summoning up of a special courage. Twice I think we were called upon to occupy the same bed, – on which occasions my age preserved me from the hard ground on which my younger companion had to stretch himself. He had stories to tell of nocturnal visitors to which I have ever been inhospital and useless, – the only wild beast that has ever attacked me being the musquito. Of musquitoes in the Transvaal I had no experience, and was told that even in summer they are not violent. We were travelling in September, which is equal in its circumstances to our March at home. So much for our beds. On our route we banqueted at times like princes, – but these were the times in which we camped out in the veld, – the open field side, – and consumed our own provisions. Never was such tea made as we had. And yet the tea in all the houses was bad, – generally so bad as to be undrinkable. We had bought our tea, as other Colonists buy theirs, at Pieter Maritzburg, and I do not think that the grocer had done anything peculiar for us. But we were determined that the water should boil, that the proper number of tea-spoon-fulls should be afforded, and that the tea should have every chance. We certainly succeeded. And surely never was there such bacon fried, or such cold tongues extracted from tin pots. It happened more than once that we were forced by circumstances to breakfast at houses on the road, – but when we did so we always breakfasted again a few miles off by the side of some spruit, – Anglice brook, – where our horses could get water and eat their forage.

The matter of forage is the main question for all travellers through these parts of South Africa. Let a man sleep where he may and eat what he will, he can go on. Let him sleep not at all and eat but little, he can have himself dragged to his destination. The will within him to reach a given place carries him safely through great hardships. But it is not so with your horse, – and is less so in the Transvaal than in any other country in which I have travelled. We soon learned that our chief care must be to provide proper food for our team, if we wished to reach Pretoria, – let alone those further towns, Kimberley and Bloemfontein. Now there are three modes in which a horse may be fed on such a journey. He may nibble the grass, – or cut his own bread and butter, – as horses do successfully in Australia; but if left to that resource he will soon cease to drag the vehicle after him in South Africa. Or he may be fed upon mealies. I hope my reader has already learned that maize or Indian corn is so called in South Africa. Mealies are so easily carried, and are almost always to be purchased along the road. But horses fed upon them while at fast work become subject to sickness and die upon the journey. If used at all they should be steeped in water and dried, but even then they are pernicious except in small quantities. Forage is the only thing. Now forage consists of corn cut green, wheat or oats or barley, – dried with the grain in it and preserved in bundles, like hay. It is cumbrous to carry and it will frequently happen that it cannot be bought on the road side. But you must have forage, or you will not get to your journey's end. We did manage to supply ourselves, sometimes carrying a large roll of it inside the cart as well as a sack filled with it outside. Every farmer grows a little of it through the country; and the storekeepers along the road, who buy it at 3d. a bundle sell it for a shilling or eighteen pence in accordance with their conscience. But yet we were always in alarm lest we should find ourselves without it. A horse requires about six bundles a day to be adequately fed for continual work. 'Have you got forage?' was the first question always asked when the cart was stopped and one of us descended to enquire as to the accommodation that might be forthcoming.

We travelled something over thirty miles a day, always being careful not to allow the horses to remain at their work above two hours and a half at a time. Then we would 'out-span', – take the horses out from the carriage, knee-hobble them and turn them loose with their forage spread upon the ground. Then all our energies would be devoted to the tea kettle and the frying pan.

As we travelled most heartrending accounts reached us of the fate of my companions from Pieter Maritzburg to Newcastle, who had pursued their journey by the mail cart to Pretoria. This conveyance is not supposed absolutely to travel night and day; – nor does it go regularly by day and stop regularly by night in a Christian fashion, but makes its progress with such diminished periods of relaxation as the condition of the animals drawing it may create. If the roads and animals be good, four or six hours in the twenty-four may be allowed to the weary passenger; – but if not, – if as at this time they both be very bad, the periods of relaxation are only those necessary for taking up the mail bags and catching the animals which are somewhere out on the veld, hobbled, and biding their time. For the mail cart the road was very bad indeed, while by our happy luck, for us it was very good. They travelled through two days and nights of uninterrupted rain by which the roads and rivers were at once made almost equally impassable; while for us, so quick are the changes effected, everything had become dry and at the same time free from dust. From place to place we heard of them, – how the three unfortunates had walked into one place fifteen miles in advance of the cart, wet through, carrying their shoes and stockings in their hands, and had then slept upon the ground till the vehicle had come up, the mules had been caught, and they had been carried on a mile or two when they had again been forced to walk. They were at this period two days late and had been travelling on these conditions for four days and four nights with the journey yet unfinished before them. Had I been one of them I think they would have been forced to leave me behind on the way side. On the road we met their conveyance coming back. It had carried them to a certain point and had thence returned. It was a miserable box on wheels with two mules whose wretched bones seemed to come through their skin. They could not raise a trot though they had no load but the black driver, and I presume some mail bags.

Nor was any one to blame for all this, – except the late Government. For two years and a half the Contractor had done the work without receiving his pay. That he should have gone on and done it at all is the marvel; – but he had persevered spending all that he could make elsewhere upon the effort. When the annexation came he was paid his arrears in lump, very much no doubt to his comfort; but then there were new tenders and a new contract and it was hardly to be expected that he should lay out his happily recovered money in providing horses and conveyances for a month or two.

I was assured, and I believe truly, that this special journey, – which I did not take, – was the most unfortunate that had ever occurred on this unfortunate road. The animals had of course gone down the hill from bad to worse, and then had come the heavy rain. It seemed to be almost a direct Providence which had rescued me from its misery.

As I passed along the road I took every opportunity that came in my way of entering the houses of the Dutch. I had heard much of the manners of the Boers, and of their low condition of life. I had been told that they were altogether unprogressive, – that the Boer farmer of this day was as his father had been, that so had been the grandfather and the great grandfather, and that so was the son about to be; that they were uneducated, dirty in their habits, ignorant of comforts, and parsimonious in the extreme. These are the main accusations brought against the Boers as a race, and they are supported by various allegations in detail; – as that they do not send their children to school; that large families live in two roomed houses, fathers mothers sons and daughters sleeping in one chamber; that they never wash, and wear their clothes day and night without changing them; that they will live upon the carcases of wild beasts and blesboks which they can shoot upon the lands so as to reduce their expenditure on food to a minimum; – that they are averse to neighbours, and that they will pay for no labour, thus leaving their large farms untilled and to a great extent unpastured. And added to all this it is said that the Boer is particularly averse to all change, resolving not only to do as his father had done before him, but also that his son shall do the like for the future.

The reader will probably perceive that these charges indicate an absence of that civilization which is produced in the world by the congregated intelligences of many persons. Had Shakespeare been born on a remote South African farm he would have been Shakespeare still; but he would not have worn a starched frill to his shirt. The Dutch Boer is what he is, not because he is Dutch or because he is a Boer, but because circumstances have isolated him. The Spaniards had proabably reached as luxurious a mode of living as any European people when they achieved their American possessions, but I have no hesitation in saying that the Spaniards who now inhabit the ranches and remote farms of Costa Rica or Columbia are in a poorer condition of life than the Dutch Boers of the Transvaal. I have seen Germans located in certain unfortunate spots about the world who have been reduced lower in the order of humanity than any Dutchmen that I have beheld. And I have been within the houses of English Free Settlers in remote parts of Australia which have had quite as little to show in the way of comfort as any Boer's homestead.

Such comparisons are only useful as showing that distance from crowded centres will produce the same falling off in civilization among one people as among another. The two points of interest in the matter are, – first the actual condition of these people who have now become British subjects, and secondly how far there is a prospect of improvement. I am now speaking of my journey from Natal up to Pretoria. When commencing that journey, though I had seen many Dutchmen in South Africa I had seen none of the Boer race; and I was told that those living near to the road would hardly be fair specimens of their kind. There was very little on the road to assist in civilizing them and that little had not existed long. From what I afterwards saw I am inclined to think that the impressions first made upon me were not incorrect.

The farmers' houses generally consisted of two main rooms, with probably some small excrescence which would serve some of the family as a sleeping apartment. In the living room there would be a fire-place, and outside the house, probably at thirty or forty yards' distance, there would be a huge oven built. The houses would never be floored, the uneven ground being sufficiently solid and also sufficiently clean for the Dutchman's purposes. There would seldom be a wall-paper or any internal painting of the woodwork. Two solid deal tables, with solid deal settees or benches, – not unfrequently with a locker under them, – would be the chief furniture. There might be a chair or two, but not more than one or two. There would always be a clock, and a not insufficient supply of cups, saucers, and basins. Knives, forks, and spoons would be there. The bedroom of course would be a sanctum; but my curiosity, – or diligence in the performance of the duty on which I was intent, – enables me to say that there is always a large bedstead, with a large feather bed, a counterpane, and apparently a pair of sheets. The traveller in Central America will see but little of such decencies among the Spanish farmers there.

Things in the Boer's house no doubt are generally dirty. An earthen floor will make everything dirty, – whether in Ireland or in the Transvaal. The Boer's dress is dirty, – and also, which is more important, that of the Boeress. The little Boerlings are all dirty, – so that, even when they are pretty, one does not wish to kiss them. The Boers are very prolific, marrying early and living a wholesome, and I think, a moral life. They are much given to marrying, the widow or the widower very speedily taking another spouse, so that there will sometimes be three or four families in the one house. The women have children very early in life, – but then they have children very late also; which seems to indicate that their manner of living is natural and healthy. I have heard them ridiculed for their speedy changes of marital affection, but it seems to me natural that a man or a woman living far apart from neighbours should require the comfort of a companion.

I am quite convinced that they are belied by the allegation which denies to them all progress in civilization. The continued increase in the number of British and German storekeepers in the country, who grow rich on their trade with the Boers, is sufficient of itself to tell one this. Twenty years since I am assured that it was a common thing for a Boer to be clad in skins. Now they wear woollen clothing, with calico. I fancy that the traveller would have to travel very far before he found a skin-clad Boer. No doubt they are parsimonious; – it might perhaps be more fair to call them prone to save. I, personally, regard saving as a mistake, thinking that the improvement of the world generally is best furthered by a free use of the good things which are earned, – and that they who do not themselves earn them should, as a rule, not have them. It is a large question, which my readers would not thank me to discuss here. But there are two sides to it; – and the parsimony of the Boer who will eat up the carcase of a wild beast till it be rotten so that he need not kill a sheep, and may thus be enabled to stock a farm for his son, will have its admirers in Great Britain, – if not among fathers at any rate among sons. These people are not great consumers, as are our farmers. They wear their clothes longer, and stretch their means further; but that the Boer of today consumes very much more than his father there can be no doubt; – and as little that his sons and daughters will consume more.

As to their educational condition I found it very difficult to ascertain facts. The distance of these homesteads one from another makes school teaching in many instances impossible. In some cases I found that great efforts were made, the mother or perhaps the mother's sister teaching the children to read. Here and there I heard of boys and girls who were sent long distances, – at an expense not only for teaching but for boarding. It has, however, to be acknowledged that the education of the country is at present very deficient. The country is now ours and when the first rudiments of stability have been fixed, so that laws may be administered and taxes collected, then I trust that the rulers of the Transvaal may find themselves able to do something towards bringing education nearer to the Boers.

I have heard the Boers spoken of as a dishonest people. I was once among certain tradesmen of the Transvaal who asserted that it was impossible to keep them from pilfering in the shops, one or two of them alleging that no Boer would make a considerable purchase without relieving the grief which was natural to him at parting with his money by pocketing some little article gratis, – a knife, or a tobacco pipe, or perhaps a few buttons. It was an accusation grievous to hear; – but there arose in the company one man, also a dealer and an Englishman, who vindicated their character, alleging that in all parts of the world petty shoplifting was so common an offence that the shopkeeper was forced to take it into account in his calculations, and asserting that the thieving Boers, few though they might be in number, would leave more impression on the shopkeeping mind than the very many Boers who would come in and out without perpetrating any dishonesty. I have heard the Boers also charged with immorality, – which always means loose conduct among the women. I am inclined to think, – though I believe that few will share my opinion, – that social morality will always stand higher in towns, where people are close to each other and watch narrowly the conduct one of another, than in far-stretching pastoral districts, where there is no one to see what is done and to question a neighbour's conduct. I do not suppose that feminine delicacy can stand very high among the Boers of the Transvaal. But on the other hand, as far as I could learn, illegitimacy is not common; and surely there never was a people more given to the honourable practice of matrimony.

I fear that the Boer families have but few recognised amusements. In the little towns or villages the people are given to dancing, and when they dance they are very merry; but the Boers do not live in the villages. The villages are but few in number over a country which is as large as Great Britain and Ireland put together, and the Boer's daughter who lives six or eight miles from her nearest neighbour can have but little dancing. The young people flirt together when they meet in the Transvaal as they do in all the parts of the world which I have visited. Their manner of flirting would probably be thought to be coarse by English mothers and daughters; but then, – if my readers will remember, – so was the manner of flirting ascribed to those most charming young ladies Rosalind and Celia. We can hardly be entitled to expect more refinement today among the Boers of South Africa than among the English of the time of Queen Elizabeth. They are very great at making love, or 'freying' as they call it, and have their recognised forms for the operation. A most amusing and clever young lady whom I met on my way up to Pretoria was kind enough to describe to me at length the proper way to engage or to attempt to engage the affections of a Boer's daughter. The young Boer who thinks that he wants a wife and has made up his mind to look for one begins by riding round the country to find the article that will suit him. On this occasion he does not trouble himself with the hard work of courtship, but merely sees what there is within the circle to which he extends his inspection. He will have dressed himself with more than ordinary care so that any impression which he may make may be favourable, and it is probable that the young ladies in the district know what he is about. But when he has made his choice, then he puts on his very best, and cleans his saddle or borrows a new one, and sticks a feather in his cap, and goes forth determined to carry his purpose. He takes with him a bottle of sugar plums, – an article in great favour among the Boers and to be purchased at every store, – with which to soften the heart of the mother, and a candle. Everything depends upon the candle. It should be of wax, or of some wax-like composition; but tallow will suffice if the proposed bride be not of very high standing. Arrived at the door he enters, and his purpose is known at once. The clean trousers and the feather declare it; and the sugar plums which are immediately brought forth, – and always consumed, – leave not a shadow of doubt. Then the candle is at once offered to the young lady. If she refuses it, which my informant seemed to think was unusual, then the swain goes on without remonstrating and offers it to the next lady upon his list. If she take it, then the candle is lighted, and the mother retires, sticking a pin into the candle as an intimation that the young couple may remain together, explaining their feelings to each other, till the flame shall have come down to the pin. A little salt, I was assured, is often employed to make the flame weak and so prolong the happy hour. But the mother, who has perhaps had occasion to use salt in her own time, may probably provide for this when arranging the distance for the pin. A day or two afterwards the couple are married, – so that there is nothing of the 'nonsense' and occasional heartbreak of long engagements. It is thus that 'freying' is carried on among the Boers of the Transvaal.

At home in England, what little is known about the Boers of South Africa, – or I might perhaps more correctly say what little has been told about them, – has tended to give a low notion of them as a race. And there is also an impression that the Boer and the English Colonist are very hostile to each other. I fear that the English Colonist does despise the Boer, but I have not found reason to think that any such hostility exists. Let an Englishman be where he may about the surface of the globe, he always thinks himself superior to other men around him. He eats more, drinks more, wears more clothes, and both earns and spends more money. He, – and the American who in this respect is the same as an Englishman, – always consume the wheat while others put up with the rye. He feeds on fresh meat, while dried or salt flesh is sufficient for his neighbours. He expects to be 'boss,' while others work under him. This is essentially so in South Africa where he is constantly brought into contact with the Dutchman, – and this feeling of ascendancy naturally produces something akin to contempt. There is no English farmer in South Africa, who would not feel himself to be vilified by being put on a par with a Dutch farmer. When an Englishman marries a Boer's daughter, the connexion is spoken of almost as a mésalliance. 'He made a mistake and married a Dutchwoman,' I have heard more than once. But, nevertheless, the feeling does not amount to hostility. The Boer in a tacit way acknowledges his own inferiority, and is conscious that the Briton is strong enough and honest enough to do him some service by his proximity.

The man whom the Dutch Boer does hate is the Hollander, and he is the man who does in truth despise the Boer. In the Transvaal a Hollander is the immigrant who has come out new from Holland, whereas the Dutchman is the descendant of those who came out two centuries since. The Dutchman is always an Africander, or one who has been born in Africa from white parents, and he has no sympathy whatever, no feeling of common country, with the new comer from the old country of his forefathers. The Hollander who thus emigrates is probably a man of no family, whereas the old Colonist can go back with his pedigree at least for two centuries and who thinks very much of his ancestors. The Hollander is educated and is said to be pedantic and priggish before those who speak his own language. And in the matter of language these new

Dutchmen or Hollanders complain much of the bad Dutch they hear in the Colony and give great offence by such complaints.

The Boers are at present much abused for cowardice, and stories without end are current in the country as to the manner in which they have allowed themselves to be scared by the smallest opposition. You will be told how a posse of twenty men sent to arrest some rebel turned and fled wildly when the rebel drew forth from his breast and presented to them a bottle of soda-water; – how they have got one Kafir to fight another on their behalf and how they have turned and run when it has been expected that they should support the Kafir and do some fighting on their own behalf. I fear that of late there has been truth in these stories and that the pluck shewn by them when they made good their hold upon the country, has been greatly dimmed by the quiet uneventful tenor of their present lives. But no one complains so bitterly of the cowardice of the Boers as the Hollander fresh from Holland. I once ventured to take the part of the Boers in a discussion on the subject, and referred back to the courage of Retief, of Potgeiter, and of Maritz. There was a gentleman from Holland in the company, and I own that I thought that politeness required me to make some defence of his Dutch brethren in his hearing. But I found myself to be altogether in the wrong. 'They are the vilest set of worthless cowards that the world has ever produced,' said the Dutchman angrily. I think I may say that there is no sympathy whatsoever between the old Dutch Colonist, and the newly-arrived immigrant from Holland.

We crossed the Vaal river at a place called Standerton or Stander's Drift, – drift being Dutch for a ford the word has by common usage become English in South Africa, – as also has the word spruit for a stream. Here there resides one General Standers from whom the place is called, an old man who commanded a party of the Dutch at the battle of Boom Platz, which was fought between the Boers and the British at a place so called in the Orange Free State in 1848. If the stories told by the English be true the Boers did not distinguish themselves by courage on the occasion. The General is a fine old man, as upright as a maypole and apparently as strong as an oak, about 80 years of age. He is now a most loyal subject of the British

throne, though there have been days in his career in which the
British name has not been very dear to him. He was finely
courteous to us, and asked us to drink coffee, as do all Boers
when they intend to be civil to their visitors. It should be
understood by travellers that their courtesy is very superior to
their coffee. No allusion is here made to the General's
establishment as we had not time to partake of his hospitality.
At Standerton we found coal burnt, which had been dug about
30 miles from the place. It was good coal, burning clearly and
without much ash.

Rising up from the Vaal river to the height of about 500 feet
the land ceases to be hilly and becomes a vast rolling plain for
many miles, without a single tree, and almost without a single
enclosure. We saw numerous herds of deer, the large blesbok
and the smaller springbok, which were near enough to be
reached by a rifle. They would stand at about 400 yards from
us and gaze at us. My friend had a smooth-bore gun with large
shot; but could not get near enough to them to make such a
weapon available. The country was very uninteresting, – but
capable of bearing wheat on almost every acre. Wheat
however there was none, and only here and there at very long
distances a batch of arable ground tilled for the purpose of
growing forage. I have said that there were but few
enclosures. Enclosures for arable or even pastoral purposes
there were none. Perhaps three or four times in a day a Boer's
farm would be seen from the road side, distinguished by a
small group of trees, generally weeping willows. This would
look like a very small oasis in a huge desert. Round the house
or on one side of it there would be from six to a dozen acres of
land ploughed, with probably a small orchard and sometimes
an attempt at a kitchen garden. There would too be some
ditching and draining and perhaps some slight arrangement
for irrigation. The Boer's farm-house I have already described. When questioned the farmer invariably declared that it
would not pay him to extend his agriculture, as he had no
labour on which to depend and no market to which he could
carry his wheat. Questions on such subjects were always
answered with the greatest courtesy, and I may almost say
with eagerness. I do not remember that I ever entered a Boer's
house in which he did not seem glad to see me.

A farm in the Transvaal is supposed to contain six thousand acres. This is so much a matter of course that when a man holds less he describes himself as possessing half a farm, or a quarter of a farm. The land is all private property, – or nearly so, very little of it remaining in the hands of the Government on behalf of the people generally, – and having been divided into these large sections, cannot now be split up into smaller sections except by sale or inheritance. The consequence has been and still is very prejudicial to the interests of the country. The farms are much too large for profitable occupation, and the farmers by the very extent of their own dominions are kept without the advantages of neighbourhood. The people are isolated in regard to schools, churches, and all the amenities of social life. They cannot assist each other in the employment of labour, or create markets for the produce of one another by their mutual wants. The boorishness of the Boer is attributable in a great degree to the number of acres of which he is the lord.

As we went along the road we met a detachment of the 13th regiment marching back from Pretoria to Newcastle. There seemed to be going on a great moving of troops hither and thither, which no doubt had been made necessary by the annexation. And these marchings were never made without accidents of flood and field. On this occasion sixteen waggon-oxen had died on the road. The soldiers had to carry their tents and belongings with them, and the bullocks therefore were essential to these movements. When I saw the big waggons, and the dead oxen, and remembered that every man there in a red coat had been extracted from our population at home with the greatest difficulty, and brought to that spot at an enorm-ous cost, and that this had been done for no British purpose, I own that I asked myself some questions as to the propriety of our position in the Transvaal which I found it difficult to answer; – as for instance whether it is necessary that the troubles of the world at large should be composed and set to rights by the soldiers of a nation so very little able to provide an army as Great Britain. But the severity of these thoughts was much mitigated when the two officers in command walked across to us while we were outspanning in the veld, and offered us bitter beer. The Transvaal would never have known even the taste of bitter beer had it not been for the British army. Talk of a fountain in the desert! What fountain can be compared to that kettle full of Bass which the orderly who followed our two new friends carried in his hand. ' Do not look at it,' said the donor as the beverage was poured out. 'The joltings of the journey have marred its brightness. But you will find that the flavour is all there.'

The only place on the road worthy to be called a town is Heidelberg and this does not contain above two or three hundred inhabitants. It is the capital of a district of the same name of which the entire population is about 2,000. The district is larger than an ordinary English county, comprising a compact area about 80 miles long by 60 broad, and yet it is returned as having no other village within its boundaries except the so called town of Heidelberg. But the place has an air of prosperity about it and contains two or three mercantile firms which are really doing a large business. In these places the shops, or stores, are very much more extensive than would be any such depôts in English villages of the same size; – so much so that comfortable fortunes may be made in a comparatively short time. As the Boers are the chief customers, it is evident that they are learning to spend their money, and are gradually departing from the old Boer law that the farm should supply everything needed for life.

At Heidelberg we found a good Inn, – a good Inn that is for the Transvaal: – but the landlord at once told us that he had got no forage. Our first work therefore was to go about into the town and beg. This we did successfully, a merchant of the place consenting to let us have enough for our immediate requirements, out of his private store. But for this we must have used the reserve supply we carried with us, and have gone on upon our road to look for more.

The Inn I have said was good. There was a large room in which a public table was kept and at which a very good dinner was provided at half-past six, and a very good breakfast at eight the next morning. There was a pretty little sitting room within which any lady might make herself comfortable. The bed and bedroom were clean and sweet. But there was only one bed tendered for the use of two of us, and a slight feeling seemed to exist that we were fastidious in requiring more. As

more was not forthcoming my unfortunate companion had to
lie upon the ground.

At Heidelberg we were nearly on the highest table ground
of the Transvaal. From thence there is a descent to Pretoria, –
not great indeed for Pretoria is 4,450 feet above the sea, – but
sufficient to produce an entire change of climate. On the High
Veld, as it is called, the characteristics of the country are all
those belonging to the temperate zone, – such, indeed, as are
the characteristics of our own country at home. Wheat will
grow if planted in the late autumn and will ripen in the
summer. But as the hill is turned, down to Pretoria, tropical
influences begin to prevail. Apples are said to thrive well, but
so also do oranges. And wheat will not live through the
droughts of the winter without irrigation. Irrigation for wheat
must be costly, and consequently but little wheat is grown.
Wheat sown in the spring is, I am told, subject to rust.
Mealies, or Indian corn, will thrive here, and almost all kinds
of fruit. The gardens will produce all kinds of vegetables,
when irrigation is used.

We descended into Pretoria throught a 'poort' or opening
between the hills and the little town with its many trees smiled
upon us in the sun. It lies in a valley on a high plateau, just as
Grahamstown does, and is surrounded by low hills. As we
were driven into the town I congratulated myself on having
come to the end of my journey. To reach Pretoria had been
my purpose, and now I was at Pretoria. My further troubles
would be confined to my journey home which I intended to
commence after a week's delay at the capital of our new
Colony. Hitherto my work had been not very uncomfortable
and certainly not unprosperous.

CHAPTER II

THE TRANSVAAL – ITS HISTORY

The Transvaal as its name plainly indicates is the district lying north and beyond the Vaal river. The Orange river as it runs down to the sea from the Diamond Fields through the inhospitable and little known regions of Bushmansland and Namaqualand used to be called the Gariep and is made up of two large rivers which, above their junction, were known as the Gariep Kye and the Knu Gariep, – the tawny and the orange coloured. The former which is the larger of the two is now known as the Vaal, and the latter as the Orange. The Vaal rises in the Drakenberg mountains and is the northern border of the Orange Free State or Republic. The country therefore beyond that river received its present name very naturally.

This southern boundary of the Transvaal has always been marked clearly enough, but on every other side there are and have been doubts and claims which are great difficulties to the administrator of the new Colony. To the west are the Zulus who are, at this moment, claiming lands which we also claim. Then above them, to the north-west are the Portuguese who are not perhaps likely to extend their demands for inland territory, but who are probably quite as much in doubt as we are as to any defined boundary between them and the natives.*
To the north I think I may say that no one yet knows how far the Transvaal goes. The maps give the Limpopo river as a boundary, but I think Sir Theophilus Shepstone will own that Great Britain cannot, should she wish to do so, make good her claim to lordship over the native races up to the Limpopo

---

* In 1964 by a treaty between the Portuguese and the Republic the Lobombo range of mountains was agreed upon as a boundary between them, but I am not aware that the natives living to the east of these mountains were ever made a party to this treaty.

19

without a considerable amount of arrangement with the
tribes. And yet the matter is one that must be settled with
accuracy because of the hut tax. From the natives living under
the protection of the British Crown in the other colonies of
South Africa a direct tax is levied – 10s., or 14s., – on each hut
occupied, and it is indispensable to the Government of the
new Colony that the same system shall be introduced there.
We cannot govern the country without a revenue, and from
our black subjects this is the only means of collecting a
revenue, – till we begin to make something out of their taste
for strong drinks. It was inaccuracy as to their northern and
north-eastern boundaries which brought the South African or
Transvaal Republic to that ruin which induced us to seize it; –
or, in other words, the lands which the Dutch claimed the
natives claimed also, and these claims were so ambiguous, so
progressive, so indefinite, that to have yielded to them would
have been to give up the whole country. Sicocoeni who was
the Chief most specially hostile to the Republic in its last days
claimed even the site on which stood Pretoria the capital,
where the Volksraad or Parliament of the Republic sat. In
dealing with the Natives as to boundaries nothing can be got
by yielding. Nor does it seem possible to trust to abstract
justice. Between Sicocoeni and Mr. Burgers, the last President of the Republic, it would have been impossible for
abstract justice to have drawn a true line so confused had the
matter become. It can only be done by a strong hand, and can
only be done well by a strong hand guided by a desire equally
strong to do what is right. As an Englishman I feel sure that
we shall have the one, and, again as Englishman, I trust that
we shall have the other. The habitations of hundreds of
thousands of Natives are concerned. I find that the coloured
population of our new Colony is variously stated at numbers
ranging from 250,000 to 800,000. It is all guess work; – but
there is no doubt that the multitude of human beings
concerned is very great. Were we to annex everything
included in the Dutch maps of the Transvaal, the true number
would probably be much greater than the larger of those
above given. You, my readers, probably think that the more
we include the better for them, even though they should be
made to pay a tax of 10s. a hut. So do I. But they

don't. They want to be independent, – as are the Zulus down on the sea coast. It is therefore impossible not to perceive a difficulty. A line to the North and North-East must be drawn; – but no possible line will satisfy the natives. To the West and North-West the matter is probably as doubtful, though not as difficult. The numbers are fewer and the people less war-like. But to the South-West there is another problem to be solved. There is a territory North by West of the Vaal river, including the little town of Bloomhof, which we, by British award declared to be independent. Governor Keate of Natal was appointed as arbitrator to draw a line between the Republic and the natives, and he declared this territory to be a portion of Bechuanaland. But the Transvaal, rejecting Governor Keate's award, took the territory and governed it. Are we now to reject it and give it back to the Bechuanas, or are we to keep it as part of the annexed Colony? This also will add something to the difficulty of defining our new possession.

The history of the European occupation of the Transvaal is the same as the history of all South Africa during this century. The Dutch have been ever running away from the English, and the English have sometimes pursued them and sometimes determined that they should go whither they would and be no longer accounted as British subjects. They have certainly been a most stiff-necked people with whom to deal, – and we by their inability to amalgamate with ourselves have been driven into vacillations which have not always been very creditable to our good sense. We have been too masterful and yet not masterful enough. In Natal as we have seen, we would not allow them to form a Republic or to throw off their British allegiance. Across the Orange river we have fought them and reduced them, – at Boom Plaats, as I shall describe when giving the little history of the Orange Free State, – and then have bid them go their own way and shift for themselves.

The Dutch of South Africa have hated our ways, though I do not think that they have hated us. What they have practically said to us is as follows. 'No doubt you are very fine fellows, and very strong. We do not intend to pit ourselves against you. We first took and cultivated and civilized this Cape Colony. But as you want it in God's name take it and use it, and do with it as you list. But let us go and do as we list

elsewhere. You don't like slavery. We do. Let us go and have
our slaves in a new land. We must encounter endless troubles
and probably death in the attempt. But anything will be better
to us than your laws and your philanthropy. ' We could not
hinder them from going. There was at one time a desire to
hinder them, and the Colonial Attorney General in 1836 was
consulted as to the law on the subject. There was an old Dutch
law, he said, forbidding the Colonists to cross the border; but
that could hardly be brought in force to prevent persons from
seeking their fortunes in other lands. We have already seen in
regard to Natal, how Lieut.-Governor Stockenstrom, when
appealed to, declared that he knew of no law which prevented
His Majesty's subjects from leaving His Majesty's dominions
and settling elsewhere. That these people must be allowed to
go away with their waggons wheresoever they might choose
was evident enough; but the British rulers could not quite
make up their minds whether it was or was not their duty to
go after the wanderers.

When the Dutch first made their way into the country now
called the Transvaal they were simply on their road to Natal.
News had reached them of the good land of Natal and they
endeavoured to get to it by going northwards across the
Orange river. While pursuing their way through what is now
the Free State they encountered a terrible savage named
Mazulekatze, who was at the head of a tribe called the
Matabele, with whom they had to fight to the death. This
warrior was a Zulu and had fought under Chaka the king of
the Zulus; – but had quarrelled with his lord and master and
fled out of Zulu Land westwards. Here he seems to have
created the tribe called Matabele, some of whom were Zulus
and some natives and some warriors who had joined him, as
being a great fighting Chief, from other tribes. He was as
terrible a savage as Chaka himself, and altogether 'ate up' the
less warlike Bechuanas who up to his time possessed the land
thereabouts. This seems to have been the way with these
tribes. They were like water running furiously in a torrent
which in its course is dashed over a rock. The stream is
scattered into infinite spray the particles of which can hardly
be distinguished from the air. But it falls again and is collected
into this stream or the other, changing not its nature but only

its name. The Zulus, the Bechuanas, the Matabeles, and the Kafirs seem to have been formed and reformed after this fashion without any long dated tribal consistency among them. When the Dutch came to the Vaal river, groping their way to Natal, they found Mazulekatze and his Matabeles who was still at war with some of these Bechuana tribes south of the Vaal river. This was in 1837, the year before the final abolition of slavery which by the law of 1834 was arranged to take place in 1838. The Dutch were nearly exterminated, but they succeeded in driving Mazulekatze out of the land. Then there was a quarrel among themselves whether they should remain in that land or go eastward to the more promising soil of Natal. They went eastward, and how they fared in Natal has already been told.

For ten or eleven years after this the 'trekking' of the Dutchmen into the Transvaal was only the onward movement of the most hardy of the class, the advanced pioneers of freedom, who would prefer to live on equal terms with the Savage, – if that were necessary, – than to have any dealings with English law. These were men at that time subject to no rule. Some were established north and west of the Vaal where Potchefstrom and Klerksdorp now are; others south and east of the Vaal. As to the latter there came an order for the appointment over them of British magistrates from Sir Henry Smith who was then the Governor of the Cape Colony. This was an offence which could not be borne. Andreas Pretorius, that most uncompromising, most stiff-necked and self-reliant of all the Dutchmen, had left Natal in disgust with this Governor and had settled himself in these parts. He instigated a rebellion against British authority, – not with the view of that moment claiming land north of the Vaal, but of asserting the independence of those who lived to the south of it. Then came the battle of Boom Plaats and the Orange sovereignty, – as will be told in the section of my Work devoted to the history of the Orange Free State. It was when flying from this battle, in 1848, that Pretorius crossed the Vaal. 'For you there is safety,' he said to his companions as he started. 'For me there is none.' Then he fled away across the river and a reward of £2,000 was set upon his head. This I think may be regarded as the beginning of the occupation of the Transvaal territory by a European or Dutch population.

A sort of Republic was at once established of which
Pretorius was at first the acknowledged rather than the elected
Chief. The most perfect freedom for the white man, – which
was supposed to include perfect equality, – was to be maintained by a union of their forces against the Natives of the
country. Mazulekatze had been ejected, and the Bechuanas
were again coming in upon their old land. Then there were
new troubles which seemed always to end in the subjection of
a certain number of the Natives to the domestic institutions of
the Dutch. The children of those who rebelled, and who were
taken as prisoners, were bound as apprentices in the families of
the Dutch farmers, – and as such were used as slaves. There
can be no doubt that such was the case. All the evidence that
there is on the subject goes to prove it, and the practice was
one entirely in accordance with Dutch sympathies and Dutch
manners. It is often pointed out to an enquirer that the
position of the little urchins who were thus brought into
contact with civilization was thereby much improved. Such an
argument cannot be accepted as worth anything until the
person using it is brought to admit that the child so
apprenticed is a slave, and the master a slave-owner. Then the
argument is brought back to the great question whether
slavery as an institution is beneficial or the reverse. But even a
Dutchman will generally avoid that position.

Such was the condition of the territory when the English
determined that they would signify to their runaway subjects
that they were regarded as free to manage themselves as they
pleased across the Vaal. Of what use could it be to follow these
Dutchmen beyond that distant river, when, if so persecuted,
they would certainly 'trek' beyond the Limpopo? Further back
than the Limpopo were the Zambesi and the Equator. And yet
as matters then stood a certain unpronounced claim was
implied by what had been done between the Orange and the
Vaal. A treaty was therefore made with the people in 1852,
and for the making of the treaty Messrs. Hogge and Owen
were despatched as Her Majesty's Commissioners to meet
Pretorius and a deputation of emigrant farmers, to settle the
terms on which the Republic should be established. There
were two clauses of special interest. One prohibited slavery in
the new Republic, – a clause so easy to put into a treaty, but

one of which it is so impossible for an outside power to exact the fulfilment! Another declared that the British would make no alliances with the natives north of the Vaal river, – a clause which we have also found to be very inconvenient. It would have been better perhaps merely to have told these Boers that if we found slavery to exist we should make it a casus belli, and to have bound ourselves to nothing. This would have been 'high-handed', – but then how much more high-handed have we been since?

Andreas Pretorius was the first President of the now established and recognised nationality which, with a weak ambition which has assisted much in bringing it to its ruin, soon called itself the South African Republic, – as though it were destined to swallow up not only the Free State but the British Colonies also. In this, however, Andreas Pretorius himself had no part. The passion of his soul seems to have been separation from the British; – not dominion over them. He died within two years, in July 1853, and his son was elected in his place. The father was certainly a remarkable man, – the one who of all his class was the most determined to liberate himself from the thraldom of English opinions. Mr. Theal in his history* of South Africa well describes how this man had become what he was by a continued reading of the Old Testament. The sanguinary orders given to the chosen people of the Lord were to him orders which he was bound to obey as were they. Mr. Theal quotes a special passage from the twentieth chapter of Deuteronomy, to which I will refer my reader – 'When thou comest nigh unto a city fight against it. ' The Israelites are enjoined either to slay or to enslave. And Pretorius felt that such were the commands given to him in reference to those natives among whom his lot had cast him. They were to him the people of the cities which were 'very far off,' and whom he had divine order to enslave, while the more unfortunate ones who would still fain occupy the lands on which it suited him and his people to dwell, were 'the Hittites and the Amorites, the Canaanites and the Perizzites, the Hivites and the Jebusites' whom the Lord had commanded him utterly to destroy. With such authority before him, and

* Vol. ii. p. 164.

while black labour was so necessary to the cultivation of the land, how could he doubt about slavery? In studying the peculiarity of the Dutch character in South Africa and the aversion of the people to our ways we have always to remember that they had been brought up for ages in the strictest belief in the letter of scripture. The very pictures in their bibles were to them true pictures, because they were there. It was so two hundred years ago with a large sect in Europe, – from which sect they had sprung. They had grown in the new land without admixture with the progressing ideas of Europe. They had neither been enlightened nor contaminated by new systems of belief, or unbelief. So it has come to pass that an institution which is so abhorrent to us as to make us feel that the man who is stained by it must be a godless sinner, is still to them a condition of things directly authorized and ordered by the Almighty. By our persistency, by our treaties, by our power, by enforcing upon their inferior condition as the very trademark of our superiority the command that slavery shall exist no longer, we have driven them to deny it, and have almost convinced them that slavery is no longer possible. But that heartfelt hatred of slavery which is now common to all of us in England has not yet reached the Dutchman of South Africa, – and is hardly as strong in the bosoms of all British South African Colonists as it might be.

After the death of the older Pretorius the Republic had by no means a quiet or a bloodless time. The capital was then at Potchefstrom, near the Vaal, while the enormous territory claimed by it to the north was almost without government. There are stories of terrible massacres amidst the records of the Republic, – of fearful revenge inflicted on the white men by the Savage whose lands had been taken from him, and of tenfold, hundredfold revenge following quick upon the heads of the wretched people. 'Thou shalt utterly destroy them!' And therefore a whole tribe was smothered and starved to death within the caves in which they had taken refuge. We read that, 'For years afterwards the supremacy of the white man was unquestioned in that part of the Transvaal, and we can easily believe it.'* But for some years the Republic hardly

* 'South Africa,' by John Noble, p. 173 B.

had any other history but that of its contests with the Natives and its efforts to extend its borders by taking land wherever its scanty European population could extend itself. The cities 'very far off' were all their legitimate prey. As the people thus followed out their destiny at great distances the seat of Government was moved from Potchefstrom to Pretoria, which city was named after the founder of the Republic.

Upon the death of Andreas Pretorius in 1853 his son became President; but in 1859 he was elected President of the Free State in the room of Mr. Bostrof, who had then retired. When at Bloemfontein he advocated measures for joining the two Republics under the name of the South African Republic. Already had risen the idea that the Dutch might oust the English from the continent, not by force of arms but by Republican sentiment, – an idea however which has never travelled beyond the brains of a few political leaders in the Transvaal. I do not think that a trace of it is to be found in the elder Pretorius. Mr. Burgers, the last President, of whom I shall have to speak presently, was so inflated by it, that it may be said to have governed all his actions. The idea is grand, for a South African Dutchman patriotic, and for a Republican Dutchman not unnatural. But such ideas must depend on their success for their vindication. When unsuccessful they seem to have been foolish thoughts, bags of gas and wind, and are held to be proof of the incompetency of the men who held them for any useful public action. Neither will Mr. Pretorius junior nor Mr. Burgers ever be regarded as benefactors of their country or as great statesmen; but the bosoms of each have no doubt swelled with the aspiration of being called the Dutch Washington of South Africa. I think I may say that Mr. Brand, who is now President of the Orange Free State, is imbued with no such vaulting ambition, whatever may be his ideas on the course of things in the womb of time. He is mildly contented to be President of the Free State, and as long as the Free State has a history to be written he will be spoken of as the man who in the midst of its difficulties made its existence possible and permanent.

The Volksraad of the Free State did not sympathise with the views of their President from the Transvaal, and in 1863 he resigned the place. He was soon re-elected President of the

Northern Republic and remained in that office till he quarrelled with his own Volksraad or was quarrelled with by
them. He struggled hard and successfully to extend the
bounds of the Empire, and claimed among other lands that
tract of land of which I have already spoken, which is far to the
south-west of the Transvaal, but still to the north or north-
west of the Vaal, where a tribe of the Griquas, a branch of the
vast tribe of the Bechuanas, were living. The question of a
boundary in that direction was submitted to Governor Keate
as umpire, and his decision, which was hostile to the claims of
the Republic, was accepted by the President. But the Volksraad repudiated their President, declaring that he had acted
without their authority, and refused to surrender the land in
question. Oddly enought after this, it is, – or it is not, – at this
moment a portion of British territory. I do not know with
what face we can hold it; – but still I feel that we shall not
abandon it. Pretorius was so disgusted with his Volksraad that
he resigned his office. This happened in 1872. Mr. Burgers,
the late President, was then elected for a term of five years,
and was sworn into office on 1st July of that year.

Mr. Burgers, whom I had the pleasure of meeting in
Capetown, is still a man in the prime of life and is entitled to
be spoken of with that courtesy which always should be
extended to living politicians who have retired from office.
Unless the proof to the contrary be so apparent as to be
glaring, – as to be impossible of refutation, – the motives of
such men should not be impugned. When a man has held high
office in his State, – especially when he has been elected to that
office by the voices of his fellow-citizens, – he is entitled to the
merit of patriotism unless the crime of selfish ambition or
unclean hands have been brought home against him by the
voices which elected him. No such charges have been subst-
antiated against Mr. Burgers, and I shall therefore speak of
him with all the respect which patriotism deserves. He was
chosen because he was supposed to be fit, and I have no reason
to doubt that he strove to do his best for his adopted country.
But the capacity of a Statesman for the office he has filled is
always open to remark, whether he be still in power or shall
have retired. In the former case it is essential to oust an
imcompetent man from his place, and in the latter to defend

the course by which such a one has been ousted. As a public man, – one who devotes himself to the service of the people, – is entitled to the most generous construction of his motives, which should be regarded as pure and honest till their impurity and dishonesty shall have been put beyond question, – so is he justly exposed to all that criticism can say as to the wisdom of his words and deeds. The work on which he is employed is too important for that good-natured reticence with which the laches of the insignificant may be allowed to be shrouded.

When Mr. Burgers was elected President of the Transvaal Republic he was, or shortly before had been, a clergyman of the Dutch Reformed Church in the Cape Colony, who had differed on matters of creed with the Church to which he belonged, and had consequently cast off his orders. He was known as an eloquent enthusiastic man, and was warmly welcomed in the Transvaal, – where, if ever, a silent, patient, unobtrusive officer was wanted for the work which had to be done in consolidating the Republic. The country at the time was very poor. The Treasury was empty, – a paper currency had been set afloat in 1865, and was of course greatly depreciated. Taxes were with difficulty collected, and the quarrels with the natives were incessant. Mr. Burgers succeeded in raising a loan, and borrowed £60,000, which the bank who lent the money will now receive from the pockets of tax-payers in England. A considerable portion of this sum has, I believe, already been repaid out of money voted by the House of Commons. He established a national flag, – which was we may suppose a cheap triumph. He had a gold coinage struck, with a portraiture of himself, – two or three hundred gold pieces worth 20s. each, – which I will not hurt his feelings by calling sovereigns. This could not have cost much as the coinage was so limited. They were too all made out of Transvaal gold. He set on foot a most high flown scheme of education, – of which the details will be given elsewhere and which might not have been amiss had it not been utterly impracticable. He attempted to have the public lands surveyed, while he did not in the least know what the public lands were and had no idea of their limits. There was to be a new code of laws, before as yet he had judges or courts. And then he resolved that a railway should at once be made from Pretoria throught the gold fields of the Transvaal down to Delagoa Bay where the Portuguese have their settlement. For the sake of raising a loan for this purpose he went in person to Holland, – just when one would have thought his presence in his own country to be indispensable, and did succeed in saddling the Republic with a debt of £100,000 for railway properties, – which debt must now, also, be paid by the British tax-payers. To all this he added, – so runs the rumour among those who were his friends in the Republic – many proud but too loudly spoken aspirations as to the future general destiny of the South African Republic. His mind seems to have been filled with the idea of competing with Washington for public admiration.

In all this there was much for which only the statesman and not the man must be blamed. The aspirations in themselves were noble and showed that Mr. Burgers had so far studied his subject as to know what things were good for a nation. But he had none of that method which should have taught him what things to put first in bestowing the blessings of government upon a people. We remember how Goldsmith ridicules the idea of sending venison to a man who is still without the necessaries of life.

'It's like sending them ruffles when wanting a shirt.'

It was certainly a shirt, and other of the simplest of garments, which the people of the Transvaal then wanted; – the ordinary calico shirt of taxation and the knee-breeches of security for property; – while Mr. Burgers was bestowing ruffles upon them in the shape of a national flag and a national gold coinage with his own portrait. Education is certainly one of the first wants of a people, but education will not be assisted at all by a law declaring that all schoolmasters shall have ample incomes, unless there be funds from which such incomes may be paid. What is so excellent as a good code of laws; – unless indeed it be some means of enforcing them, without which the best code in the world must be ineffective? A code of laws is to be had with comparatively little difficulty, – almost as easily as the flag. There are so many that an aspiring President need only choose. But that regular system of obedience to the laws which has to found itself on a well-collected Revenue, and which is the very essence of government, should come first, and in such a country as that which Mr. Burgers was called upon to govern, the establishment of this system should have been the care of the Governor before he had thought of a new code. Mr. Burgers rushed at once to the fruition of all the good things which a country can possess without stopping to see whether they were there, to be enjoyed. Such was his temperament. Nothing more plainly declares the excessive wealth of France and of England than the plenty of their gold coinage; – therefore certainly let us have some gold pieces in the Transvaal. How proud are the citizens of the United States of their Stars and Stripes! Therefore let us have a flag. How grand is the education of Prussia! Therefore let us have schools everywhere!

I myself think that the measure most essential for the development of the resources of the Transvaal is a railway to Delagoa Bay. I cannot therefore quarrel with Mr. Burgers for holding the same opinion. But it was characteristic of the enthusiasm of the man that he, leaving his country in uttermost confusion, should himself rush off to Europe for a loan, – characteristic of his energy that he should be able to raise, if not a large sum of money, railway plant representing a large sum – and characteristic of his imprudence that all this should have been done without any good result whatever. A railway to a country is a great luxury, the most comfortable perhaps that it can enjoy; but Mr. Burgers does not seem to have understood that a nation like a man, should be able to provide for itself the neccessaries of life before it looks for luxuries.

As in this I am accusing Mr. Burgers, so also am I defending him from many of the charges which have been brought against him. His fault hitherto has been an ambition to make his country great before it had been made secure; but in what he so did there is no trace of any undue desire for personal aggrandizement. As a nation rises in the world, so will its rulers rise. That a President of a young Republic should be aware of this and feel that as honour and wealth come to his people so will they come to him, is fair enough. It is but human. I believe that Mr. Burgers thought more of his country than of himself. That he was sanguine, unsteady, and utterly deficient in patience and prudence was the fault of those who elected him rather than of himself.

All these follies, if they were follies, could have been nothing to us but for our close proximity to the borders of the Transvaal. While the gold was being coined and the flag was being stitched, there were never-ending troubles with the Natives. The question of the right to territory in a country which was inhabited by native races when it was invaded by Europeans is one so complex that nothing but superior force has as yet been able to decide it. The white races have gradually obtained possession of whatever land they have wanted because they have the braver and the stronger people. Philanthropy must put up with the fact, and justice must reconcile herself to it as best she may. I venture to express an opinion that to the minds of all just men, who have turned this matter in their thoughts with painful anxiety, there has come a solution, – which has by no means satisfied them, but which has been the only solution possible, – that God Almighty has intended that it should be as it is. The increasing populations of the civilized world have been compelled to find for themselves new homes; and that they should make these homes in the lands occupied by people whose power of enjoying them has been very limited, seems to have been arranged— by Destiny. That is the excuse which we make for ourselves; and if we do not find verbal authority for it in Deuteronomy as do the Boers, we think that we collect a general authority from the manifested intention of the Creator.

But in the midst of all this the attempts to deal justly with the original occupants of the soil have of late years been incessant. If we buy the land than it will be ours of right. Or if we surrender and secure to the Natives as much as the Native wants, then are we not a benefactor rather than a robber? If we succour the weak against the strong then shall we not justify our position? If in fact we do them more good than harm may we not have quiet consciences? So we have dealt with them intending to be just, but our dealings have always ended in coercion, annexation, dominion and masterdom.

In these dealing who has been able to fix a price or to decide where has been the right to sell? A few cattle have been given for a large territory or even a few beads; and than it has turned out that the recipient of the cattle or beads has had no title to dispose of the land. But the purchaser if he be strong-handed will stick to his purchase. And then come complications as to property which no judge can unravel. Shall the law of the Native prevail or European laws? and if the former who shall interpret it, – a Native or a European? Some years ago a Zulu king conquered a native tribe which lived on lands which are now claimed as part of the Transvaal and then sold them for a herd of cattle to the Dutch Republic. Time went by and the conquered people were still allowed to live on the land, but the Dutch still claimed it as a part of their empire. Then there arose a warrior among the tribe which had been conquered; and the number of the tribe had increased with peace; and the warrior said that he was then on his own territory and not there by sufferance. And now that he was brave and strong he declared that all the land that had once belonged to his tribe should be his. And so there came war. The warrior was Secocoeni, the son of Sequani who had been conquered by Dingaan the King of the Zulus, and the war came up in the time of Mr. Burgers and has been the cause of our annexation of the Republic. It should have been the first duty of Mr. Burgers to have settled this affair with Secocoeni. His title to the land in question was not very good, but he should have held it or yielded it. If not all he might have yielded some. Or he might have shown himself able to conquer the Native, as Dutchmen and Englishmen have done before, – and have consoled himself with such justification as that I have mentioned. But with his coins and his flags and his railway he seems to have lost that power of inducing his Dutchmen to fight which the Dutch leaders before his time have always possessed. There was fighting and the Dutch had certain native allies, who assisted them well. The use of such allies has become quite customary in South Africa. At the very moment in which I am writing we are employing the Fingos against Kreli and the Galekas in Kafraria. But Mr. Burgers with his allies could not conquer Secocoeni although he was again and again rebuked by our Secretary of State at home for the

barbarity with which he carried on the war. It is thus that Lord
Carnarvon wrote to our Governor at the Cape on the 25th
January 1877. 'I have to instruct you once more to express to
him,' – President Burgers, – 'the deep regret and indignation
with which H.M. Government view the proceedings of the
armed force which is acting in the name and under the
authority of the Transvaal Government, and that he is rapidly
making impossible the continuance either of those sentiments
of respect and confidence towards him, or of those friendly
relations with him as the Chief of a neighbouring Government, which it was the earnest hope of H.M. Government to
preserve.' This was a nice message for a President to receive,
not when he had quelled the Natives by the 'armed force
which is acting in the name and under the authority of the
Transvaal Government,' – and which was undoubtedly the
Transvaal army fighting for the just and unjust claims of the
country, – but when that armed force had run away after an
ineffective effort to drive the enemy from his stronghold!

Whether Mr. Burgers ever received that message I do not
know. It was not written till a day or two after the arrival of
Sir Theophilus Shepstone at Pretoria, – to which place he had
then gone up as British Commissioner, and could hardly have
been handed to the President much before the final overthrow
of his authority. Under these circumstances we may hope that
he was spared the annoyance of reading it. But other annoyan-
ces, some from the same source, must surely have been
enough to crush any man, even one so sanguine as Mr.
Burgers. During all the latter period of his office he was
subjected to a continued hail-storm of reproaches as to slavery
from British authorities and British newspapers. These
reached him generally from the Cape Colony, and Mr.
Burgers, who had come from the Cape, must have known his
own old Colony well enough himself to have been sure that if
not refuted they would certainly lead to disaster. I do not
believe that Mr Burgers had any leaning towards slavery. He
was by no means a Boer among Boers, but has come rather of
a younger class of men and from a newer school. But he could
only exist in the Transvaal by means of the Boers, and in his
existing condition could not exert himself for the fulfillment
of the clause of the treaty which forbad slavery.

Then he had against him a tribe of natives whom he could not conquer, and at the same time the British Government and British feeling. And he had not a shilling in the Treasury. Nominal taxes there were; – but no one would pay them. As they were all direct taxes, it was open to the people to pay them or to decline to do so. And they declined. As no one had any confidence in anything, why should any one pay five or ten pounds to a tax gatherer who had no constable at his back to enforce payment? No one did do so, and there was not a shilling in the Treasury. This was the condition of the South African Republic when Sir Theophilus Shepstone arrived at Pretoria on January 22nd, 1877, with six or seven other gentlemen from Natal and a guard of 25 mounted policemen.

CHAPTER III

THE TRANSVAAL – ANNEXATION

I have endeavoured in the last chapter to tell very shortly the story of the South African Republic and to describe its condition at the moment when our Secretary of State at home took the unusual step of sending a British Commissioner, – not with orders to take possession of the land but with orders which have been held to justify the act when done. I doubt whether there is a precedent for so high-handed a deed in British history. It is as though the rulers of Germany were to say that in their opinion the existence of a Switzerland in Europe was deleterious and dangerous, and that therefore they would abolish Switzerland as a Republic, and annex its territory. It will be said that the case would be different because Switzerland is well governed and prosperous. But the Germans in such a case would say that they thought otherwise, – which is what we say here, – and that they therefore took it. It was we who found fault with the management of that other Republic and we who have taken possession of the land. It is well that the whole truth as to the matter should be understood. If we had done this act in compliance with the expressed wish of the inhabitants generally, that would be a justification. But it cannot fairly be said that such was the case here. A nation with a popular parliament can only be said to express its opinion to another nation by the voices of its parliament; – and the Volksraad of the Transvaal was altogether opposed to the interference of Great Britain. I will touch upon this matter again presently when alluding to the words of the Commission given to the British Commissioner by the Secretary of State at home; – but I think it must be acknowledged that no other expression of opinion, unless it be a general rising of a people, can be taken as national. In nine cases out of ten petitions ought to be held to mean nothing.

They cannot be verified. They show the energy of the instigators of the petition and not of the petitioners. They can be signed by those who have and by those who have not an interest in the matter. The signatures to them can be readily forged. At home in England the right of petitioning is so dear to us from tradition that we still cling to it as one of the bulwarks of our freedom; but there cannot be a statesman, hardly a Member of Parliament among us, who does not feel that pen and ink and agitating management have become so common that petitions are seldom now entitled to much respect.

It may perhaps be said that we have repeatedly done the same thing in India. But a little thinking will show that our Indian annexations have been quite of a different nature. There we have gone on annexing in opposition to the barbarism and weakness of native rule against which our presence in India has, from the first, been a protest. Each annexation has been the result of previous conquest and has been caused by non-compliance with the demands of the conquerors. In the Transvaal we have annexed a dominion which was established by ourselves in express obedience to our own requisitions, which was in the possession of European rulers, which was altogether independent, and as to the expediency of annexing which we have had nothing to guide us but our own judgement and our own will. It is as though a strong boy should say to a weak one, 'It is better that I should have that cricket bat than you,' and should therefore take it.

The case will seem to be still stronger if it shall appear, as I think it will, that Sir Theophilus Shepstone, the Commissioner appointed to this work, did what he did do without complete authority. It is evident that there was doubt in the Colonial Office at home. The condition of the Transvaal was very bad. Slavery was rampant. The Natives were being encouraged to rebellion. The President was impotent. The Volksraad was stiff-necked and ignorant. There was no revenue, no order, no obedience. The Dutch seemed to have forgotten even the way to fight. What were we to do with such neighbours, – for whose inefficiency we were in a measure responsible, having ourselves established the Republic? That we must interfere for our own protection in regard to the Natives seemed to be necessary. As has been said so often, there was a house on fire next door to us, in the flames of which we might ourselves be enveloped. Remonstrances had been frequent and had been altogether ineffectual. The Republic was drifting, – nay, had drifted into Chaos. If any other people could have assisted us in putting out the fire, French, Germans, or Italians, – so that we might not seem to tyrannise, – it would have been so comfortable! But in South Africa we had none to help us. And then though this Republic was more than half Dutch it was also only less than half English.

Something must be done; and therefore an order was sent out directing Sir Theophilus Shepstone to go to Pretoria and see what he could do. Sir Theophilus was and for many years had been Minister for Native Affairs in the Colony of Natal, and was credited, – no doubt correctly, – with knowing more about the Natives than any other European in South Africa. He was a man held in special respect by the King of the Zulus, and the King of the Zulus was in truth the great power whom both Dutch and English would dread should the natives be encouraged to rebel. When men have talked of our South African house being in danger of fire, Cetywayo the King of the Zulus has been the fire to whom they have alluded. So Sir Theophilus started on his journey taking his Commission in his pocket. He took a small body of policemen with him as an escort, but advisedly not a body that might seem by its number to intimidate even so weak a Government as that of the South African Republic.

The writing of the Commission must have been a work of labour, requiring much thought, and a great weighing of words. It had to be imperative and yet hemmed in by all precautions; giving clear instruction, and yet leaving very much to the Commissioner on the spot who would have his work to do in a distant country not connected with the world by telegraph wires. The Commission is long and I will not quote it all; but it goes on to say that 'if the emergency should seem to you to be such as to render it necessary, in order to secure the peace and safety of Our said Colonies and of Our subjects elsewhere that the said territories, or any portion or portions of the same, should *provisionally and pending the* *announcement of Our pleasure,** be administered in Our name and on Our behalf, then *and in such case only** We—' authorize you to annex so much of any such territories as aforesaid.

But the caution against such annexing was continued much further. 'Provided first – that' – no such annexation shall be made – 'unless you shall be satisfied that the inhabitants thereof, *or a sufficient number of them, or the Legislature thereof** desire to become Our subjects, nor if any conditions unduly limiting Our power and authority are sought to be imposed. And secondly, that, unless the circumstances are such as in your opinion to make it necessary to issue a Proclamation forthwith, no such Proclamation shall be issued by you until the same has been submitted to and approved by——' the Governor of the Cape Colony, all whose titles are given at great length.

Could anything be more guarded, or less likely one would say on the mere perusal of the document, to lean to an immediate and permanent annexation of the whole country. The annexation if made at all was to be provisional only and pending the Queen's pleasure, and then it was only to be made if the inhabitants, or a sufficient number of them, or the Legislature should wish it. What the sufficient number might be was left to the discretion of the Commissioner. But he was only to do this in compliance with the wishes of the people themselves. He was to take temporary possession, – only temporary possession, – of a part of the Transvaal should the people desire it, and in the event of such a measure being approved by a distant Governor, – unless the circumstances were such as to make him think it expedient to do it without such approval. Such was the nature of the Order, and I think that any one reading it before the event would have said that it was not intended to convey an authority for the immediate and permanent annexation of the whole country.

But Sir Theophilus, after a sojourn of ten weeks at Pretoria, in which the question of the annexation was submitted to the Volksraad and in which petitions and counter-petitions were signed, did annex the whole country permanently, without any question of provisional occupation, and without, as far as

* The italics are my own

I have been able to learn, any sanction from the Governor of the Cape Colony. As to conditions limiting Her Majesty's power, the mere allusion to such a condition of things seems to be absurd now that we know what has been done. 'Now therefore I do . . . . proclaim and make known that from and after the publication hereof the territory heretofore known as the South African Republic . . . . shall be, and shall be taken to be, British territory.' These are the words which contain the real purport of the Proclamation issued by Sir Theophilus Shepstone at Pretoria on 12th April, 1877. Was ever anything so decided, so audacious, and apparently so opposed to the spirit of the instructions which the Commissioner had received? When the Secretary of State received a telegram from Madeira, the nearest telegraph station, saying that the Transvaal had been annexed, which he did in the following May, he surely must have been more surprised than any other man in England at what had been done.

Was the deed justifiable? Has it been justified by what has occurred since? And if so how had come about a state of things which had made necessary a proceeding apparently so outrageous? The only man I have met in all South Africa who has questioned the propriety of what has been done is Mr. Burgers, the ousted President. Though I have discussed the matter wherever I have been, taking generally something of a slant against Sir Theophilus, – as I must seem to have done in the remarks I have just made, and to which I always felt myself prompted by the high-handedness of the proceeding, – I have never encountered even a doubtful word on the subject, except in what Mr Burgers said to me. And Mr Burgers acknowledged to me, not once or twice only, that the step which had been taken was manifestly beneficial, to the Natives, to the English, – and to the Dutch. He thought that Sir Theophilus had done a great wrong, – but that the wrong done would be of great advantage to every one concerned. He made various complaints; – that the Natives around him had been encouraged to rebel in order that an assumed difficulty might be pleaded; – that no national petition, and indeed no trustworthy petition, had been sent forward praying for annexation; – that the deed was uncalled for and tyrannical; – and that the whole proceeding was one in which the courtesy due to a weaker nation was neglected and omitted. He then asserted that fresh emigrants would not flock into a land governed under a European crown as they would have done into a Republic. But he repeated his admission that for Dutchmen, Englishmen, and Natives as at present settled in the country, the British rule would be the best.

He alleged as to himself that when Sir Theophilus stated to him his intentions, three courses appeared to be open to him. He might use his influence and his words in assisting the transference of the country to the British. This as President of the Republic he could not do; – and the less so as he did not think that it should be done. Or he might cause Sir Theophilus and his twenty-five policemen to be marched back over the border, treating them on their way as unauthorized intruders. This he would not do, he said, because he knew it to be useless to wage war with Great Britain. Or he might yield and remonstrate; – yield to power while he remonstrated against injustice. This, he said, that he did do. The words and personal bearing of the man recommended themselves to me much. Whether he is to be regarded as a banished patriot or a willing placeman must depend on a delicate question which has not as far as I know yet been answered, though it has been broached, – to which, delicate as it is, I will refer again before I have ended my story.

I had not the pleasure of meeting Sir Theophilus and have the less repugnance therefore to surmise the condition of his mind when he received the order to go to Pretoria. Had he told me his mind I might have been unable to publish my own surmises. He knew that the native races of the Transvaal unless convinced of the superiority of their white neighbours would ever struggle to prove them inferior, and that such inferiority if proved would at once be their death-warrant. The Natives had long learned to respect the English and to hate the Dutch; – but even that respect would not restrain them if once they had asserted their masterhood to a white race. And now this state of things was at hand. He was aware that though English troops could be supplied to maintain English authority, English troops would not be lent to fight the battles of the Dutch. There might, nay there probably would be, a native triumph just across our borders which he as

a minister in Natal could not interfere to quell, – but which,
when a rumour of it should spread among the Zulus on our
border, might induce 300,000 coloured subjects to think that
they could free themselves by a blow from 20,000 white
masters. And he knew the condition which I have attempted
to explain, – that these Dutch people in the Transvaal would
not pay a stiver of tax, that there was in fact no government,
that the gaols were unlocked in order that prisoners might find
elsewhere the bread which their gaolers could not get for
them, that the posts could not be continued because the
Contractors were not paid, that no one would part with a coin
which he possessed, that property was unsaleable, that industry was unprofitable, that life was insecure, that Chaos was
come upon the land. I do not suppose that Sir Theophilus
doubted much when he read the Commission which had been
sent to him, or that he thought very much of all the safeguards
and provisions. He probably felt, as did everybody else, that
the South African Republic had from the first been a failure, –
almost a farce, – and that the sooner so expensive a failure
could be brought to an end, the better. If indeed the Volksraad
would have voted their own extermination that would have
been very well; but he could hardly have expected it. As for
petitions, and the wish of a 'sufficient number' of the inhabitants, – I should imagine that he must have been a little
indifferent to that. His mind was probably made up, – with a
resolve to give the Volksraad what time might be needed for
their deliberations. They did not deliberate, – only deliberated
whether they would deliberate or not, and then declined even
to deliberate. Whereupon Sir Theophilus said that then and
from thenceforth the Transvaal should be British property. So
he put up the Queen's flag; – and the Transvaal is and probably
will remain British property.

I have to acknowledge, with all my sympathies strongly
opposed to what I call high-handed political operations, that I
think Sir Theophilus was justified. A case of such a kind must
in truth be governed by its own merits, and cannot be
subjected to a fixed rule. To have annexed only a part of the
Transvaal would have been not only useless, but absurd. Not
only would the part which we had spared have been hostile to
us, but the Dutch within our assumed borders would have

envied the independence we had left to others. We shall have
trouble enough now in settling our boundaries with the
Natives. We should then have had the worse trouble of
settling them with the Dutch. To have waited for authority
from the Governor of the Cape Colony would have shown a
weakness in his own authority which might have been fatal to
Sir Theophilus as he was then placed. No other Governor
could know the condition of the matter as well as he did. To
get the authority needed he must have wasted six weeks
during which it would have been known to every member of
the Volksraad that he was waiting. To carry him through it
was needed that the Boers should understand that when he
said that the land should be annexed, Great Britain was saying
so. They did so believe. The President so believed. And
therefore the surrender was made without a struggle.

So much for Sir Theophilus and his instructions. In the
larger matter which regards Great Britain and her character,
we have to enquire whether this arbitrary act has been justified
by what has occurred since. In discussing this there are at least
four parties concerned, if not more. Mr. Burgers spoke of
three, and in South Africa it is natural that reference should be
made to those three only. As regards the Natives there can be
no question. No friend of theirs can wish it to be otherwise
unless they have a friend so foolish as to desire for them an
independence which can be obtained only by the extermination or banishment of the European races. That the Natives
generally respect the English and do not respect the Dutch is
certain. This had come to such a pitch in the Transvaal that it
had produced war, – and that war if continued would have
meant the destruction of the tribe which was waging it.
Permanent success against white men is impossible for
Natives in South Africa. Every war between a tribe and its
white neighbours ends in the destruction of the tribe as an
independent people. And here, if Secocoeni had been successful against the Dutch, – if the English could have allowed
themselves to sit by and see the house all in flames, –
Cetywayo, the King of the Zulus, would at once have been at
war with Secocoeni. As far as the Natives were concerned, it
would indeed have been to 'let slip the dogs of war.' It has
been one of our great objects in dealing with the Natives, –

perhaps that in accomplishing which we should be most proud
of what we have done, – to save the tribes from being
hounded on to war among themselves by their Chiefs. The
Dutch rule in the Transvaal was an incentive to war which was
already operating. The house was on fire and could only have
been put out by us.

As to the good done to the English of the Transvaal it is
hardly necessary that any arguments should be used. We had
abandoned the country to Dutch rule in 1852, and it was
natural that the Dutch should consider only themselves – and
the Natives. After what we had done we clearly had no right
to take back the Transvaal by force in order that we might
protect the interests of Englishmen who were living there. But
it is matter of additional satisfaction that we have been enabled
to re-establish a basis of trade in the country; – for the trade of
the country has been in the hands of English, Germans, or
newly arrived Hollanders, and not in those of the Boers to
whom the country was given up. I do not remember to have
found a shop or even an hotel all through the Transvaal in the
hands of a Dutch Boer.

But the man who has cause to rejoice the most, – and who
as far as I could learn is wide awake to the fact, – is the Boer
himself. He is an owner of land, – and on the first of January
1877 his land was hardly worth having. Now he can sell it,
and such sales are already being made. He was all astray even
as to what duty required of him. Ought he to pay his taxes
when no one around him was paying? Of what use would be
his little contribution? Therefore he did not pay. And yet he
had sense enough to know that when there are no taxes, then
there can be no government. Now he will pay his taxes.
Ought he to have fought, when those wretched Natives, in
their audacity, were trying to recover the land which he had
taken from them? Of what use could fighting have been when
he had no recognised leader, – when the next Boer to him was
not fighting? Now he knows that he will have a leader. Why
cultivate his land, or more of it than would feed himself? Why
shear his sheep if he could not sell his wool? Now there are
markets for him. It was to this condition of not paying, not
fighting, and not working that he was coming when British
annexation was suggested to him. He could not himself ask to

be expatriated; but it may well be understood that he should thoroughly appreciate the advantage to himself of a measure for which as a Dutchman he could not ask. What was wanted was money and the credit which money gives. England had money and the Boer knew well enough that English money could procure for him that which a national flag, and a gold coinage, and a code of laws, and a promised railway could not achieve. It was almost cruel to ask him to consent to annexation, but it would have been more cruel not to annex him.

But the condition of the fourth party is to be considered. That fourth party is the annexing country. It may be very well for the Natives and for the Dutch, and for the English in the Transvaal, but how will it suit the English at home? It became immediately necessary for us to send a large military force up to the Transvaal, or to its neighbourhood. Something above two regiments have I believe been employed on the service, and money has been demanded from Parliament for the purpose of paying for them. Up to this time England has had to pay about £125,000 for the sake of procuring that security of which I have spoken. Why should she pay this for the Boers, – or even for the English who have settled themselves among the Boers? And then the sum I have named will be but a small part of what we must pay. Hitherto no violent objection has been made at home to the annexation. In Parliament it has been almost as well received by the Opposition as by the Government. No one has said a word against Lord Carnarvon; and hardly a word has been said against Sir Theophilus. But how will it be when other and larger sums are asked for the maintenance of the Transvaal? Surely some one will then arise and say that such payments are altogether antagonistic to our colonial policy, – by which our Colonies, as they are required to give nothing to us, are also required to support themselves.

The answer to this I think must be that we have been compelled thus to deviate from our practice and to put our hands deeply into our pockets by our folly in a former generation. It is because we came to a wrong judgement of our position in 1852, – when we first called upon the Dutch Boers to rule themselves, – that we are now, twenty-five years afterwards, called upon to pay for the mistake that has since occurred. We then endeavoured to limit our responsibility, saying to ourselves that there was a line in South Africa which we would not pass. We had already declined to say the same thing as to Natal and we ought to have seen and acknowledged that doctrine of the house on fire as clearly then as we do now. The Dutch who trekked across the Vaal were our subjects as much as though they were English. Their troubles must ultimately have become our troubles, – whereas their success, had they been successful, might have been as troublesome to us as their trouble. We repudiated two territories, and originated two Republics. The first has come back upon our hands and we must pay the bill. That is the Transvaal. The other, which can pay its own bill, will not come back to us even though we should want it. That is the Orange Free State. I have now answered the three questions. I think the annexation was justifiable. I think that it has been justified by the circumstances that have followed it. And I have given what in my opinion has been the cause for so disagreeable a necessity.

There is one other matter to be mentioned, – that delicate matter to which I have alluded. A report has been spread all through South Africa that the late President of the South African Republic is to be gratified by a pension of £750 per annum out of the revenues of Great Britain. I trust for every one's sake that that report may not be true. The late President was the chief officer of his country when the annexation was made, and I cannot think that it would be compatible with his honour to receive a pension from the Government of the country which has annihilated the Republic over which he had been called on to preside. When he says that he yielded and remonstrated he takes a highly honourable position and one which cannot be tarnished by any incapability for ruling which he may have shown. But were he to live after that as a pensioner on English bounty, – the bounty of a country which had annihilated his own, – then I think that he had better at least live far away from the Transvaal, and from the hearing of the sound of a Dutchman's voice.

And why should we pay such a pension? Is it necessary that we should silence Mr. Burgers? Have we done him an injustice that we should pay him a compensation for the loss of his office? It is said that we pay dethroned Indian Princes. But we take the revenues of dethroned Indian Princes, – revenues which have become their own by hereditary descent. Mr. Burgers had a month or two more of his Presidency to enjoy, with but little chance of re-election to an office the stipend of which could not have been paid for want of means. But this argument ought not to be required. An expensive and disagreeable duty was forced upon us by a country which could not rule itself, and certainly we should not convict ourselves of an injustice by giving a pension to the man whose incompetence imposed upon us the task. I trust that the rumour though very general has been untrue.

CHAPTER IV

THE TRANSVAAL – PRETORIA

Pretoria itself, the capital of our new country, is a little town, lying in a basin on a plateau 4,500 feet above the level of the sea – lat. 25° 45′, S., long. 28° 49′, E. From its latitude it would be considered to be semitropical, but its altitude above the sea is so great as to make the climate temperate. In regard to heat and cold it is very peculiar, – the changes being more rapid and violent than I have experienced in any other place. I was there during the last days of September, which would answer to the last days of March on our side of the equator. The mornings were very fine, but somewhat chilly, – not so as to make a fire desirable but just to give a little sting to the water. The noon-day was hot, – not too hot for exercise; but the heat seemed to increase towards the afternoon, the level rays of the sun being almost oppressive. Then suddenly there would come an air so cold that the stranger who had not expected the change and who was wearing perhaps his lightest clothes would find that he wanted a great coat and a warm cravat round his neck. It was not till I was about to leave the place that I became alive to its peculiarities. I caught a cold every evening in consequence of my ignorance, becoming quite hoarse and thinking of hot water externally and internally as I went to bed; – but in the morning I was always quite well again. I was assured, however, that the climate of Pretoria was one which required great care from its inhabitants. It is subject to very violent storms, and deaths from lightning are not uncommon. The hailstorms, when they come, are very violent, the stones being so large as not unfrequently to batter the cattle to death. I was glad to find that they were infrequent, and that my good fortune saved me from experiencing their effects. 'What does a man do if he be out in the veld?' I asked when I heard these frightful stories.

'Put his saddle over his head,' was the answer, showing much as to the custom of a people who seldom walk to any distance always having horses at command. 'But if he have not a saddle?' 'Ah, then indeed, he would be badly off.' My informants, for I was told of the hailstorms and the necessary saddles more than once, seemed to think that in such a dilemma there would be no hope for a man who, without a saddle, might chance to be beyond the reach of a roof. I could not, however, learn that people were often killed. I therefore accepted the Pretorian hailstones with a grain of salt.

The first President of the Colony was named Pretorius and hence the name of the town, which became the capital in the time of his son who was the second President. The old man was one of the pioneer farmers who first entered in upon the country under circumstances already described, and the family now is very numerous in the Transvaal, occupying many farms. Potchefstroom, – a hundred miles to the south-west of Pretoria, – was the first capital and is still the bigger town; but President Pretorius the second thought it well to move the seat of Government more to the centre of the large district which the Republic was then claiming, and called the little city Pretoria, after the name of his father.

I am quite unable to say what is the population of the capital, as those of whom I inquired could only guess at it from their own point of view. I should think it might amount to two thousand exclusive of the military. At the time I was there it was of a very shifting nature, and will be so for some months. It has lately become the seat of a British Government, and people have flocked into it knowing that money will be flying about. Money has flown about very readily, and there are hands of course to receive it. Six hundred British soldiers are stationed there under tents, and soldiers, though their pay is low, are great consumers. A single British soldier will consume as much purchased provender as a whole Boer family. But as people are going in, so are they going out. The place therefore in its present condition is like a caravansary rather than an established town. All menial services are done by a Kafir population, – not permanently resident Kafirs who can be counted, but by a migratory imported set who are caught and used as each master or mistress of a family may find it possible to catch and use them. 'They always go when you have taught them anything,' one poor lady said to me. Another assured me that two months of continuous service was considered a great comfort. And yet they have their domestic jealousies. I dined at a house at which one of our British soldiers waited at table, an officer who dined there having kindly brought the much-needed assistance with him. The dinner was cooked by a Kafir who, as the lady of the house told me, was very angry because the soldier was allowed to interfere with the gala arrangements of the day. He did not see why he should not be allowed to show himself among the company after having undergone that heat of the fray. These Kafirs at Pretoria, and through all those parts of the Transvaal which I visited, are an imported population, – the Dutch having made the land too hot to hold them as residents. The Dutch hated them, and they certainly have learned to hate the Dutch in return. Now they will come and settle themselves in Pretoria for a short time and be good-humoured and occasionally serviceable. But till they settle themselves there permanently it is impossible to count them as a resident population.

Down many of the streets of the town, – down all of them that are on the slope of the descent, – little rivulets flow, adding much to the fertility of the gardens and to the feeling of salubrity. Nothing seems to add so much to the prettiness and comfort of a town as open running water, though I doubt whether it be in truth the most healthy mode of providing for man the first necessary of life. Let a traveller, however, live for a few days but a quarter of a mile from his water supply and he will learn what is the comfort of a rivulet just at his door-step. Men who have roughed it in the wilderness, as many of our Colonists have had to do, before they have settled themselves into townships, have learned this lesson so perfectly that they are inclined perhaps, to be too fond of a deluge. For purposes of gardening in such a place as Pretoria there can be no doubt about the water. The town gardens are large, fertile, and productive, whereas nothing would grow without irrigation.

The streets are broad and well laid out, with a fine square in the centre, and the one fact that they have no houses in them is the only strong argument against them. To those who know

the first struggling efforts of a colonial town, – who are
familiar with the appearance of a spot on which men have
decided to begin a city but have not as yet progressed far, the
place with all its attributes and drawbacks will be manifest
enough. To those who have never seen a city thus struggling
into birth it is difficult to make it intelligible. The old faults of
old towns have been well understood and thoroughly avoided.
The old town began with a simple cluster of houses in close
contiguity, because no more than that was wanted. As the
traffic of the day was small, no provision was made for broad
spaces. If a man could pass a man, or a horse a horse, – or at
most a cart a cart, – no more was needed. Of sanitary laws
nothing was known. Air and water were taken for granted.
Then as people added themselves to people, as the grocer came
to supply the earlier tanner, the butcher the grocer, the
merchant tailor his three forerunners, and as a schoolmaster
added himself to them to teach their children, house was
adjoined to house and lane to lane, till a town built itself after
its own devise, and such a London and such a Paris grew into
existence as we who are old have lived to see pulled down
within the period of our own lives. There was no foresight and
a great lack of economy in this old way of city building.

But now the founder has all these examples before his eyes,
and is grandly courageous in his determination to avoid the
evils of which he has heard and perhaps seen so much. Of
course he is sanguine. A founder of cities is necessarily a
sanguine man, or he would not find himself employed on such
a work. He pegs out his streets and his squares bravely, being
stopped by no consideration as to the value of land. He clings
to parallelograms as being simple, and in a day or two has his
chief thoroughfare a mile long, his cross streets all numbered
and named, his pleasant airy squares, each with a peg at each
corner, out in the wilderness. Here shall be his Belgravia for
the grandees, and this his Cheapside and his Lombard Street
for the merchants and bankers. We can understand how
pleasant may be the occupation and how pile upon pile would
rise before the eyes of the projector, how spires and minarets
would ascend, how fountains would play in the open places,
and pleasant trees would lend their shade to the broad sunny
ways.

Then comes the real commencement with some little hovel at the corner of two as yet invisible streets. Other hovels arise always at a distance from each other and the town begins to be a town. Sometimes there will be success, but much more often a failure. Very many failures I have seen, in which all the efforts of the sanguine founder have not produced more than an Inn, a church, half a dozen stores, and twice as many drinking booths. And yet there have been the broad streets, – and the squares if one would take the trouble to make enquiry. Pretoria has not been a failure. Among recent attempts of the kind Pretoria is now likely to be a distinguished success. An English Governor is to live there, and there will be English troops, – I fear, for many years. Balls will be given at Pretoria. Judges will hold their courts there, and a Bishop will live in a Pretorian Bishopstowe. But the Pretoria of today has its unknown squares, and its broad ill defined streets about which houses straggle in an apparently formless way, none of which have as yet achieved the honours of a second storey. The brooks flow pleasantly, but sometimes demand an inconvenient amount of jumping. The streets lie in holes, in which when it rains the mud is very deep. In all such towns as these mud assumes the force of a fifth element, and becomes so much a matter of course that it is as necessary to be muddy, as it is to be smoke-begrimed in London. In London there is soap and water, and in Pretoria there are, perhaps, clothes-brushes; but a man to be clean either in one place or the other must always be using his soap or his clothes-brush. There are many gardens in Pretoria, – for much of the vacant spaces is so occupied. The time will come in which the gardens will give place to buildings, but in the mean time they are green and pleasant-looking. Perhaps the most peculiar feature of the place is the roses. There are everywhere hedges of roses, hedges which are all roses, – not wild roses but our roses of the garden though generally less sweet to the smell. And with the roses, there are everywhere weeping willows, mourning gracefully over the hitherto unaccomplished aspirations of the country. This tree, which I believe to have been imported from St. Helena, has become common to the towns and homesteads of the Transvaal. To the eye that is strange to them the roses and weeping willows are very pretty; but, as with everything else in the world, their very profusion and commonness detracts from their value. The people of Pretoria think no more of their roses, than do those of Bermuda of their oleanders.

In such towns the smallness of the houses is not the characteristic which chiefly produces the air of meanness which certainly strikes the visitor, nor is it their distance from each other, nor their poverty; but a certain flavour of untidiness which is common to all new towns and which is, I fear, unavoidable. Brandy bottles and sardine boxes meet the eye everywhere. Tins in which pickled good things have been conveyed accumulate themselves in corners. The straw receptacles in which wine is nowadays conveyed meet the eye constantly, as do paper shirt-collars, rags, old boots, and fragments of wooden cases. There are no dust holes and no scavengers, and all the unseemly relics of a hungry and thirsty race of pioneers are left open to inspection.

And yet in spite of the mud, in spite of the brandy bottles, in spite of the ubiquitous rags Pretoria is both picturesque and promising. The efforts are being made in the right direction, and the cottages which look lowly enough from without have an air of comfort within. I was taken by a gentleman to call on his wife, – an officer of our army who is interested in the gold fields of the Transvaal, – and I found that they had managed to gather round them within a very small space all the comforts of civilized life. There was no front door and no hall; but I never entered a room in which I felt myself more inclined to 'rest and be thankful.' I made various calls, and always with similar results. I found internal prettiness, with roses and weeping willows outside which reconciled me to sardine boxes, paper collars, and straw liquor-guards.

In the middle of Pretoria is a square, round which are congregated the public offices, the banks, hotels, and some of the chief stores, or shops of the place, and in which are depastured horses of such travellers as choose to use the grass for the purpose. Ours, I hope, were duly fed within their stables; but I used to see them wandering about, trying to pick a bit of grass in the main square. And here stands the Dutch Reformed Church, – in the centre, – a large building, and as ugly as any building could possibly be made. Its clergyman, quite a young man, called upon me while I was in Pretoria, and told me that his congregation was spread over an area forty miles round. The people of the town are regular attendants; for the Dutchman is almost always a religious father of a family, thinking much of all such services as were reverenced by his fathers before him. But the real congregation consists of the people from the country who flock into the Nichtmaal, or Lord's Supper, once in three months, who encamp or live in their waggons in the square round the Church, who take the occasion to make their town purchases and to perform their religious services at the same time. The number attending is much too large to enter the church at once, so that on the appointed Sunday one service succeeds another. The sacrament is given, and sermons are preached, and friends meet each other, amid the throng of the waggons. The clergyman pressed me to stay and see it; – but at this time my heart had begun to turn homewards very strongly. I had come out to see Pretoria and, having seen it, was intent upon seeing London once again.

There are various other churches, – all of them small edifices, – in the place, among which there is a place of worship for the Church of England. And there is a resident English clergyman, a University man, who if he live long enough and continue to exercise his functions at Pretoria will probably become the 'clergyman of the place.' For such is the nature of Englishmen. Now that the Transvaal is an English Colony there can be no doubt but that the English clergyman will become the 'clergyman of the place.'

I would fain give as far as it may be possible an idea to any intending emigrant of what may be the cost of living in Pretoria. Houses are very dear, – if hired; cheap enough if bought. When I was there in September, 1877, the annexation being then four months old, a decent cottage might be bought for seven or eight hundred pounds, for which a rental of seven of eight pounds a month would be demanded. A good four-roomed house with kitchen &c. might be built, land included, for a thousand pounds, the rent demanded for which would be from £150 to £175 a year. Meat was about 6d. a pound, beef being cheaper and I think better than mutton. Butter, quite uneatable, was 2s. a pound. Eggs a shilling a dozen. Fowls 1s. 6d. each. Turkeys, very good, 7s. 6d. to 9s. 6d. each. Coals 10s. a half hundredweight, – and wood for fuel about £2 for a load of two and a half tons. These prices for fuel would add considerably to the cost of living were it not that fires are rarely necessary except for the purpose of cooking. Bread is quoted at 1s. a loaf of two pounds, but was I think cheaper when I was there. Potatoes were very dear indeed, the price depending altogether on the period of the year and on the season. I doubt whether other vegetables were to be bought in the market, unless it might be pumpkins. Potatoes and green vegetables the inhabitant of Pretoria should grow for himself. And he should be prepared to live without butter. Why the butter of South Africa should be almost always uneatable, culminating into an acme of filth at Pretoria, I cannot say; – but such was my experience. After all men and women can live without butter if other things be in plenty.

Then comes that difficult question of domestic service. All that the inhabitant of Pretoria will get in this respect will cost him very much less than in Europe, very much less indeed than in England, infinitely less than in London. With us at home the cost of domestic service has become out of proportion to our expenditure in other respects, partly because it has become to be thought derogatory to do anything for ourselves, and partly because our servants have been taught by their masters and mistresses to live in idle luxury. Probably no man earning his bread eats so much meat in proportion to the work he does as the ordinary London footman. This is an evil to those who live in London from which the inhabitant of Pretoria will find himself free. He will get a 'boy' or perhaps two boys about the house, – never a girl let the mistress of the family coming out to the Transvaal remember, – to whom he will pay perhaps 10s. a month and whom he will feed upon mealies. The 'boy's' wages and diet will cost perhaps £12 per annum. But indeed they will not cost him so much, for the 'boy' will go away, and he will not be able to get another just when he wants one. These boys he will find will be useful, good humoured, and trustworthy, – if only he could keep them. They will nurse his baby, cook his dinner, look after his house, make his bed, and dig his garden. That is they will half do all these things, – with the exception of nursing the baby, whom the Kafir is never known to neglect or injure. The baby perhaps may serve to keep him a whole twelvemonth, for he is very fond of a white baby. The wife of the British gentleman who thus settles himself at Pretoria will, at first, be struck with horror at the appearance of the Kafir, who will probably wear an old soldier's jacket with a ragged shirt under it and no other article of clothing; and she will not at first suffer the Savage to touch her darling. But she will soon become reconciled to her inmate and the darling will take as naturally to the Kafir man as though he were some tenderest, best instructed old English nurse out of a thoroughly well-to-do British family. And very soon she will only regret the reckless departure of the jet black dependent who had struck her at first with unmingled disgust.

Gradually I suppose these people will learn to cling to their work with some better constancy. I, as a stranger, was tempted to say that better diet, better usage, and better wages would allure them. But I was assured that I was wrong in this, and that any attempts in that direction only spoilt 'the Native'. No doubt if you teach a Native to understand that he is indispensable to your comfort you raise his own estimation of himself, and may do so in such a manner as to make him absurdly fastidious. He is still irrational, still a Savage. He has to be brought by degrees to bend his neck to the yoke of labour and to learn that continued wages are desirable. That the thing will be done by degrees I do not at all doubt, and do not think that there is just cause of dissatisfaction at the rate of the present progress. The new comer to Pretoria to whom I am addressing myself will doubtless do something towards perfecting the work. In the meantime his domestic servants will cost him very much less than they have done in England.

A man with a wife and family and £500 a year would I think live with more comfort, certainly with more plenty in Pretoria, than in England. The inhabitants of Pretoria will demur to this, for it is a matter of pride to the denizens of every place to think that the necessaries of life are dearer there than elsewhere. But the cheapness of a place is not to be reckoned only by what people pay for the articles they use. The ways of the country, the requirements which fashion makes, the pitch to which the grandeur of Mrs Smith has aroused the ambition of Mrs Jones, the propensities of a community to broadcloth or to fustian, – these are the causes of expensive or economical living. A gentleman in Pretoria may invite his friends to dinner with no greater establishment than a Kafir boy to cook the dinner and another to hand the plates, whereas he does not dare to do so in London without paying 10s. for the assistance of the greengrocer.

As, however, men with £500 a year will not emigrate in great numbers to Pretoria it would be more important to say how the labouring man might live in the Transvaal. With him his condition of life does not depend so much on what he will have to pay for what he consumes as on the wages which he may receive. I found that an artizan can generally earn from 10s. to 12s. a day at almost any trade, – if the work of the special trade be required. But I am far from saying that amidst so small a community all artizans would find an opening. At the present moment bricklayers and carpenters are in demand at Pretoria, – and can live in great plenty on their wages.

As to workmen, who are not artizans but agricultural labourers, I hardly think that there is any opening for them in the Transvaal. Though the farmers all complain that they cannot plough their lands because there is no labour, yet they will not pay for work. And though the Kafir is lazy and indifferent, yet he does work sufficiently to prevent the white man from working. As I have said before the white men will not work along with the Kafir at the same labour. If there be but a couple of black men with him he presumes that it is his business to superintend and not to work. This is so completely the case in the Transvaal that it is impossible to name any rate of wages as applicable to white rural labour. Sons work for their fathers or brothers may work together; – but wages are not paid. The Dutchman has a great dislike to paying wages.

The capital of the Transvaal is all alive with soldiers. There are 600 redcoats there, besides artillery, engineers and staff. These men live under canvas at present, and are therefore very visible. Barracks however are being built, with officers' quarters and all the appurtenances of a regular military station. It was odd enough to me to see a world of British tents in the middle of a region hazily spoken of at home six months ago as the South African Republic; but how much stranger must it be to the Dutch Boers who certainly anticipated no such advent. I had the honour of being invited to dine at the mess, and found myself as well entertained as though I had been at Aldershott. When I was sitting with the officers in their uniform around me it seemed as though a little block of England had been cut out and transported to the centre of South Africa.

It may be as well to say a few words here as elsewhere as to the state of education in our new Colony. The law on this matter as it stood under the Republic is the law still. Now, as I write, it is hardly more than six months since the annexation and there has not been time for changes. On no subject was the late President with his Cabinet more alive to the necessity of care and energy, on no subject were there more precise enactments, and on no subject were the legislative enactments, more pretentious and inefficacious. There are three classes of schools, – the High Schools, the District Schools, and the Ward Schools, the whole being under the inspection of a Superintendent General of Education. The curriculum at the High Schools is very high indeed, including Dutch, English, French, German, Latin, Greek, geometry, algebra, and all the ologies, together with logic, music, drawing, and astronomy. The law enacts that the principal master at a High School shall receive £400 a year, and the Assistant Masters £250 each; – but even at these salaries teachers sufficiently instructed could not be found, and when the Superintendent made his last return there was but one High School in the Transvaal, and at that school there were but five pupils. At the High School, the pupils paid 30s. a month, which, presuming there to be two months of holidays in the year, would give £15 per annum. There would be therefore £75 towards maintaining a school of which the Head Master received £400. But the reality of the failure was worse even than this. The law required that all boys and girls should pay the regular fees, but in order to keep up the number of pupils gratuitous instruction was offered. Three months after annexation the five High School pupils had dwindled down to two, and then the school was closed by order of the British Governor. The education no doubt was far too advanced for the public wants; and as it was given by means of the Dutch language only it did not meet the needs of those who were most likely to make use of it. For, even while the Transvaal was a Dutch Republic, the English language was contending for ascendancy with that of the people. In this contention the President with his Government did his best to make Dutch, and Dutch only, the language of the country. For this we cannot blame him. It was naturally his object to maintain the declining nationality of his country. But the parents and pupils who were likely to profit by such a school as I have described were chiefly English.

At the District and Ward schools the nature of the instruction proposed to be given is lower. The District schools are held in the chief towns, – such as they are, – and the Ward schools in sub-divisions of the Districts. They too have failed for the same reasons. They are too expensive and pretentious. The Salaries, – i.e. the lowest salaries permitted by law, – are £200 and £100 for head masters at the two classes of schools, and £125 and £30 for assistant masters. According to the last return there were 236 pupils at the District schools, and 65 at the Ward schools. The pupils pay varying fees, averaging 7s. a month or about £3 10s. per annum each. There are six District schools and two Ward schools, at which the masters' salaries alone would amount to £1,700 per annum, – presuming there to be no assistant masters, – while the total of fees would be about £1,050 per annum. As the Government had been for many months penniless, it need hardly be explained further that the schools must have been in a poor condition. The nominal cost to the State during the last years of the Republic was about £3,500, being more than £11 per year for each pupil over and above the fees. What was still due under the head had of course to be paid out of British taxes when the country was annexed.

But all this does not show the extent of the evil. The white population of the country is supposed to be 45,000, of which about a tenth or 4,500 ought to be at school. The public schools at present show 300. There are some private schools as to which I could obtain no trustworthy information; but the pupils educated at them are few in number.

The average Boer is generally satisfied in regard to education if his children can be made to read the Bible. To this must be added such a knowledge of the ritual of the religion of the Dutch Reformed Church as will enable the children to pass the

examination necessary for confirmation. Until this ceremony
has been completed they cannot marry. So much, by hook or
by crook, is attained, and thus the outermost darkness of
ignorance is avoided. But the present law as to education does
not provide for even this moderate amount of religious
instruction, and is therefore, and has been, most unpopular
with the Boers. It must be understood that on all religious
matters the late Government was at loggerheads with the bulk
of the population, the President being an advocate of free-
thinking and absolute secularism, – of an education from
which religion should be as far as possible removed; whereas
the Boer is as fanatic, as conservative, and as firmly wedded to
the creed of his fathers as an Irish Roman Catholic Coadjutor.
It may, on this account, be the easier for the Colonial
Government to reconcile the population to some change in the
law.

A few of the better class of farmers, in the difficulty which
at present exists, maintain a schoolmaster in their houses for a
year or two, paying a small salary and entertaining the
teachers at their tables. I have not met more than one such a
schoolmaster in a Boer's house. In the course of my travels I
found an Englishman in the family of a Dutchman who could
not speak a word of English, – and was astonished to find so
much instructed intelligence in such a position. Formerly there
existed a class of itinerant schoolmasters in the Transvaal, who
went from house to house carrying with them some rudiments of education, and returning now and again on their tract
to see how the seed had prospered. These were supported by
the Government of the day, but the late Government in its
ambitious desire to effect great things, discontinued this
allowance. It is not improbable that the renewal of some such
scheme may be suggested.

It will be imperative on the Colonial Government to do
something as the law now existing has certainly failed altogether. But there are great difficulties. It is not so much that
education has to be provided for the children of a people
numbering 45,000; – but that it has to be done for children
dispersed over an area as big as Great Britain and Ireland. The
families live so far apart, owing to the absurdly large size of
the farms, that it is impossible to congregate them in schools.

When I was at Pretoria I rode out with four companions to see a wonderful spot called the 'Zoutpan' or saltpan. It is 28 miles from the town and the journey required that we should take out a tent and food, and that we should sleep in the veld. I was mounted on an excellent horse who was always trying to run away with me. This tired me much, and the ground was very hard. While turning myself about upon the ground I could not but think how comfortable the beds are in London. The saltpan, however, was worth the visit. That it had been a volcanic crater there could be no doubt, but unlike all other volcanic craters that I have seen it was not an aperture on the apex of a mountain. We went north from Pretoria and crossing through the spurs of the Magaliesberg range of hills found ourselves upon a plain which after a while became studded with scrub or thorn bushes. Close to the saltpan, and still on the plain, we came to the residence of a Boer who gave us water, – the dirtiest that ever was given me to drink, – with a stable for our horses and sold us mealies for our animals. As one of our party was a doctor and as the Boer's wife was ill, his hospitality was not ill repaid. A gentle rise of about 200 feet from the house took us to the edge of the pan, which then lay about 300 feet below us, – so as to look as though the earthwork around the valley and had been merely thrown out of it as earth might be thrown from any other hole. And this no doubt had been done, – by the operation of nature.

The high outside rim of the cup was about 2¼ miles round, with a diameter of 1,500 yards; and the circle was nearly as perfect as that of a cup. Down thence to the salt lake at the bottom the inside of the bowl fell steeply but gradually, and was thickly covered with bush. The perfect regularity of shape was, to the eye, the most wonderful feature of the phenomenon. At the bottom to which we descended lay the shallow salt lake, which at the time of our visit was about half full, – or half covered, I might better say, in describing the gently shelving bottom of which not more than a moiety was under water. In very dry weather there is no water at all, – and then no salt. When full the lake is about 400 yards across.

Some enterprising Englishman had put up a large iron pan 36 feet by 20, and 18 inches deep, with a furnace under it, which, as everything had been brought out from England at a great cost for land transit, must have been an expensive operation. But it had been deserted because the late Government had been unable to protect him in the rights which he attempted to hire from them. The farmers of the neighbourhood would not allow themselves to be debarred from taking the salt, – and cared nothing for the facts that the Government claimed the privilege of disposing of the salt and that the Englishman had bought the privilege. The Englishman therefore withdrew, leaving behind him his iron pan and his furnace, no doubt with some bitter feelings.

It is probably, I believe, that another Englishman, – or a Scotchman, – will now commence proceedings there, expecting that Downing Street will give better security than a Republican President. In the meantime our friend the Boer pays £50 per annum to the Government, and charges all comers some small fine per load for what they take. Baskets are inserted into the water and are pulled up full of slush. This is deposited on the shore and allowed to drain itself. On the residuum carbonate of soda rises, with a thick layer, as solid cream on standing milk; – and below this there is the salt more or less pure, – very nasty, tasting to me as though it were putrid, – but sufficing without other operation for the curing of meat and for the use of cattle. I was told by one of our party that the friable stone which we found all around is soda-feldspar from which, as it melts in the rain, the salt is brouhgt down. Here, at this place, there is but one crater; – whereas at other places of a like nature, as in New Zealand and Central America, I have seen various mouths crowded together, like disjected fragments of a great aperture down into the earth. Here there is but the one circle, and that is as regular as though it had been the work of men's hands.

Such saltpans in South Africa are common, though I saw none other but the one which I have described. The northern district of the Transvaal is called Zoutpansberg from the number of saltpans, – and there are others in other parts of the country. I do not know that there is much else particularly worthy of notice in the neighbourhood of Pretoria, unless it be the wonderboom, – a pretty green over-arching tree, which makes for its visitors a large bower capable of holding perhaps 50 persons. It is a graceful green tree; – but not very wonderful.

CHAPTER V

THE TRANSVAAL: ITS CONDITION
AND PRODUCTS

Among the products of the Transvaal gold must be reckoned first, because gold in itself is so precious and so important a commodity, that it will ever force itself into the first rank, – and because notice was first attracted to the Transvaal in Europe, or at any rate in England, by the discovery of gold in the country and by the establishment of gold fields. But I believe that the gold which has hitherto been extracted from the auriferous deposits of the country has been far from paying the expenses incurred in finding them and bringing them into the market. Gold is a product of the earth which will be greedily sought, even when the seeker lose by his labour. I doubt even whether the Australian gold would be found to have paid for itself if an accurate calculation were made. I know that the promotors in Australian gold enterprises and the shareholders in Australian Gold Companies would attempt to cover me with ridicule for expressing such an opinion were I to discuss the matter with them. But these enterprising and occasionally successful people hardly look at the question all round. Before it can be answered with accuracy account must be taken not only of all the money lost, but of the time lost also in unsuccessful search, and of such failures the world takes no record. Be that as it may gold has done very much to make the fortune of the Australian Colonies. This has not been done by the wealth of the gold-finders. It is only now and then, – and I may say that the nows and thens are rare, – that we find a gold-seeker who has retired into a settled condition of wealth as a result of his labours among the Gold Fields. But great towns have sprung up, and tradesmen have become wealthy, and communities have grown into compact forms, by the expenditure which

63

the gold-seekers have created. Melbourne is a great city and
Ballarat is a great city, not because the Victorian gold-diggers
have been rich and successful; – but because the trade of
gold-finding creates a great outlay. If the gold-diggers themselves have not been rich they have enriched the bankers and
the wine-merchants and the grocers and the butchers and the
innkeepers who have waited upon them. While one gold-
digger starves or lives upon his little capital, another drinks
champagne. Even the first contributes something to the
building up of a country, but the champagne-drinker contributes a great deal. There is no better consumer to the
tradesman, no more potent consumer, than the man who is
finding gold from day to day. Gold becomes common to him,
and silver contemptible.

I say this for the purpose of showing that though the gold
trade of the Transvaal has not as yet been remunerative, –
though it may perhaps never be truly remunerative to the
gold-seekers, – it may nevertheless help to bring a population
to the country which will build it up, and make it prosperous.
It will do so in the teeth of the despair and ruin which
unsuccessful speculations create. There is a charm and a power
about gold which is so seductive and inebriating that judgement and calculation are ignored by its votaries. If there be
gold in a country men will seek it though it has been sought
there for years with disastrous effects. It creates a sanguine
confidence which teaches the gold-dreamer to believe that he
will succeed where hundreds have failed. It despises climate,
and reconciles the harshness of manual labour to those who
have been soft of hand and luxurious of habit. I am not now
intending to warn the covetous against the Gold Fields of
South Africa; – but am simply expressing an opinion that
though these gold regions have hitherto created no wealth,
though henceforth they should not be the source of fortune to
the speculators, they will certainly serve to bring white
inhabitants into the country.

Gold as a modern discovery in South Africa was first found
at Tatin in 1867. That there had been gold up north, near the
Eastern coast, within the tropics, there can be little doubt.
There are those who are perfectly satisfied that Ophir was here
situated and that the Queen of Sheba came to Solomon's court

from these realms. As I once wrote a chapter to prove that the Queen of Sheba reigned in the Isle of Ceylon and the Ophir was Point de Galle, I will not now go into that subject. It has no special interest for the Transvaal which as a gold country must sink or swim by its own resources. But Tatin though not within the Transvaal, is only just without it, being to the north of the Limpopo river which is the boundary of our Colony in that direction.

The Limpopo is an unfortunate river as much of its valley with a considerable district on each side of it is subjected by nature to an abominable curse, – which population and cultivation will in the course of years probably remove but which at present is almost fatal to European efforts at work within the region affected. There is a fly, – called the Tsetse fly, – which destroys all horses and cattle which come within the regions which it selects for its own purposes. Why it should be destructive to a party of horses or to a team of oxen and not to men has I believe to be yet found out. But as men cannot carry themselves and their tools into these districts without horses or oxen, the evil is almost overpowering. The courses of the fly are so well known as to have enabled geographers to mark out on the maps the limits of the Tsetse country. The valley of the Limpopo river may be taken as giving a general idea of the district so afflicted, the distance of the fly-invested region varying from half a dozen to 60 and 80 miles from the river. But towards the East it runs down across the Portuguese possessions never quite touching the sea but just reaching Zululand.

Tatin is to the north west of this region, and though the place itself is not within the fly boundary, all ingress and egress must have been much impeded by the nuisance. The first discovery there of gold is said to have been made by Mauch. There has been heavy work carried on in the district and a quartz-crushing machine was used there. When I was in the Transvaal these works had been abandoned, but of the existence of gold in the country around there can be no doubt. In 1868 the same explorer, Mauch, found gold at a spot considerably to the south east of this, – south of the Limpopo and the Tsetse district, just north of the Olifant's river and in the Transvaal. Then in 1871 Mr Button found gold at Marabas

Stad, not far to the west of Mauch's discovery, in the neighbourhood of which the mines at Eesteling are now being
worked by an English Company. On the Marabas-Stad gold
fields a printed report was made by Captain Elton in 1872, and a
considerable sum of money must have been spent. The Eesteling reef is the only one at present worked in the neighbourhood. Captain Elton's report seems to promise much on the
condition that a sufficient sum of money be raised to enable the
district to be thoroughly 'prospected' by an able body of fifty
gold-miners for a period of six months. Captain Elton no doubt
understood his subject, but the adequate means for the search
suggested by him have not yet been raised. And, indeed, it is
not thus that gold fields have been opened. The chances of
success are too small for men in cold blood to subscribe money
at a distance. The work has to be done by the gambling energy
of men who rush to the spot trusting that they may individually
grasp the gold, fill their pockets with the gold, and thus have in
a few months, perhaps in a few days or hours, a superabun-
dance of that which they have ever been desiring but which has
always been so hard to get! The great Australian and Califor-
nian enterprises have always been commenced by rushes of
individual miners to some favoured spot, and not by companies
floated by subscription. The companies have come afterwards,
but individual enterprise has done the pioneering work.

In 1873 gold was found in the Lydenburg district which is
south of the Olifant's river. Here are the diggings called
Pilgrim's Rest, and here the search for gold is still carried on, –
not as I am told with altogether favourable results. One nugget
has been found weighing nearly 18 pounds. Had there been a
few more such treasures brought to light the Lydenburg gold
fields would have been famous. There are two crushing
machines now at work, and skilled European miners are
earning from 10s. to 12s. a day. The place is healthy, and though
tropical is not within the tropics. A considerable number of
Kafirs are employed at low rates of wages, but they have not as
yet obtained a reputation as good miners. The white employer
of black labour in South Africa does not allow that the Kafir
does anything well.

Among other difficulties and drawbacks to gold mining in
South Africa the want of fuel or steam is one. Wood of course is

used, but I am told that wood is already becoming scarce and dear. And then the great distance from the coast, the badness of the roads, and the lack of the means of carriage exaggerates all the other difficulties. Machinery, provisions, and the very men themselves have to be brought into the country at a cost which very materially interfered with the chances of a final satisfactory result. If there be a railway from Pretoria to Delagoa Bay, – as at some not very remote date there probably will be, – then that railway will pass either through or very near to the Lydenburg district, and in that case the Lydenburg gold fields will become all alive with mining life.

Attempts are always made to show what gold fields have done in the way of produce by Government records of the gold exported. In the second great exhibition of London we saw an enormous yellow pyramid near the door, and were told that the gold taken out of Victoria would if collected make a pyramid of just that size. To enable the makers of the pyramid to arrive at that result it was necessary that they should know how much gold had been taken from Victoria. I presume that the records of the Colony did tell of so much, – but if so the gold found must have been considerably more. For gold is portable and can be carried away in a man's pocket without any record. And as that which was recorded was taxed, it is probable that very much was taken away, untaxed, in some private fashion. As to the Transvaal gold a record of that supposed to be exported has been kept at the Custom House in Natal, which shows but very poor results. It is as follows: –

1873	735
1874	4,710
1875	28,443
1876 (first six months)	13,650
	£47,538

This sum can have done but little more than paid for the necessary transport of the machinery and other matters which have been carried up from the coast. It certainly cannot also have paid for the machinery itself. The bulk of the gold found

has, however, been probably carried down to the coast at Fort
Elizabeth or Capetown without any record.

Such is all that I have to say respecting the Gold Fields of the
Transvaal, – and it is very little. I did not visit them, and had I
done so I do not know that I could have said much more. I
conscientiously inspected many Gold mines in Australia,
going down into the bowels of the earth 500 feet here and 600
feet there at much personal inconvenience, and some danger to
one altogether unused to mining operations; but I do not
know that I did any good by this exercise of valour and
conscience. A man should be a mineralogist to be able to take
advantage of such inspections. Had I visited Pilgrim Rest, I
could have said how the men looked who were there working,
and might have attempted to guess whether they were contented with their lot; – but I could have said nothing as to the
success of the place with more accuracy than I do now.

The Transvaal is said, and I believe correctly, to be very rich
in other minerals besides gold; – but the travellers in new
countries are always startled by sanguine descriptions of
wealth which is not in view. Lead and cobalt are certainly
being worked. Coal is found in beds all along the eastern
boundary of the country, and will probably some day be the
most valuable product of the country. Did I not myself see it
burning at Stander's Drift? Iron is said to be plentiful in almost
every district of the Colony and has been long used by the
natives in making weapons and ornaments. Copper also has
been worked by the natives and is now found in old pits,
where it has been dug to the depth of from 30 to 40 feet. A
variety of copper ornaments are worn by the Kafirs of the
northern parts of the Transvaal who have known how to
extract the metal from the mineral and to smelt it into pure
ore. No mining operations in search of copper have, as I
believe, yet been carried on by white men in the country. At
an Agricultural Show which was held in 1876 at Potchefstroom, the chief town in the southern part of the Transvaal,
prizes were awarded for specimens of the following minerals
found in the country itself. Gold–bearing quartz, alluvial gold,
copper, tin, lead, iron, plumbago, cobalt, and coal. The
following is an extract from a report of the Show, which I
borrow from Messrs. Silver's South African Guide Book. 'We

believe there is no other country in the whole world that could have presented to the public gaze such a variety of minerals as were seen in the room set apart for their exhibition and which upon first entering reminded one of a charming museum; and all these minerals and earthy substances, we are informed, were the products of this country. We saw gold both quartz and alluvial, – not in small quantities but pounds in weight; coal by the ton, – silver, iron, lead. We do not know what to say about this last mineral; but there it was, not in small lumps, as previously exhibited, but immense quantities of ore, and molten bars by the hundred.'

This is somewhat flowery, but I believe the statements to be substantially true. The metals are all there, but I do not know whether any of them have yet been so worked as to pay for expenses and to give a profit. All the good things in the Transvaal seem to be so hard to come at, that it is like looking and longing for grapes, hanging high above our reach. But when grapes are really good and plentiful, ladders are at last procured, and so it will be with the grapes of the Transvaal.

The ladder which is especially wanted is of course a Railway. President Burgers among his other high schemes was fully aware of this and made a journey to Europe during the days of his power with the view of raising funds for this purpose. Like all his schemes it was unsuccessful, but he did raise in Holland a sum of £90,958 for this purpose, which has been expended on railway materials, or perhaps tendered to the Republic in that shape. These are now lying at Delagoa Bay, and the sum above named is part of the responsibility which England has assumed in annexing the Republic.

The question of a Railway is of all the most vital to the new Colony. The Transvaal has no seaboard, and no navigable rivers, and no available outlet for its produce. Pretoria is about 450 miles from Durban, which at present is the seaport it uses, and the road to Durban is but half made and unbridged. The traffic is by oxen, and oxen cannot travel in dry weather because there is no grass for them to eat. They often cannot travel in wet weather because the rivers are unpassable and the mud is overwhelming. If any country ever wanted a Railway it is the Transvaal.

But whence shall the money come? Pretoria is about 300 miles distant from the excellent Portuguese harbour at Delagoa Bay, and it was to this outlet that President Burgers looked. But an undertaking to construct a railway through an unsurveyed country at the rate of £1,000 a mile was manifestly a castle in the air. If the absolute money could have been obtained, hard cash in hand, the thing could not have been half done. But President Burgers was one of those men who believe that if you can only set an enterprise well on foot the gods themselves will look after its accomplishment, – that if you can expend money on an object other money will come to look after that which has been expended. But here, in the Transvaal, he could not get his enterprise on foot; and I fear that certain railway materials lying at Delagoa Bay, and more or less suited for the purpose, are all that England has to show for the debt she has taken upon her shoulders.

I am not very anxious to offer an opinion as to the best route for a railway out from the Transvaal to the sea. Ne sutor ultra crepidam; – and the proper answering of such a question is, I fear, beyond the reach of my skill. But the reasons I have heard for the Delagoa Bay seem to me to be strong, – and those against it to be weak. The harbour at the Bay is very good, – perhaps the only thoroughly good harbour in South Africa, whereas that at Durban is at present very bad. Expensive operations may improve it, but little or nothing has as yet been done to lessen the inconvenience occasioned by its sand-bar. Durban is 450 miles from the capital of the Transvaal, whereas Delagoa Bay is only two-thirds of that distance. The land falls gradually from Pretoria to the Bay, whereas in going to Durban the line would twice have to be raised to high levels. And then the route to the Bay would run by the Gold Fields, whereas the other line would go through a district less likely to be productive of traffic. It is alleged on the other hand that as Delagoa Bay belongs to the Portuguese, and as the Portuguese will probably be unwilling to part with the possession, the making of a railway into their territory would be inexpedient. I cannot see that there is anything in this argument. The Americans of the United States made a railway across the Isthmus of Panama with excellent financial results, and in Europe each railway enterprise has not been stopped by the bounds of the country which it has occupied. The Portuguese have offered to take some share in the construction, and by doing so would lessen the effort which the Colony will be obliged to make. It is also alleged that Lorenço Marques, the Portuguese town at Delagoa Bay, is very unhealthy. I believe that it is so. Tropical towns on the sea board are apt to be unhealthy, and Lorenço Marques though not within the tropics is tropical. But so is Aspenwall, the terminus of the Panama Railway, unhealthy, being peculiarly subject to the Chagres fever. But in the pursuit of wealth men will endure bad climate. That at Delagoa Bay is by no means so bad as to frighten passengers, though it will probably be injurious to the construction of the railway. To the ordinary traffic of a constructed railway it will hardly be injurious at all.

If the Natal Colony would join the Transvaal in the cost, making the railways up to its own boundary, then the Natal line would no doubt be the best. The people of the Transvaal would compensate themselves for the bad harbour at Durban by the lessening of their own expenditure, and the line as a whole would be better for British interests in general than that to the Portuguese coast. But there is but little probability of this. Natal wants a line from its capital to its coast, and will have such a line almost by the time that these words are published. But it cares comparatively little for a line through 175 miles of its country up to its boundary at Newcastle, over which the traffic would be for the benefit of the Transvaal rather than for that of Natal. Estcourt and Newçastle which are in Natal would no doubt be pleased, but Natal will not spend its money for the sake of Estcourt and Newcastle.

But when the route for the railway shall have been decided, whence shall the money come? No one looking at the position of the country will be slow to say that a railway is so necessary for the purposes of the Colony that it must expend its first and its greatest energies in achieving that object. It is as would be the possession of a corkscrew to a man having a bottle of wine in the desert. There is no getting at the imprisoned treasure without it. The farms will not be cultivated, the mines will not be worked, the towns will not be built, the people will not come without it. President Burgers, prone as he was to build castles in the air, saw at any rate, when he planned the railway, where the foundations should be laid for a true and serviceable edifice. But then we must return to the question, – whence shall the money come?

Well-to-do Colonists find no difficulty in borrowing money for their own purposes at a moderate rate of interest, – say 4 per cent. Victoria and New South Wales have made their railways most successfully, and New Zealand has shown what a Colony can do in borrowing. But the Transvaal is not as yet a well-to-do Colony, and certainly could not go into the money market with any hope of success with the mere offer of her own security, – such as that security is at this moment. This is so manifestly the case that no one proposes to do so. Mr. Burgers went home for the purpose and succeeded only in getting a quantity of material, – for which, in the end, the British Government will have to pay probably more than twice the value.

I think I am justified in saying that the idea among those who are now managing the Colony is to induce the Government at home to guarantee a loan, – which means that the Transvaal should be enabled to borrow on the best security that the world has yet produced, that namely of the British nation. And perhaps there is something to warrant this expectation on their part. The annexation, distasteful as the idea is at home of a measure so high-handed and so apparently unwarrantable, has been well received. It has been approved by our Secretary of State, who is himself approved of in what he has caused to done by Parliament and the nation. The Secretary of State must feel a tenderness for the Transvaal, as we all do for any belonging of our own which has turned out better than we expected. The annexation has turned out so well that they who are now concerned with its affairs seem to expect that the British Government and the British Parliament will assent to the giving of such security. It may be that they are right. Writing when and where I am now I have no means of knowing how far the need for such a loan and the undoubted utility of such a railway may induce those who have the power in their hands to depart from what I believe to be now the established usage of the mother country in regard to its Colonies, – viz., that of sanctioning loans only when they can be floated on the security of the Colony itself.

If I may venture to express an opinion on the subject, I think that that usage should be followed in this case. No doubt the making of the railway would be postponed in this way, – or rather would be accelerated if the British name and British credit were to be pawned for Transvaal purpose; but I doubt the justice of risking British money in such a cause. The Transvaal colonist in making such an application would in fact be asking for the use of capital at British rates of interest with the object of making colonial profits. The risk would attach wholly to the mother country. The profits, if profits should come, would belong wholly to the Colony.

Money, too, with nations and with colonies is valued and used on the same principles as with individuals. When it has been easily got, without personal labour, proffered lightly without requirement of responsibility or demand for security, it is spent as easily and too often is used foolishly. Lend a man money on security and he will know that every shilling that he spends must come at last out of his own pocket. If money for the purpose required were at once thrown into the Transvaal, – as might be the case tomorrow if the British Government were to secure the loan, – there would immediately arise a feeling that wealth was being scattered about broadcast, and that a halcyon time had come in which parsimony and prudence were no longer needed. The thing would have been too easy, – and easy things are seldom useful and are never valued.

At the present moment Great Britain is paying the Transvaal bill. The marching to and fro of the soldiers, the salaries of the Governors and other officials, the debts of the late Government, the interests on loans already made, the sums necessary for the gradual redemption of loans, I fear even a pension for the late President, are provided or are to be provided out of British taxes. The country was annexed on 12th April. On 8th June a letter was written from the Colonial Office to the Treasury, showing that we had annexed an existing debt of £217,158 for which we were responsible, and that we had expended £25,000 in marching troops up to the Transvaal for the sake of giving safety to the inhabitants and their property. The report then goes on to its natural purpose. 'Lord Carnarvon is of opinion that it may be possible to meet

the more immediate requirements of the moment if their
Lordships will make an advance of £100,000 in aid of the
revenues of the Transvaal, *to be repaid as soon as practicable*.
Unless aid is given at once the new province would be obliged
to endeavour to borrow at a ruinously high rate of interest.' I
doubt whether the idea of repayment has taken so strong a
hold on the people in the Transvaal, as it has of the officials in
Downing Street. In a former paragraph of the report the
Secretary of State thus excuses himself for making the application. 'It is with great unwillingness that Lord Carnarvon
feels himself compelled to have recourse to the assistance of
the Imperial Treasury in this matter, but he is satisfied that the
Lord Commissioners of Her Majesty's Treasury will readily
acknowledge that in this most difficult case he has had no
alternative. The annexation of the Transvaal with all its
consequent liabilities, political as well as financial, *has been
neither coveted nor sought by him*;' – the italics here and above are
my own; – 'and it is only a sincere conviction that this step was
necessary in order to prevent most serious danger to Her
Majesty's Colonies in South Africa which has persuaded him
to approve the late action of Sir. T. Shepstone.'

The £100,000 was advanced, if not without a scruple at least
without a doubt, whatever might be the expectations of the
Treasury as to speedy repayment; and there can be little doubt,
I fear, that further advances will be needed and made before
the resources of the country in the shape of collected taxes will
suffice to pay the expenses of the country, including the
gradual redemption of the Dutch loans. But if the country
cannot do this soon the annexation will certainly have been a
failure. Great as is the parliamentary strength of the present
Ministry, Parliament would hardly endure the idea of paying
permanently for the stability and security of a Dutch population out of the British pocket. I do believe myself that the
country will be able to pay its way in the course of some years;
– but I do not believe that the influx of a large loan on easy
terms, the expenditure of which must go to a great measure be
entrusted to the Colony, would hasten the coming of this
desirable condition. There would be a feeling engendered, – if
that can be said to be engendered which to some extent already
exists, – that 'nunky pays for all.' Neither for Colony nor for

Mother Country can it be well that nunky should either pay or be supposed to pay through the nose.

When it shall once be known that the Transvaal is paying its own bill, governing itself and protecting itself out of its own revenues, then the raising of a sufficient loan for its railway on its own security will not be difficult. It may even then, – when that day comes, – have to pay a percentage something higher than it would have to give under a British guarantee; but the money will be its own, brought into use on its own security, and will then be treated with respect and used with care. The Transvaal no doubt wants a railway sorely, but it has no right to expect that a railway shall be raised for it, as by a magician's wand. Like other people, and other countries the Transvaal should struggle hard to get what it wants, and if it struggles honestly no doubt will have its railway and will enjoy it when it has it.

'The Transvaal may in truth be called the "corn chamber" of South Eastern Africa, for no other Colony or State in this part of the world produces wheat of such superior quality or offers so many and varied advantages to farming pursuits.' This is extracted from Mr. Jeppe's excellent Transvaal Directory. The words are again somewhat flowery, as is always the nature of national self-praise expressed in national literature. But the capability of the Transvaal for producing wheat is undoubted; as are also the facts that it has for years past fed itself, – with casual exceptions which amount to nothing, – and that it has done something towards feeding the great influx of population which has been made into the Diamond Fields. It has also continually sent a certain amount of flour and corn into Natal over its northern and western borders for the use of those wandering Europeans, who are seeking their fortunes among the distant tribes of South Africa. In esti- mating the wheat produce of the country these are I know but idle words. A great deal of wheat, – when the words are written and printed, – means nothing. It is like saying that a horse is a very good horse when the owner desires to sell him. The vendor should produce his statistics as to the horse in the shape of the opinion from a veterinary surgeon. If Mr Jeppe had given statistics as to the wheat-produce of the Transvaal during the last few years it would have been better. Statistics are generally believed and always look like evidence. But unless Mr Jeppe had created them himself, he could not produce them, – for there are none. I think I may say that a very large portion of the country, – all of it indeed which does not come under tropical influences, with the exception of regions which are mountainous or stoney, – is certainly capable of bearing wheat; but I have no means whatever of telling the reader what wheat is already produced.

It is certain, however, that the cereal produce of the country is curtailed by most pernicious circumstances against which the very best of governments though joined by the very best of climates can only operate slowly. One of these circumstances is the enormous size of the existing farms. The great colonial quidnunc and speculator in colonial matters, Gibbon Wakefield, enunciated one great truth when he declared that all land in new countries should be sold to the new comers at a price. By this he meant that let the price be what it might land should not be given away, but should be parted with in such a manner as to induce in the mind of the incoming proprietor a feeling that he had paid for it its proper price, and that he should value the land accordingly. The thing given is never valued as is the thing bought, – as is the thing for which hard-earned money has been handed over, money which is surrendered with a pang, and which leaves behind a lasting remorse unless he who has parted with it can make himself believe that he has at least got for it its full worth. Now the land in the Transvaal generally has never been sold, – and yet it has almost entirely become the property of private occupiers. The Dutchmen who came into the country brought with them ideas and usages as to the distribution of land from the Cape Colony, and following their ideas and usages they divided the soil among themselves adjudging so much to every claimant who came forward as a certified burgher. The amount determined on as comprising a sufficient farm for such an individual was 3,000 morgen, – which is something more than 6,000 acres. The Dutchman in South Africa has ever been greedy of land, feeling himsself to be cribbed, cabined, and confined if a neighbour be near to him. It was in great measure because land was not in sufficient plenty for him that he 'trekked' away from the Cape Colony. Even there

3,000 'morgen' of land had been his idea of a farm, – which farm was to satisfy his pastoral as well as his much smaller agricultural needs. When at last he found his way into the Transvaal and became a free Republican, his first ambition was for land to fulfil the lust of his heart. The country therefore was divided into 6,000-acre farms, – many of which however contained much more than that number of acres, – and in many cases more than one farm fell into the hands of one Dutchman. The consequences are that there is not room for fresh comers and that nevertheless the land is not a quarter occupied.

Nor is this the only or perhaps the greatest evil of the system which I have attempted to describe. The Boer has become solitary, self-dependent, some would say half savage in his habits. The self-dependent man is almost as injurious to the world at large as the idle man. The good and useful citizen is he who works for his own comfort of others and requires the work of others for his own comfort. The Boer feels a pride in his acres, though his acres may do nothing for him. He desires no neighbours though neighbours would buy his produce. He declares he cannot plough his fields because he cannot get labour, but he will allow no Kafirs to make their kraals on his land. Therefore he wraps himself up in himself, eats his billetong, – strips of meat dried in the sun, – and his own flour, and feels himself to be an aristocrat because he is independent.

If the farms in the Transvaal could be at once divided, and a moiety from each owner taken away without compensation, not only would the country itself be soon improved by such an arrangement, but the farmers also themselves from whom the land had been taken. Their titles, however, are good, and they are lords of the soil beyond the power of any such arbitrary legislation. But all the influences of government should be used to favour subdivision. Subdivisions no doubt are made from day to day. As I went through the country I heard of this man having half a 'plaats' and that man a quarter. These diminished holdings had probably arisen from family arrangements, possibly from sales. Farms frequently are sold, – freehold lands passing from hand to hand at prices varying from 1s. an acre upwards. Land therefore is very vile, – what I would call cheap if it were to be found in the market when wanted and in the quantities wanted. In our Australian Colonies land is not as a rule sold under 20s. an acre; but it is being sold daily, because men of small means can always purchase small areas from the Government, and because the Governments afford easy terms. But the land in the Transvaal is locked up and unused, – and not open to new comers. Therefore it is that the produce is small, that the roads are desolate, and that the country to the eye of the traveller appears like a neglected wilderness.

What may be the remedy for this I am not prepared to say after the sojourn of but a few weeks in the country; but it is probable that a remedy may be found by making the transfer of land easy and profitable to the Boers.

As this land will produce wheat, so will it also other cereals – such as barley, oats, and Indian corn. Hay, such as we use at home, is unknown. The food given to stabled cattle is Indian corn or forage, such as I have before mentioned, – that is young corn, wheat, oats, or barley, cut before fully grown and dried. This is considered to be the best food for horses all through South Africa.

The fruits of the country are very plentiful; – oranges, lemons, figs, grapes, peaches, apricots, apples, pears, and many others. The climate is more tropical than ours, so as to give the oranges and lemons, but not so much so at to exclude pears and apples.

No doubt it may, – as far as its nature is concerned, – become a land flowing with milk and honey, if the evil effects of remoteness and of a bad beginning can be removed.

CHAPTER VI

THE TRANSVAAL – PRETORIA TO THE DIAMOND FIELDS

On the 1st of October I and my friend started from Pretoria for the Diamond Fields, having spent a pleasant week at the capital of the Transvaal. There was, however, one regret. I had not seen Sir Theophilus Shepstone though I had been entertained at his house. He, during the time, had been absent on one of those pilgrimages which Colonial Governors make through their domains, and would be absent so long that I could not afford the time to wait his return. I should much have liked to discuss with him the question of the annexation, and to have heard from his own lips, as I had heard from those of Mr Burgers, a description of what had passed at the interviews between them. I should have been glad, also, to have learned from himself what he had thought of the danger to which the Dutch community had been subject from the Kafirs and Zulus, – from Secocoeni and Cetywayo, – at the moment of his coming. But the tale which was not told to me by him was, I think, told with accuracy by some of those who were with him. I have spoken my opinion very plainly, and I hope not too confidently of the affair, and I will only add to that now an assurance of my conviction that had I been in Sir Theophilus Shepstone's place and done as he did, I should have been proud of the way I had served my country.

We started in our cart with our horses as we thought in grand condition. While at Pretoria we had been congratulated on the way in which we had made our purchases and travelled the road surmounting South African difficulties as though we had been at the work all our lives. We had refilled our comissariat chest, and with the exception that my companion had shied a bottle of brandy, – joint property, – at the head of a dog that would bite him, – not me, – as we were packing the

cart, there had been as yet no misfortune. Our Cape-boy
driver had not once been drunk and nothing material had been
lost or broken. We got off at 11 A.M.; and at half past one P.M.,
– having travelled about fifteen miles in the normal two and
half hours, – we spanned out and shared our lunch with a very
hungry-looking Dutchman who squatted himself on his
haunches close to our little fire. He was herding cattle and
seemed to be very poor and hungry. I imagined him to be
some unfortunate who was working for low wages at a
distance from his home. But I found him to be the lord of the
soil, the owner of the herd, and the possessor of a homestead
about a mile distant. I have no doubt that he would have given
me what he had to give if I had called at his house. As it was he
seemed to be delighted with fried bacon and biscuits, and was
aroused almost to enthusiasm over a little drop of brandy and
water.

On our road during this day we stopped at an accomodation
house, as it is called in the country, – or small Inn, kept by an
Englishman. Here before the door I saw flying a flag intended
to represent the colours of the Transvaal Dutch Republic. The
Englishman, who was rather drunk and very civil, apologized
for this by explaining that he had his own patriotic feelings,
but that as it was his lot in life to live by the Boers it was
necessary that he should please the Boers. This was, however,
the only flag of the Republic which I saw during my journey
through the country, and I am inclined to think that our
countryman had mistaken the signs of the time. I have
however to acknowledge in his favour that he offered to make
us a present of some fresh butter.

We passed that night at the house of a Boer, who was
represented to me as being a man of wealth and repute in the
country and as being peculiarly averse to English rule, – Dutch
and republican to his heart's core. And I was told soon after by
a party who had travelled over the same road, among whom
there were two Dutchmen, that he had been very uncourteous
to them. No man could have been more gracious than he was
to us, who had come in as strangers upon his hospitality, with
all our wants for ourselves our servants and our horses. I am
bound to say that his house was very dirty, and the bed of a
nature to make the flesh creep, and to force a British occupant

of the chamber to wrap himself round with further guards of his own in the shape of rugs and great coats, rather than divest himself of clothes before he would lay himself down. And the copious mess of meat which was prepared for the family supper was not appetising. But nothing could be more grandly courteous than the old man's manner, or kinder than that that of his wife. With this there was perhaps something of an air of rank, – just a touch of consciousness of superiority, – as there might be with some old Earl at home who in the midst of his pleasant amenities could not quite forget his ancestors. Our host could not speak a word of English, – nor we of Dutch; but an Englishman was in the house, – one of the schoolmasters of whom I have before spoken, – and thus we were able to converse. Not a word was said about the annexation; – but much as to the farming prospects of the country. He had grown rich and was content with the condition of the land.

He was heartily abused to us afterwards by the party which contained the two Dutchmen as being a Boer by name and a boor by nature, as being a Boer all round and down to the ground. These were not Hollanders from Holland, but Dutchmen lately imported from the Cape Colony; – and as such were infinitely more antagonistic to the real Boer than would be any Englishman out from Europe. To them he was a dirty, ignorant, and arrogant Savage. To him they were presumptuous, new-fangled, vulgar upstarts. They were men of culture and of sense and of high standing in the new country, – but between them and him there were no sympathies.

I think that the English who have now taken the Transvaal will be able, after a while, to rule the Boers and to extort from them that respect without which there can be no comfort between the governors and the governed; – but the work must be done by English and not by Dutch hands. The Dutch Boer will not endure over him either a reforming Hollander from Europe, or a spick-and-span Dutch Africander from the Cape Colony. The reforming Hollander and the spick-and-span Dutch Africander are very intelligent people. It is not to be supposed that I am denying them any good qualities which are to be found in Englishmen. But the Boer does not love them.

Soon after starting from our aristocratic friend's house one of our horses fell sick. He was the one that kicked, – a bright bay little pony, – and in spite of his kicking had been the favourite of the team. We dined that day about noon at a Boer's house, and there we did all that we knew to relieve the poor brute. We gave him chlorodyne and alum, – in accordance with advice which had been given to us for our behoof along the road, – and when we started we hitched him on behind, and went the last stage for that day with a unicorn team. Then we gave him whisky, but it was of no use. That night he could not feed, and early the next morning he laid himself down when he was brought out of the stable and died at my feet. It was our first great misfortune. Our other three horses were not the better or the brighter for all the work they had done, and would certainly not be able to do what would be required of them without a fourth companion.

The place we were now at is called Wonder Fontein, and is remarkable, not specially for any delightfully springing run of water, but for a huge cave, which is supposed to go some miles underground. We went to visit it just as sunset, and being afraid of returning in the dark, had not time to see all of it that is known. But we climbed down into the hole, and lit our candles and wandered about for a time. Here and there, in every direction, there were branches and passages running under ground which had hitherto never been explored. The son of the Boer who owned the farm at which we were staying, was with us, and could guide us through certain ways; – but other streets of the place were unknown to him, and, as he assured us, had never yet been visited by man. The place was full of bats, but other animals we saw none. In getting down, the path was narrow, steep, low and disagreeable enough; – but when once we were in the cave we could walk without stooping. At certain periods when the rains had been heavy the caves would become full of water, – and then they would drain themselves when the rains had ceased. It was a hideously ugly place; and most uninteresting were it not that anything not customary interests us to some extent. The caves were very unlike those in the Cango district, which I described in the first volume.

At Wonder Fontein there were six or seven guests besides the very large family with which the Boer and his wife were blessed, and we could not therefore have bedrooms apiece; – nor even beds. I and my young friend had one assigned to us, while the Attorney General of the Colony, who was on circuit and to whom we had given a lift in our cart to relieve him for a couple days of the tedium of travelling with the Judge and the Sheriff by ox wagon, had a bench assigned to him in a corner of the room. In such circumstances a man lies down, but does not go to bed. We lay down, – and got up at break of day, to see our poor little horse die.

On leaving these farm houses the Boers, if asked, will make a charge for the accomodation afforded, generally demanding about 5s. for the supper, a night's rest, and breakfast if the traveller chooses to wait for it. Others, English and Germans, will take nothing for their hospitality. Both the one and the other expect to be paid for what the horses may consume; and we thought we observed that forage with the English and Germans was dearer than with the Boers, – so that the cost came to much the same with the one as with the other. At the English houses, – or German, – it was possible to go to bed. In a Boer's establishment we did not venture to do more than lie down.

Starting on the following day with our three horses we reached Potchefstroom, which, though not the capital, is the largest town in the Transvaal. The road all along had been of the same nature, and the country nearly of the same kind as that we had seen before reaching Pretoria. Here and there it was stony – but for the most part capable of cultivation. None of it, however, was cultivated with the exception of small patches round the farm houses. These would be at any rate ten miles distant one from each other, and probably more. The roads are altogether unmade, and the 'spruits' or streams are unbridged. But the traffic, though unfrequent, had been sufficient to mark the way and to keep it free from grass. Travelling in wet weather must often be impossible, – and in windy weather very disagreeable. We were most fortunate in avoiding both mud and dust, either of which, to the extent in which they sometimes prevail in the Transvaal, might have made our journey altogether impossible.

At Potchefstroom we found a decent hotel kept by an Englishman, – at which we could go to bed, though not indulged with the luxury of a room for each of us. The assizes were going on and we found ourselves to be lucky in not being forced to have a third with us. Here our first care was to buy a horse so as once again to complete our team. We felt that if we loudly proclaimed our want, the price of horses in Potchefstroom would be raised at once; – and yet it was difficult to take any step without proclaiming our want. We had only one day to stay in the town, and could not therefore dally with the difficulty as is generally the proper thing to do when horse-flesh is concerned. So we whispered our need into the landlord's ear and he undertook to stand our friend, – acknowledging, however, that a horse in a hurry was of all things the most difficult to be had at Potchefstroom. Nevertheless within two hours of our arrival an entire team of four horses was standing in the hotel yard, from which we were to be allowed to choose one for £30. I had refused to have anything to do with the buying in regard to terms; but consented to select the one which should be bought, if we could agree as to price. When I went forth to make the choice I found that in spite of our secrecy a congregation of horse-fanciers had come to see what was being done. Four leaner, poorer, skinnier brutes I never saw standing together with halters round their necks; – but of the four I did pick one, guided by the bigness of his leg bones and by the freedom of his pace. Everybody was against me, – our driver preferring a younger horse, and the vendor assuring me that in passing over an old grey animal I was altogether cutting my own throat. But I was firm, and then left the conclave, desiring my young friend to go into the money question.

The seller at first seemed to think that the price was a thing settled. Had he not told the landlord that we might select one for £30; – and had not the selection been made? He assumed a look of injured innocence as though the astute Briton were endeavouring to get the better of the poor Dutchman most dishonourably. Eventually, however, he consented to accept £23, and the money was paid. Then came the criticism of the bystanders thick and hard upon us. £23 for that brute! Was it true that we had given the man £23 for an animal worth at the most £7 10s.? They had allowed the seller to have his luck while the sale was going on, but could not smother their envy when the money was absolutely in his pocket. However we had our horse, whose capabilities were much better than his appearance, and who stood to us gallantly in some after difficulties in which his co-operation was much needed.

Potchefstroom may probably contain something over 2,000 white inhabitants. In saying this, however, I have nothing but guess work to guide me. It is a town covering a very large area, with streets nearly a mile in length; – but here again is a great deficiency of houses. In some of those streets a wanderer might fancy himself to be roaming through some remote green lane in England, overshadowed through its whole length by weeping willows. The road way under his feet will be exactly that of a green lane; – here a rut, and there a meandering path worn by children's feet, and grass around him everywhere. Now and again he will come across a cottage, – hardly more than a cabin, – with half a dozen dirty children at the door. Such are the back streets at Potchefstroom. And here too, as at Pretoria, there are hedges of roses, long rows of crowded rose-bushes round the little houses of the better class. There are spots so picturesque as almost to make the wanderer fancy that it would be pleasant to live in a place so pretty, so retired, and so quiet. But weeping willows and rose hedges would, I fear, after a time become insufficient, and the wanderer who had chosen to sojourn here under the influence of these attractions, might wish himself back in some busier centre of the world's business.

Here also there is a great square in the centre of the town, with the Dutch church in the midst of it, – by no means so ugly as the church at Pretoria. The square is larger and very much more picturesque, – while the sardine boxes and paper shirt-collars, so ubiquitous at the newer town, are less obtrusive. The square when I was there was green with grass on which horses were grazing, and here and there were stationed the huge waggons of travellers who had 'spanned out' their oxen and were resting here under the tent coverings erected on their vehicles. The scene as I saw it would have made an exquisite subject for a Dutch landscape painter, and was especially Dutch in all its details.

At one corner of the square the Judge was holding the Court in a large room next to the Post-office which is kept for that and other public services. The Judge I had met at Pretoria, and had been much struck by his youth. One expects a judge to be reverend with years, but this was hardly more than a boy judge. He had been brought from the Cape Bar to act as Judge in the Transvaal before the annexation, – when the payment even of a judge's salary must have been a matter of much doubt. But the annexation came speedily and the position of the new comer was made sure by British authority. He at any rate must approve the great step taken by Sir Theophilus Shepstone. I was assured when at Pretoria that the Colony generally had every reason to be satisfied with the choice made by the Republic. He will no doubt have assistant Judges and become a Chief Justice before long and may probably live to be the oldest legal pundit under the British Crown. I went into the Court to look at him while at work, but was not much edified as the case then before him was carried on in Dutch. Dutch and English have to be used in the Court as one or the other language may be needed. An interpreter is present, but as all the parties concerned in the case, including the Judge and jury, were conversant with Dutch, no interpreter was wanted when I was there.

From Potchefstroom to Klerksdorp our horses, including the new purchase, did their work well. Here we found a clean little Inn kept by an Englishman with a very nice English wife, – who regaled us with lamb and mint-sauce and boiled potatoes, and provided clean sheets for our couches. Why such a man, and especially why such a woman, should be at such a place it is difficult to understand. For Klerksdorp is a town consisting perhaps of a dozen houses. The mail cart passes but once a week, and the other traffic on the road is chiefly that of ox-waggons.

On the following day, a Saturday, we travelled 50 miles, and, with our horses very tired, reached a spot across the 'Maquasie Spruit,' at which a store or shop is kept and where we remained over the Sunday, hospitably entertained by the owners of the establishment. Here we were on land which has been claimed and possessed by the Transvaal Republic; but which was given over to the Batlapin natives by a division generally known in the later-day history of South African affairs as the Keate award. The Batlapins are a branch of the great Bechuana tribe. Mr Keate in 1871 was Lieut.-Governor of Natal, and undertook, at the instance of the British Government, to make an award between the Transvaal Republic and the Batlapin Kafirs, whose Chief is and was a man called Gassibone. I should hardly interest or instruct my readers by going deeply into the vexed question of the Keate award. To Europeans living in South Africa it is always abominable that anything should be given up or back to the natives, and whatever is surrendered to them in the way of territory is always resumed before long by hook or crook. There is a whole district of the Transvaal Republic, – a county as we should say, – lying outside or beyond the 'Maquasie Spruit', – called Bloomhof, with two towns, Bloomhof and Christiana, each having perhaps a dozen houses, – and this the Transvaal never did surrender. Governor Keate's award was repudiated by the Volksraad of the Transvaal, and a Dutch Landroost, – or magistrate, – who however is an Englishman, was stationed at Christiana and still remains there. This was a matter of no great trouble to us while the Republic stood on its own legs. Though a Governor of ours had made the award we were not bound to remedy Dutch injustice. But now what are we to do? Are we to give back the country with its British and Dutch inhabitants, – a dozen families at Bloomhof and a dozen more at Christiana, – and the farmers here and there to the dominion of Gassibone and his Batlapins? I think I may say that most certainly we shall do nothing of the kind, – but with what excuse we shall escape the necessity I do not see so clearly. In the meantime there is the Landroost at Christiana, – now paid with British gold, who before the annexation was paid with Transvaal notes worth 5s. to the nominal pound. When I talked to him of Keate's award and of Gassibone's line, he laughed at me. Annexation to British rule with all the beauties of British punctuality was a great deal too good a thing to be sacrificed to a theory of justice in favour of such a poor race of unfighting Kafirs as the Batlapins! I have no doubt that he was right, and that the Transvaal Colony will maintain a Landroost at Christiana as long as Landroosts remain in that part of South Africa.

But the question was a very vital one in that neighbourhood. As I was passing over the Vaal in a punt to the Orange

Free State a Boer who had heard my name, and who paid me the undeserved compliment of thinking my opinion on such a matter worth having, consulted me on this peculiar case. After the Keate award, when by the decision then made the portion of territory in question had been adjudged to the property of Gassibone and his tribe, this Boer had bought land of the Kafirs. The land so procured had also been distributed by the Transvaal Republican Government to those claiming it under the law as to burgher's rights. The rulers of the Transvaal Republic would not recognise any alienation of land by contract with the Kafirs. Now, upon the annexation, my friend had thought that the Keate award would be the law, and that his purchase from the Kafirs would hold good. There was I, a grey-bearded Englishman of repute, travelling the country. What did I think of it? I could only refer him to the Landroost. The Landroost, he said, was against him. 'Then,' said I, 'you may be sure that the facts will be against you, for the Landroost will have the decision in his hands.'' He assented to my opinion as though it had come direct from Minos, merely remarking that it was very hard upon him. I did not pity him much because it is probable that he only gave the Kafirs a few head of cattle, and that he bought the land from Kafirs who had no right of selling it away from their tribe. At the 'Maquasie Spruit', where we first entered this debateable land, the storekeepers were also anxious to know what was to happen to them; but they were Scotchmen and were no doubt quite clear in their own minds that the entire country would remain British soil.

The next day we reached Bloomhof and on the day following Christiana. This last place we entered anything but triumphantly, two of our horses being so tired that we had to take them off the cart, and walk into the place driving them before us. Two more days would take us to Kimberley according to our appointed time, but these two days would be days of long work. And here we heard for the first time that there was a long and weary region of sand before us in the portion of the Orange Free State through which we must pass. It was evident to us that we could not do it all with our own horses, and therefore we resolved to hire. This was at first pronounced to be impossible, but the impossibility vanished.

Though there were certainly not more than twelve houses in the place one belonged to a man who, oddly enough, had two spare horses out in the veld. He had brought to us, and I shall never forget the look of dismay and bewilderment which came across his countenance when he was told that he must decide at once whether he would allow his horses to be hired. 'He must,' he said, as he seated himself near a bottle of Cape brandy, – 'he must have time to think about it!' When he was again pressed, he groaned and shook himself. The landlord told us that the man was so poor that his children had nothing to eat but mealies. The money no doubt was desirable; – but how could he make up his mind in less than two or three hours to what extent he might so raise his demand as not to frighten away the customers which Providence has sent him, and yet secure the uttermost sum after due chaffering and bargaining? At last words were extracted from him. We should have two horses for sixteen miles, for, – well, say, for the incredibly small sum of £2. We hurriedly offered him 30s., and he was at last bustled into the impropriety of agreeing to our terms without taking a night's rest to sleep upon it. He was an agonised man as he assented, having been made to understand that we must them and there make up our minds, whether we would proceed early on the next day or stay for twenty-four hours to refresh our stud. The latter alternative would, however, have been destructive to us, as our horses had already eaten up all the forage to be found in Christiana.

At seven the next morning two wretched little ponies were brought in from the veld, one of which was lame. All Christiana was standing in the street to watch us. I flicked the lame animal with the driver's long whip to see if he could trot, and then pronounced in his favour. I fear I felt that his lameness would not matter if he could be made to take us as far as 'Blignaut's punt' which was now his destination. He was harnessed in, and on we went with the two most infirm of our own team following behind us. We made the stage with great success, – and whatever may have been the future state of that pony he went out of harness apparently a much sounder animal than he went in. From hence, after discussing the matter of Keate's award with the injured Dutchmen, we went on across the arid lands of the Orange Free State to a Boer's house in the wilderness, where we were assured that we should be made welcome for that night. Our horses could hardly take us there; – but they did do it, and we were made welcome. The Boer was very much like the other Boers of the Transvaal, – a burly, handsome, dirty man, with a very large, dirty family, and a dirty house, – but all the manners of the owner of a baronial castle. He also had a private tutor in his family, a Dutchman who had come out to make money, who knew German and English, but who had failed in his career, and had undertaken his present duties at the rate of £12 a month, besides his board and lodging. I have known English gentlemen who have not paid so highly for their private tutors. This farm was altogether in the wilderness, the land around being a sandy, stony desert, and not a shrub, hardly a blade of grass, being visible. But we knew that our host had grown rich as a farmer on it, owning in fee about 12,000 acres.

On the next morning we were up early, but we could not get on without the Boer's assistance. One of our horses was again dying or seemed to be dying. He was a pretty bay pony, the very fellow of the one we had lost at Wonder Fontein. He had not ate his food all night, and when we took him out at five in the morning he would do nothing but fall down in the veld at our feet. He suffered excruciating agonies, groaning and screaming as we looked at him. We gave him all that we had to give, – French brandy and Castor oil. But nothing seemed to serve him. Then there came to us a little Dutchman from a neighbouring waggon who suggested that we should bleed our poor pony in the ear. The little Dutchman was accordingly allowed the use of a penknife, and the animal's ear was slit. From that moment he recovered, – beginning at once to crop what grass there was. I have often known the necessity of bleeding horses for meagrims or staggers, by cutting the animal on the palate of the mouth. But I had never before heard of operating on a horse's ear; and I think I may say that our pony was suffering, not from meagrims or from staggers, but from cholic. I leave the fact to veterinary surgeons at home; but our pony, after having almost died and then been bled on the ear, travelled on with us bravely though without much strength to help us.

On this day we did at last reach the Diamond Fields, but our journey was anything but comfortable. It was very hot and the greater part of the road was so heavy with sand that we were forced to leave the cart and walk. The Boer at whose house we had slept, lent us a horse to help us for the first eight miles. Then we came to a little Dutch roadside public house, the owner of which provided us with two horses to help us on to Kimberley, – a distance of 27 miles, – for £2, sending with us a Kafir boy to lead our tired horses and bring back his own. Eight miles on we reached a hut in the wilderness where a Dutchman had made a dam, and he allowed us to water our cattle charging us one and sixpence. From thence on to Kimberley, through the heavy sand, there was not a drop of water. We went very slowly ourselves, trudging on foot after the cart; but the Kafir boy could not keep up with us, and he with the two poor animals remained out in the veld all night. We did reach the town about sunset, and I found myself once again restored to the delights of tubs, telegrams, and bed linen.

Here we parted with our cart, horses, and harness which, – including the price of the animal purchased at Potchefstroom, – had cost us £243, – selling them by auction and realising the respectable sum of £100 by the sale. The auctioneer endeavoured to raise the speculative energy of the bidders by telling them that the horses had all been bred at 'Orley Farm' for my own express use, 'Orley Farm' being the name of a novel written by me many years ago; – but I do not know that this romance much affected the bidding. We had intended to have taken our equipage on to Bloemfontein, the capital of the Orange Free State, which is about 80 miles from Kimberley; but my travelling companion was summoned back to Capetown, and I would not make the journey, or undertake the nuisance of the sale alone. We were of course told that, as things were at present, horses were a mere drug at the Diamond Fields, and that a Cape cart in Kimberley was a thing of no value at all. In my ignorance I would have taken £10 for my share, and therefore when I heard what the auctioneer had done for us I almost felt that my fortune had been made for ever. I certainly think that if the purchaser had seen the team coming into Kimberley he would have hesitated before he made his last bid.

I have endeavoured to give the reader the results so far of my experience of South African travel. As regards money and time no doubt both are to some extent sacrificed by the buying and selling of a private carriage or cart. We had our horses on the road a month.

They cost us about 7s. 6d. a day each for their keep, or	45
The expenses of the Cape boy who drove us amounted to about	15
The cart and horses and harness, as above shown, cost	143
Total	£203

which, as we were two, must be divided, making our expense £101 10s. each for about 700 miles. There are public conveyances over the whole road which would carry a passenger with his luggagee for about £40. We travelled when on the road 30 miles a day on an average, whereas the public carts make an average of 90. This seems to be all in favour of the mail carts. And then it has to be acknowledged that the responsibilities and difficulties of a private team are very wearing. Horses in South Africa are peculiarly liable to sickness; and, though they do a very large average of work, seem when tired to be more incapable of getting over the ground than any other horses. The necessity of providing forage, – sometimes where no forage is to be had, – and of carrying large quantities on the cart; the agony of losing a horse, and the nuisance of having to purchase or hire others; the continual fear of being left as it were planted in the mud; – all these things are very harassing, and teach the traveller to think that the simplicity of the Mail Cart is beautiful. If misfortune happen to a public conveyance the passenger is not responsible. He may be left behind, but he always has the satisfaction of demanding from others that he shall be carried on. On our route we encountered two sets of travellers who had been left on the road through the laches of the Cart Contractors; but in both cases the sufferers had the satisfaction of threatening legal proceedings and of demanding damages. When one's own horse dies on the road, or one's own wheel flies off the axle, there is nobody to threaten, and personal loss is added to personal misery. All this seems to be in favour of the simple Mail Cart.

But there is another side to the question which I attempted

to describe when I told the tale of those unfortunate wretches who were forced to wander about in the mud and darkness between Newcastle and Pretoria. Such a journey as those gentlemen were compelled to make would in truth kill a weakly person. Some of these conveyances travel day and night, for four, five, six consecutive days, – or stop perhaps for three or four hours at some irregular time which can hardly be turned to account for rest. Such journeys if they do not kill are likely to be prejudicial, and for the time are almost agonizing. We with our own cart and horses could get in and out when we pleased, could stop when we liked and as long as we liked, and encountered no injurious fatigue. In addition to this I must declare that I never enjoyed my meals more thoroughly than I did those which we prepared for ourselves out in the veld. Such comfort, however, must depend altogether on the nature of the companion whom the traveller may have selected for himself. I had been, in this respect, most fortunate. We had harassed minds when our horses became sick or when difficulties arose as to feeding them; but our bodies were not subjected to torment.

These are the pros and cons, as I found them, and which I now offer for the service of any gentleman about to undertake South African travel. Ladies, who make long journeys in these parts only when their husbands or fathers have selected some new and more distant site for their homes, are generally carried about on ox-waggons, in which they live and sleep and take their meals. They progress about 16, 20, or sometimes 24 miles a day, and find the life wearisome and uncomfortable. But it is sure, and healthy, and when much luggage has to be carried, is comparatively inexpensive.

I had by no means finished my overland travels in South Africa on reaching Kimberley. I had indeed four or five hundred miles still before me, of which I shall speak as I go on. But I had learned that the coaches to Bloemfontein, and thence down to Grahamstown were more christian in their nature, and more trustworthy than those which had frightened me in the Transvaal. Partly on this account and partly because my friend was deserting me I determined to trust myself to them; – and therefore have given here this record of my experiences as to a Cape cart and private team of horses.

GRIQUALAND WEST

CHAPTER VII

GRIQUALAND WEST – WHY WE TOOK IT

Griqualand West is the proper, or official, name for that part of South Africa which is generally known in England as the Diamond Fields, and which is at the period of my writing, – the latter part of 1877, – a separate Colony belonging to the British Crown, under the jurisdiction of the Governor of the Cape Colony, but in truth governed by a resident administrator. Major Lanyon is now the occupier of the Government House, and is 'His Excellency of Griqualand' to all the Queen's loyal British subjects living in and about the mines. This is the present position of things; – but the British Government has offered to annex the Province to the Cape Colony, and the Cape Colony has at length agreed to accept the charge, – subject to certain conditions as to representation and other details. Those conditions are, I believe, now under consideration, and if they be found acceptable, – as will probably be the case, – the Colonial Office at home being apparently anxious to avoid the expense and trouble of an additional little Colony, – Griqualand West and the Diamond Fields will become a part of the Cape Colony in the course of 1878. The proposed conditions offer but one member for the Legislative Council, and four for the Assembly, to join twenty-one members in the former house, and sixty-eight in the latter. It is alleged very loudly and perhaps correctly at the Fields that this number is smaller than that to which the District is entitled if it is to be put on the same footing with other portions of the Colony. It is alleged also that a class of the community which has shown itself to be singularly energetic should be treated at any rate not worse than its neighbours who have been very much more slow in their movements, and less useful by their industry to the world at large. Whether such remonstrances will avail anything I doubt much. If they do not, I presume that the annexation will almost be immediate.

The history of Griqualand West does not go back to a distant antiquity, but it is one which has given rise to a singularly large amount of controversy and hot feeling, and has been debated at home with more than usual animation and more than usual acerbity. In the course of last year (1877) the 'Quarterly' and the 'Edinburgh Reviews' warmed themselves in a contest respecting the Hottentot Waterboer and his West Griquas, and the other Hottentot Adam Kok and his East Griquas, till South African sparks were flying which reminded one of the glorious days of Sidney Smith and Wilson Croker. Such writings are anonymous, and though one knows in a certain sense who were the authors, in another sense one is ingorant of anything except that an old-fashioned battle was carried on about Kok and Waterboer in our two highly esteemed and reverend Quarterlies. But as the conduct, not only of our Colonial Office, but of Great Britain as an administrator of Colonies, was at stake, – as on one side it was stated that an egregious wrong had been done from questionable motives, and on the other that perfect statecraft and perfect wisdom had been combined in the happy manner in which Griqualand West with its diamonds had become British territory, I thought it might be of interest to endeavour to get at the truth when I was on the spot. But I have to own that I have failed in the attempt to find any exact truth or to ascertain what abstract justice would have demanded. In order to get at a semblance of truth and justice in the matter it has to be presumed that a Hottentot Chief has understood the exact nature of a treaty with the accuracy of an accomplished European diplomate; and it has to be presumed also that the Hottentot's right to execute a treaty binding his tribe or nation is as well defined and as firmly founded as that of a Minister of a great nation who has the throne of his Sovereign and the constitutional omnipotence of his country's parliament at his back. In our many dealings with native tribes we have repeatedly had to make treaties. These treaties we have endeavoured to define, have endeavoured to explain; but it has always been with the conviction that they can be trusted only to a certain very limited extent.

The question in dispute is whether we did an injustice to the Orange Free State by taking possession of Griqualand West in 1871 when diamonds had already been discovered there and the value of the district had been acknowledged. At that time it was claimed by the Orange Free State whose subjects had inhabited the land before a diamond had been found, and which had levied taxes on the Boers who had taken up land there as though the country had belonged to the Republic. Since the annexation has been effected by us we have, in a measure, acknowledged the claim of the Free State by agreeing to pay to it a sum of £90,000 – as compensation for what injustice we may have done; and we have so far admitted that the Free State has had something to say for itself.

The district in question at a period not very remote was as little valuable perhaps as any land on the earth's surface lying adjacent to British territory. The first mention I find of the Griquas is of their existence as a bastard Hottentot tribe in 1811 when one Adam Kok was their captain. The word Griqua signifies bastard, and Adam Kok was probably half Dutchman and half Hottentot. In 1821 Adam Kok was dismissed or resigned, and Andreas Waterboer was elected in his place. Kok then went eastwards with perhaps half the tribe, and settled himself at a place which the reader will find on the map, under the name of Philipolis, north of the Orange river in the now existing Orange Free State. Then some line of demarcation was made between Waterboer's lands and Kok's lands, which line leaves the Diamond Fields on one side or, – on the other. Adam Kok then trekked further eastward with the Griquas of Griqualand East, as they had come to be called, to a territory south of Natal, which had probably been depopulated by the Zulus. This territory was then called No Man's Land, but is now marked on the maps as Adam Kok's Land. But he gave some power of attorney enabling an agent to sell the lands he left behind him, and under this power his lands were sold to the Orange Free State which had established itself in 1854. The Free State claims to have bought the Diamond Fields, – diamonds having been then unknown, – under this deed. But it is alleged that the deed only empowered the agent to sell the lands in and around Philipolis on which Adam Kok's Griquas had been living. It is certain, however, that Adam Kok had continued to exercise a certain

right of sovereignty over the territory in question after his de-
position or resignation, and that he made over land to the Boers
of the Free State by some deed which the Boers had accepted as
giving a good title. It is equally certain that old Waterboer's son
had remonstrated against these proceedings and had objected to
the coming in of the Boers under Kok's authority.

We will now go back to old Andreas Waterboer, who for a
Hottentot seems to have been a remarkably good sort of
person, and who as I have said had been chosen chief of the
Griquas when Adam Kok went out. In 1834 Sir Benjamin
D'Urban, that best and most ill-used of Cape Colony Governors, made a treaty with old Andreas undertaking to recognise
him in all rights, and obtaining a promise from the Hottentot
to assist in defending the British border from the hordes of
savagery to the north. There was also a clause under which the
Hottentot was to receive a stipend of £150 per annum. This
treaty seems to have been kept with faith on both sides till
Waterboer died in December, 1852. The stipend was
punctually paid, and the Hottentot did a considerable quantity
of hard fighting on behalf of the British. On his death his son
Nicholas Waterboer came to reign in his stead. Nicholas is a
Christian as was his father, and is comparatively civilised; –
but he is by no means so good a Christian as was the old man,
and his father's old friends were not at first inclined to keep up
the acquaintance on the same terms.

Nicholas, no doubt mindful of the annual stipend, asked to
have the treaty renewed in his favour. But other complications
had arisen. In 1852 Messrs. Hogge and Owen had acted as
Commissioners for giving over the Transvaal as a separate
Republic and in the deed of transference it was agreed that
there should not be any special treaties between the Cape
Colony and the Natives north of the Orange river, as it was
thought that such treaties would interfere with the independence of the Republic. Poor Nicholas for a time suffered under
this arrangement, but in 1858 a letter was written to him
saying that all that had been done for his father should be done
for him, – and the payment of the £150 per annum was
continued though no treaty was made.*

---

* I believe he did receive the stipend all through.

In the mean time, in 1854, the severance had been made of the Orange Free State from the Colony, the bounds of which were not then settled with much precision. Had they been declared to be the Orange and the Vaal rivers in reference to the North, East, and South, the Diamond Fields would have been included, – or the greater part of the Diamond Fields. But that would not have settled the question, as England could not have ceded what she did not possess. Thus there was a corner of land as there have been many corners in South Africa, respecting which there was doubts as to ownership. Waterboer alleged that the line which his father and old Adam Kok had made so long ago as 1821, – with what geometrical measures they might then have, – gave him a certain apparently valueless tract of land, and those again who assumed a right to Adam Kok's land, asserted that the line gave it to them. The Kokites, however, had this point in their favour, that they had in some sort occupied the land, – having sold it or granted leases on it to Dutch Boers who paid taxes to the Orange Free State in spite of Waterboer's remonstrances.

But the matter at the time was in truth unimportant. Encroachments were made also into this very district of Griqualand from the other Republic also. In speaking of the Transvaal I have already described the position there to which such encroachments had led. A treaty became necessary to check the Transvaal Boers from establishing themselves on Griqualand, and the Transvaal authorities with the native Chiefs, and our Governor at the Cape, agreed that the matter should be referred to an umpire. Mr. Keate, the Lieut. Governor of Natal, was chosen and the Keate award was made. But the land in question was not valuable; diamonds had not yet been found, and the question was not weighty enough to create determined action. The Transvaal rejected the treaty, and the Transvaal Boers, as well as those from the Free State, continued to occupy land in Griqualand West. Now the land of the Transvaal Republic has come back into our hands, and there is one little difficulty the more to solve.

Then, in 1869, the first diamond was found on a farm possessed by an Orange Free State Boer, and in 1871 Nicholas Waterboer, claiming possession of the land, and making his claim good to British colonial intellects, executed a treaty ceding to the British the whole district of Griqualand West, – a tract of land about half as big as Scotland, containing 17,800 square miles. There had by this time grown up a vast diamond seeking population which was manifestly in want of government. Waterboer himself could certainly do nothing to govern the free, loudspeaking, resolute body of men which had suddenly settled itself upon the territory which he claimed. Though he considered himself to be Captain of the Country, he would have been treated with no more respect than any other Hottentot had he shown himself at the diggings. Yet he no doubt felt that such a piece of luck having turned up on what he considered to be his own soil, he ought to get something out of it. So he made a treaty, ceding the country to Great Britain in 1871. In 1872 his stipend was raised to £250, – in 1873 to £500; and an agreement has now been made, dated I think in October 1877, increasing this to d1,000 a year, with an allowance of £500 to his widow and children after his death. It was upon this deed that we took possession of Griqualand West with all its diamonds; but the Orange Free State at once asserted its claim, – based on present possession and on the purchase of Adam Kok's rights.

I think I shall not be contradicted when I say that amidst such a condition of things it is very hard to determine where is precisely the truth and what perfect abstract justice would have demanded. I cannot myself feel altogether content with the title of a country which we have bought from a Hottentot for an allowance of £1,000 a year with a pension of £500 to his wife and children. Much less can I assent to the title put forward by the Free State in consequence of their negotiation with Adam Kok's Agent. The excuse for annexation does not in my mind rest on such buyings and sellings. I have always felt that my sense of justice could not be satisfied as to any purchase of territory by civilized from uncivilized people, – first because the idea of the value of the land is essentially different in the minds of the two contracting parties; and secondly because whatever may be the tribal customs of a people as to land I cannot acknowledge the right of a Chieftain to alienate the property of his tribe, – and the less so when the price given takes the form of an annuity for life to one or two individuals.

The real excuse is to be found in that order of things which has often in the affairs of our Colonies made a duty clear to us, though we have been unable to reconcile that duty with abstract justice. When we accepted the cession of the Province in 1871 the Free State was no doubt making an attempt to regulate affairs at the Diamond Fields; but it was but a feeble attempt. The Republic had not at its back the power needed for saying this shall be law, and that shall be law, and for enforcing the laws so enacted. And if the claim of Great Britain to the land was imperfect, so was that of the Free State. The persons most interested in the matter prayed for our interference, and felt that they could live only under our Government. There had no doubt been occupation after a kind. A few Boers here and there had possessed themselves of the lands, buying them by some shifty means either from the Natives or from those who alleged that they had purchased them from the Natives. And, as I have said, taxes were levied. But I cannot learn that any direct and absolute claim had ever been made to national dominion, – as is made by ourselves and other nations when on a new-found shore we fly our national flags. The Dutch had encroached over the border of the Griquas and then justified their encroachment by their dealings with Adam Kok. We have done much the same and have justified our encroachment by our dealings with Nicholas Waterboer. But history will justify us because it was essentially necessary that an English speaking population of a peculiarly bold and aggressive nature should be made subject to law and order.

The accusation against our Colonial Office of having stolen the Diamond Fields because Diamonds are peculiarly rich and desirable can not hold water for an instant. If that were so in what bosom did the passion rise and how was it to be gratified? A man may have a lust for power as Alexander had, and Napoleon, – a lust to which many a British Minister has in former days been a prey; but, even though we might possibly have a Colonial Secretary at this time so opposed in his ideas to the existing theories and feelings of our statesmen as to be willing to increase his responsibilities by adding new Colonies to our long list of dependencies, I cannot conceive that his ambition should take the shape of annexing an additional digging population. Has any individual either claimed or received glory by annexing Griqualand West? From the operation of such a Province as the Diamond Fields it is not the mother country that reaps the reward, but the population whether they be English, Dutch, or Americans, the difficult task of ruling whom the mother country is driven to assume.

It is known to all Englishmen who have watched the course of our colonial history for the last forty years that nothing can be so little pleasant to a Secretary of State for the Colonies as the idea of a new Colony. Though they have accrued to us, one after the other, with terrible rapidity there has always been an attempt made to reject them. The Colonial Secretary has been like an old hen to whose large brood another and another chick is ever being added, – as though her powers of stretching her wings were unlimited. She does stretch them, like a good old mother with her maternal instincts, but with most unwilling efforts, till the bystander thinks that not a feather of protection could be given to another youngling. But another comes and the old hen stretches herself still wider, – most painfully.

New Zealand is now perhaps the pet of our colonial family; and yet what efforts were made when Lord Normanby and afterwards when Lord John Russell were at the Colonies to stave off the necessity of taking possession of the land! But Englishmen had settled themselves in such numbers on her shores that England was forced to send forth the means of governing her own children. The same thing happened, as I have attempted to tell, both in British Kafraria and Natal. The same thing happened the other day in the Fiji Islands. The same feeling, acting in an inverse way, – repudiating the chicks instead of taking them in, – induced us to give over the Transvaal and the Orange Free State to Republicanism. Our repudiation of the former had lasted but for a quarter of a century, and there are many now of British race to be found in South Africa who are confident that we shall have to take the Orange Free State in among the brood in about the same period from her birth. British rule in distant parts, much as it is abused, is so precious a blessing that men will have it, and the old hen is forced to stretch her poor old wings again and still again.

This I hold to be the real and unanswerable excuse for what we have done in Griqualand West and not our treaty with Waterboer. As far as right devolving from any treaty goes I think that we have the best of it, – but not so much the best, that even I could recognize those treaties as conveying all they are held to convey, I should declare our title to be complete. But, that such treaties are for the most part powerless when pressure comes, is proved by our own doings and by those of other nations all round the world. We have just annexed the Transvaal, – with the approbation of both sides in the House of Commons. Our excuse is that though the Transvaal was an independent State she was so little able to take care of herself that we were obliged to enter in upon her, as the law does on the estate of a lunatic. But how would it have been if the Transvaal instead of the Orange Free State had been our competitor for the government of the Diamond Fields? If we can justify ourselves in annexing a whole Republic surely we should not have scrupled to take the assumed dependency of a Republic. In such doings we have to reconcile ourselves to expedience, however abhorrent such a doctrine may be to us in our own private affairs. Here it was expedient that a large body, chiefly of Englishmen, should, for their own comfort and well being, be brought under rule. If in following out the doctrine any abstract injustice was done, it was not against the Orange Free State, but against the tribes whom no Waterboer and no Adam Kok could in truth be authorized to hand over either to British or to Dutch Republican rule.

For a while I was minded to go closely into the question of Kok v. Waterboer and to put forward what might probably have been a crude expression of the right either of the one Hottentot or of the other to make over at any rate his power and his privilege of government. But I convinced myself, when on the spot, that neither could have much right, and that whatever right either might have, was so far buried in the obscurity of savagery in general, that I could not possibly get at the bottom of it so as to form any valid opinion. Books have been written on the subject, on the one side and on the other, which have not I think been much studied. Were I to write no more than a chapter on it my readers would pass it by. The intelligence of England will not engage itself on unravelling the geographical facts of a line of demarcation made between two Hottentot Chieftains when the land was comparatively valueless, and when such line could only be signified by the names of places of which the exact position can hardly even now be ascertained. When subsequently I read the report which the Secretary of State for the Colonies made to the Governor of the Cape Colony on 5 August 1876, informing the Governor of the terms under which he and the President of the Orange Free State had agreed to compromise the matter, I was glad to find that he, in his final discussions with the President, had come to the same conclusion. I here quote the words in which Lord Carnarvon expressed himself to Sir Henry Barkly; – and I would say that I fully agree with him were it not that such testimony might seem to be impertinent. 'At the earlier interviews Mr. Brand repeatedly expressed his desire to submit proof of the claim preferred by his Government to a great part of Griqualand West. I had however determined from the first that there would be no advantage in entering upon such an enquiry. It was obvious that there could be no prospect of our coming to an agreement on a question which teemed with local details and personal contentions.'

The Secretary of State goes on to explain the circumstances under which the £90,000 are to be given. I will confess for myself that I should almost have preferred to have stuck to the territory without paying the money. If it be our 'destiny' to rule people I do not think that we ought to pay for assuming an office which we cannot avoid. The Secretary of State in this report strongly reasserts the British right to Griqualand West, – though he acknowledges that he cannot hope by mere eloquence to convince President Brand of that right. 'As you think you are wronged', the Secretary goes on to argue, 'we will consent to compensate the wrong which we feel sure you have not suffered, but which you think you have endured, so that there need be no quarrel between us.' Probably it was the easiest way out of the difficulty; but there is something in it to regret. It must of course be understood that the £90,000 will not be paid by the British taxpayer, but will be gathered from the riches of Griqualand West herself.

On the 27 October 1871 the Diamond Fields were declared to be British territory. But such a declaration, even had it not

been opposed by the Free State and the friends of the Free
State, would by no means have made the course of British rule
plain and simple. There have, from that day to this, arisen a
series of questions to settle and difficulties to solve which, as
they crop up to the enquirer's mind, would seem to have been
sufficient to have overcome the patience of any Colonial
Secretary even though he had not another Colony on his
shoulders. If there was any Colonial sinner, – Secretary,
Governor, or subordinate, – who carried away by the lust of
empire had sought to gratify his ambition by annexing
Griqualand West, he must certainly have repented himself in
sackcloth and ashes before this time (the end of 1877) when the
vexed question of annexation or non-annexation to the Cape
Colony is hardly yet settled. When the territory was first
accepted by Great Britain it was done on an understanding
that the Cape Colony should take it and rule it, and pay for it,
– or make it pay for itself. The Colonial Secretary of the day
declared in an official dispatch that he would not consent to
the annexation unless, 'the Cape Parliament would personally
bind itself to accept the responsibility of governing the
territory which was to be united to it, together with the entire
maintenance of any force which might be necessary for the
preservation of order.' It must be presumed therefore that the
lust for empire did not exist in Downing Street. The Cape
Parliament did so far accede to the stipulation made by the
Secretary of State, as to pass a resolution of assent. They
would agree, – seeing that British rule could not in any other
way be obtained. But an intermediate moment was necessary,
– a moment which should admit of the arrangment of terms, –
between the absolute act of assumption by Great Britain and
the annexation by the Colony. That moment has been much
prolonged, and has not yet, as I write, been brought to an end.
So that the lust for rule over the richest diamond fields in the
world seems hardly to be very strong even in the Colony.
Though the Parliament of the Colony had assented to the
requisition from Downing Street, it afterwards, – not
unnaturally, – declined to take the matter in hand till the
Government at home had settled its difficulties with the
Orange Free State. The Free State had withdrawn whatever
officers it had had on the Fields, and had remonstrated. That

difficulty is now solved; – and the Cape Colony has passed a bill shewing on what terms it will annex the territory. The terms are very unpopular in the district, – as indeed is the idea of annexation to the Cape Colony at all. Griqualand would very much prefer to continue a separate dependency, with a little Council of its own. The intention however of the mother country and of the Colony has been too clearly expressed for doubt on that subject. They are both determined that the annexation shall take place, and the Colony will probably be able to dictate the terms.

But there have been other difficulties sufficient almost to break the heart of all concerned. Who did the land belong to on which the diamonds were being found, and what were the rights of the owners either to the stones beneath the surface, or to the use of the surface for the purpose of searching? The most valuable spot in the district, called at first the Colesberg Kopje, – Kopje being little hill, – and now known as the Kimberley mine, had been on a farm called Vooruitzuit belonging to a Dutchman named De Beer. This farm he sold to a firm of Englishmen for the very moderate sum of £6,600,* – a sum however which to him must have appeared enormous, – and the firm soon afterwards sold it to the Government for £100,000. To this purchase the Government was driven by the difficulties of the position. Diggers were digging and paying 10s. a month for their claims to the owners of the soil, justifying themselves in that payment by the original edict of the Free State, while the owners were claiming £10 a month, and asserting their right to do as they pleased with their own property. The diggers declared their purpose of resisting by force any who interfered with them; – and the owners of the soil were probably in league with the diggers, so as to enhance the difficulties, and force the Government to purchase. The Government was obliged to buy and paid the enormous sum of £100,000 for the farm.

---

* The purchasers were in treaty for De Beer's farm at the time when the first diamond was found by a lady's parasol on the little hill where is now the Kimberley mine, and £600 was added to the purchase money in consequence. It is calculated that diamonds to the value of £12,000,000 have since been extracted from the mine.

Many stories could be told of the almost inextricable complexities which attended the settlement of claims to property while the diggers were arming and drilling and declaring that they would take the law into their own hands if they were interfered with in their industry.

In 1872 the population had become so great, – and, as was natural in such circumstances, so unruly, – that the Governor of the Cape Colony, who is also High Commissioner for all our South African territories, was obliged to recommend that a separate Lieutenant Governor should be appointed, and Mr. Southey who had long held official employment in the Cape Colony was sent to fill the place. Here he remained till 1875, encumbered by hardships of which the difficulty of raising a sufficient revenue to pay the expenses of the place was not the least. Diamonds were being extracted worth many millions, but the diamonds did not come into the pocket of the Government. In such localities the great source of revenue, – that which is generally most available, – is found in the Custom duties levied on the goods consumed by the diggers. But here, though the diggers consumed manfully, the Custom duties levied went elsewhere. Griqualand West possessed no port and could maintain no cordon of officers to prevent goods coming over her borders without taxation. The Cape Colony which has been so slow to annex the land got the chief advantages from the consumption of the Diamond Fields, sharing it, however, with Natal. Mr. Southey is said to have had but thirty policemen with him to assist in keeping the peace, and was forced to ask for the assistance of troops from the Cape. Troops were at last sent from Capetown, – at an expense of about £20,000 to Griqualand West. During all this time it may easily be conceived that no British aggressor had as yet obtained the fruition of that rich empire for which he is supposed to have lusted when annexing the country.

The Lieutenant Governor with his thirty policemen, – and the sudden influx of about 300 soldiers from the Cape – was found to be too expensive for the capabilities of the place. 'In 1875,' says the Colonial Office List for 1877, 'the condition of the finances rendered it necessary to reduce the civil establishment, and the office of Lieutenant Governor, as well as that of Secretary of Government, was discontinued, and an administrator appointed.' That administrator has been Major Lanyon who has simply been a Lieutenant Governor with a salary somewhat less than that of his predecessor. That the difficulty of administering the affairs of the Colony have been lessened during his period of office, may in part be due to circumstances and the more settled condition of men's minds. But with such a task as he has had not to have failed is sufficient claim for praise. There have been no serious outrages since he reached the Fields.

Annexation to the Cape Colony will probably take place. But what will come next? The Province does not want annexation; – but specially wants an adequate, we may say a large share in the constituencies of the joint Colonies should annexation be carried out. I sympathise with Griqualand West in the first feeling. I do not think that the diggers of the Diamond Fields will be satisfied with legislation carried on at Capetown. I do not think that a parliamentary majority at Capetown will know how to manage the diggers. Kimberley is so peculiar a place, and so likely to shew its feeling of offence against the Government if it be offended, that I fear it will be a very thorn in the side of any possible Cape Colony Prime Minister. That Downing Street should wish to make over to the Colony the rich treasure, which we are told has been acquired with so much violence and avarice, I am not surprised, – though such annexation must be prejudicial to that desire for South African Confederation which is now strong in Colonial Office bosoms; – but that the Colony should accept the burden while she already possesses that which generally makes such burdens acceptable, – viz., the Custom duties on the goods consumed by the people, – is to me a marvel. It may be that the Cape Parliament was induced to give its first assent by the strongly expressed wishes of the Secretary of State at home, and that it can hardly now recede from the promise it then made.

But in regard to the share which Griqualand claims in the two legislative Houses of the future combined Colonies I cannot at all wish her to prevail. It may be natural that a community should desire to be largely represented without looking forward to all the circumstances by which such representation may be affected. The population of the

Diamond Fields is supposed to consist of about 15,000 whites and 30,000 natives. Of the latter number about 12,000 are men employed in the mines. The other 18,000 natives who are living on their own lands may be eliminated from our present enquiry. Of the 15,000 white persons we will say that a half are men who would be entitled to vote under the present franchise of the Cape Colony. The number would show a very large proportion of adult males, but a digging population will always have an excessive population of men. But the 12,000 natives would, with a very small deduction on account of women, all be enabled to claim a right to be registered.

The Cape Colony franchise is given to all men with certain qualifications. One qualification, and that the broadest, – is that a man shall be earning wages at the rate of £25 a year and his diet. And he must either have been born a British subject, or born in a Dutch South African territory taken over by the British Government. The latter clause was inserted no doubt with the intention of saving from exclusion any men then still living who might have been born when the Cape of Good Hope was a Dutch Colony; but in justice must be held to include also those born in the Transvaal when the Transvaal was a Dutch Republic. The meaning is that all shall vote, who are otherwise qualified, who have been born English subjects or have become English subjects by annexation from Dutch rule. The majority of the Kafirs now working at the Diamond Fields have been born in the Transvaal; some indeed at Natal, some few in Zululand which is not English, and some few beyond the Limpopo, on native territory which has never been either Dutch or English. But the great majority are from the distant parts of the Transvaal; – and, with a Kafir as with a white man who should asssert himself to be born an English subject or a Transvaalian, the onus probandi would be with those who objected to, or denied, the claim. Every Kafir about the mines earns at the lowest 10s. a week, or £26 10s. per annum and his diet, and it would be found I think impossible to reject their claim to be registered as voters if their names were brought up on the lists.

There will be those at home who say, – why should they not vote if they are industrious labourers earning wages at so high a rate? But no white man who has been in South Africa

and knows anything of South Africa, will say that. A very
eminent member of the House of Commons, – a friend of my
own whom I respect as a politician as highly as any man of the
present day, – gently murmured a complaint in discussing the
South African permissive bill as to the statement which had
been made by the Secretary of State 'that until the civilization
of the Natives throughout South Africa had made considerable progress it would be desirable that they should not have
direct representation in the Legislative Assembly of the
Union;' – that is in the Confederated Union sanctioned by the
permissive bill. My friend's philanthropic feelings were hurt
by the idea that the coloured man should be excluded from the
franchise. But the suggestion contained in this speech that the
Kafir should have a vote is received by Europeans in South
Africa simply with a smile. Were it granted and could it be
generally used at the will and in accordance with the judgment
of the Kafir himself all Europeans would at once leave the
country, and South Africa would again become the prey of the
strongest handed among the Natives then existing. That
Englishmen should live under a policy devised or depending
upon Negroes I believe to be altogether impossible. Nor will
such an attempt be made. Let the law say what it will as to
suffrage that state of things will be avoided, – if not otherwise,
then by force.

It is not that I think that the Kafirs about the Diamond
Fields will at once swarm to the poll as soon as the franchise of
the Cape Colony shall make it possible for them to do so. That
is not the way the evil will show itself. They will care nothing
for the franchise and will not be at the trouble to understand its
nature. But certain Europeans will understand it, – politicians
not of the first class, – and they will endeavour to use for their
own purposes a privilege which will have been thoughtlessly
conferred. Such politicians will not improbably secure election
by Kafir votes, and will cause to be done exactly that which
the most respectable employers of labour in the place will
think most prejudicial to the interests of the place. And after a
while the Negroes of Griqualand West will learn the powers
which they possess as have the Negroes of the Southern
American States, and thus there will spring up a contest as to
the party in which is to be vested the political power of the

district. I do not doubt how the contest would end. The white men would certainly prevail however small might be their numbers, and however great the majority of the Kafirs. But I am sure that no part of South Africa would willingly subject itself to the possibility of such a condition. I think that the franchise of the Cape Colony has been, – I will not say fixed too low, but arranged injudiciously in regard to the population of the Colony itself; – but I am even more strongly of opinion that that franchise is not at all adapted to the population of the Diamond Fields. Considering the nature of the task it may be doubted whether the country of the diamonds would not be best ruled as a Crown Colony.

At the present moment, pending annexation, the Government is carried on by an administrator with a Council of seven besides himself, – eight in all. Four are appointed and enjoy salaries, while four are elected and are not paid. If necessary for a majority the administrator has two votes. But a quorum of five is necessary of which quorum two must be elected members. The consequence is that unless two of the elected members are staunch to the Government, every thing is liable to be brought to a stand still. One or two elected members take up their hats and walk out, – and all business is at an end for the day. This, to say the least of it, is awkward. The evil would be much remedied, if it were required that in forming the quorum of five one elected member would be sufficient. Out of eight a quorum of four might be held to suffice of which one might be an elected member.

CHAPTER VIII

THE STORY OF THE DIAMOND FIELDS

The first known finding of a diamond in South Africa was as recent as 1867; – so that the entire business which has well nigh deluged the world of luxury with precious stones and has added so many difficulties to the task of British rule in South Africa is only now, – in 1877, – ten years old. Mr Morton, an American gentleman who lectured on the subject before the American Geographical Society in the early part of 1877 tells us that 'Across a mission map of this very tract printed in 1750 is written, "Here be Diamonds;"' – that the Natives had long used the diamonds for boring other stones, and that it was their practice to make periodical visits to what are now the Diamond Fields to procure their supply. I have not been fortunate enough to see such a map, nor have I heard the story adequately confirmed, so as to make me believe that any customary search was ever made here for diamonds even by the Natives. I am indeed inclined to doubt the existence of any record of South African diamonds previous to 1867, thinking that Mr Morton must have been led astray by some unguarded assertion. Such a map would be most interesting if it could be produced. For all British and South African purposes, – whether in regard to politics, or geological enquiry the finding of the diamond in 1867 was the beginning of the affair.

And this diamond was found by accident and could not for a time obtain any credence. It is first known to have been seen at the house of a Dutch farmer named Jacobs in the northern limits of the Cape Colony, and South of the Orange river. It had probably been brought from the bed of the stream or from the other side of the river. The 'other side' would be, in Griqualand West, the land of diamonds. As far as I can learn there is no idea that diamonds have been deposited by nature in the soil of the Cape Colony proper. At Jacobs' house it was seen in the hands of one of the children by another Boer named Van Niekerk, who observing that it was brighter and also heavier than other stones, and thinking it to be too valuable for a plaything offered to buy it. But the child's mother would not sell such a trifle and gave it to Van Niekerk. From Van Niekerk it was passed on to one O'Reilly who seems to have been the first to imagine it to be a diamond. He took it to Capetown where he could get no faith for his stone, and thence back to Colesberg on the northern extremity of the Colony where it was again encountered with ridicule. But it became a matter of discussion and was at last sent to Dr Atherstone of Grahamstown who was known to be a geologist and a man of science. He surprised the world of South Africa by declaring the stone to be an undoubted diamond. It weighed over 21 carats and was sold to Sir P. Wodehouse, the then Governor of the Colony, for £500.*

In 1868 and 1869 various diamonds were found, and the search for them was no doubt instigated by Van Niekerk's and O'Reilly's success; – but nothing great was done nor did the belief prevail that South Africa was a country richer in precious stones than any other region yet discovered. Those which were brought to the light during these two years may I believe yet be numbered, and no general belief had been created. But some searching by individuals was continued. The same Van Niekerk who had received the first diamond from the child not unnaturally had his imagination fired by his success. Either in 1868 or 1869 he heard of a large stone which was then in the hands of a Kafir witchdoctor from whom he succeeded in buying it, giving for it as the story goes all his sheep and all his horses. But the purchase was a good one, – for a Dutchman's flocks are not often very numerous or very valuable, – and he sold the diamond to merchants in the neighbourhood for £11,200. It weighed 83 carats, and is said to be perfect in all its appointments as to water, shape, and whiteness. It became known among diamonds and was

---

* I find the story told with slight variation by different persons. I have taken the version published in the second edition of Messrs. Silver's Handbook, having found ample reason to trust the accuracy of that compilation. See p. 378 of that volume.

christened the Star of South Africa. After a law suit, during which an interdict was pronounced forbidding its exportation or sale, it made its way to the establishment of Messrs. Hunt and Rosskill from whom it was purchased for the delight of a lovely British Countess.

Even then the question whether this part of South Africa was diamondiferous* had not been settled to the satisfaction of persons who concern themselves in the produce and distribution of diamonds. There seems to have been almost an Anti-South African party in the diamond market, as though it was too much to expect that from a spot so insignificant as this corner of the Orange and Vaal rivers should be found a rival to the time-honoured glories of Brazil and India. It was too good to believe, – or to some perhaps too bad, – that there should suddenly come a plethora of diamonds from among the Hottentots.

It was in 1870 that the question seems to have got itself so settled that some portion of the speculative energy of the world was enabled to fix itself on the new Diamond Fields. In that year various white men set themselves seriously to work in searching the banks of the Vaal up and down between Hebron and Klipdrift, – or Barkly as it is now called, and many small parcels of stones were brought from Natives who had been instigated to search by what they had already heard. The operations of those times are now called the 'river diggings' in distinction to the 'dry diggings', which are works of much greater magnitude carried on in a much more scientific manner away from the river, – and which certainly are in all respects 'dry' enough. But at first the searchers confined themselves chiefly to the river bed and to the small confluents of the river, scraping up into their mining cradles the shingles and dirt they had collected, and shaking and washing away the grit and mud, till they could see by turning the remaining stones over with a bit of slate on a board whether Fortune had sent on that morning a peculiar sparkle among the lot.

* This is an abominable word, coined as I believe for the use of the British Diamond Fields; – but it has become so common that it would be affectation to avoid the use of it.

I was taken up to Barkly 'on a picnic' as people say; and a very nice picnic it was, – one of the pleasantest days I had in South Africa. The object was to shew me the Vaal river, and the little town which had been the capital of the diamond country before the grand discovery at Colesberg Kopje had made the town of Kimberley. There is nothing peculiar about Barkly as a South African town, except that it is already half deserted. There may be perhaps a score of houses there most of which are much better built than those at Kimberley. They are made of rough stone, or of mud and whitewash; and, if I do not mistake, one of them had two storeys. There was an hotel, – quite full although the place is deserted, – and clustering round it were six or seven idle gentlemen all of whom were or had been connected with diamonds. I am often struck by the amount of idleness which persons can allow themselves whose occupations have diverged from the common work of the world.

When at Barkly we got ourselves and our provisions into a boat so that we might have our picnic properly, under the trees at the other side of the river, – for opposite to Barkly is to be found the luxury of trees. As we were rowed down the river we saw a white man with two Kafirs poking about his stones and gravel on a miner's ricketty table under a little tent on the bench. He was a digger who had still clung to the 'river' business; a Frenchman who had come to try his luck there a few days since. On the Monday previous, – we were told, – he had found a 13 carat white stone without a flaw. This would be enough perhaps to keep him going and almost to satisfy him for a month. Had he missed that one stone he would probably have left the place after a week. Now he would go on through days and days without finding another sparkle. I can conceive no occupation on earth more dreary, – hardly any more demoralizing than this of perpetually turning over dirt in quest of a peculiar little stone which may turn up once a week or may not. I could not but think, as I watched the man, of the comparative nobility of the work of a shoemaker who by every pull at his thread is helping to keep some person's foot dry.

After our dinner we walked along the bank and found another 'river' digger, though this man's claim might perhaps be removed a couple of hundred yards from the water. He was an Englishman and we stood awhile and talked to him. He had one Kafir with him to whom he paid 7s. a week and his food, and he too had found one or two stones which he shewed us, – just enough to make the place tenable. He had got upon an old digging which he was clearing out lower. He had, however, in one place reached the hard stone at the bottom, in, or below, which there could be no diamonds. There was however a certain quantity of diamondiferous matter left, and as he had already found stones he thought that it might pay him to work through the remainder. He was a most good-humoured well-mannered man, with a pleasant fund of humour. When I asked him of his fortune generally at the diggings, he told us among other things that he had broken his shoulder bone at the diggings, which he displayed to us in order that we might see how badly the surgeon had used him. He had no pain to complain of, – or weakness; but his shoulder had not been made beautiful. 'And who did it?' said the gentleman who was our Amphytrion at the picnic and is himself one of the leading practitioners of the Fields. 'I think it was one Dr. ——,' said the digger, naming our friend whom no doubt he knew. I need not say that the doctor loudly disclaimed ever having had previous acquaintance with the shoulder.

The Kafir was washing the dirt in a rough cradle, separating the stones from the dirt, and the owner, as each sieve-full was brought to him, threw out the stones on his table and sorted them through with the eternal bit of slate or iron formed into the shape of a trowel. For the chance of a sieve-full one of our party offered him half a crown – which he took. I was glad to see it all inspected without a diamond, as had there been anything good the poor fellow's disappointment must have been great. That halfcrown was probably all that he would earn during the week – all that he would earn perhaps for a month. Then there might come three or four stones in one day. I should think that the tedious despair of the vacant days could hardly be compensated by the triumph of the lucky minute. These 'river' diggers have this in their favour, – that the stones found near the river are more likely to be white and pure than those which are extracted from the mines. The Vaal itself in the neighbourhood of Barkly is pretty, – with rocks in its bed and islands and trees on its banks. But the country around, and from thence to Kimberley, which is twenty-four miles distant, is as ugly as flatness barrenness and sand together can make the face of the earth.

The commencement of diamond-digging as a settled industry was in 1872. It was then that dry-digging was commenced, which consists of the regulated removal of ground found to be diamondiferous and of the washing and examination of every fraction of the soil. The district which we as yet know to be so specially gifted extends up and down the Vaal river from the confluence of the Modder to Hebron, about 75 miles, and includes a small district on the east side of the river. Here, within 12 miles of the river, and within a circle of which the diameter is about 2½ miles, are contained all the mines, – or dry diggings, – from which have come the real wealth of the country. I should have said that the precious diamond yet produced, one of 288 carats, was found close to the river about 12 miles from Barkly. This prize was made in 1872.

It is of the dry diggings that the future student of the Diamond Fields of South Africa will have to take chief account. The river diggings were only the prospecting work which led up to the real mining operations, – as the washing of the gullies in Australia led to the crushing of quartz and to the sinking of deep mines in search of alluvial gold. Of these dry diggings there are now four, Du Toit's Pan, Bultfontein, Old De Beers, – and Colesberg Kopje or the great Kimberley mine, which though last in the Field has thrown all the other diamond mines of the world into the shade. The first working at the three first of these was so nearly simulatneous, that they may almost be said to have been commenced at once. I believe however that they were in fact opened in the order I have given.

Bultfontein and Du Toit's Pan were on two separate Boer farms, of which the former was bought the first, – as early as 1869, – by a firm who had even then had dealings in diamonds and who no doubt purchased the land with reference to diamonds. Here some few stones were picked from the surface, but the affair was not thought to be hopeful. The diamond searchers still believed that the river was the place. But the Dutch farmer at Du Toit's Pan, one Van Wyk, finding that precious stones were found on his neighbour's land, let out mining licences on his own land, binding the miners to give him one fourth of the value of what they found. This however did not answer and the miners resolved to pay some small monthly sum for a licence, or to 'jump' the two farms altogether. Now 'jumping' in South African language means open stealing. A man 'jumps' a thing when he takes what does not belong to him with a tacit declaration that might makes right. Appeal was then made to the authorities of the Orange Free State for protection; – and something was done. But the diggers were too strong, and the proprietors of the farms were obliged to throw open their lands to the miners on the terms which the men dictated.

The English came, – at the end of 1871, – just as the system of dry digging had formed itself at these two mines, and from that time to this Du Toit's Pan and Bultfontein have been worked as regular diamond mines. I did not find them especially interesting to a visitor. Each of them is about two miles distant from Kimberley town, and the centre of the one can hardly be more than a mile distant from the centre of the other. They are under the inspection of the same Government officer, and might be supposed to be part of one and the same enterprise were it not that there is a Mining Board at Du Toit's Pan, whereas the shareholders at Bultfontein have abstained from troubling themselves with such an apparatus. They trust the adjustment of any disputes which may arise to the discretion of the Government Inspector.

At each place there is a little village, very melancholy to look at, consisting of hotels or drinking bars, and the small shops of the diamond dealers. Everything is made of corrugated iron and the whole is very mean to the eye. There had been no rain for some months when I was there, and as I rode into Du Toit's Pan the thermometer showed over 90 in the shade, and over 150 in the sun. While I was at Kimberley it rose to 96 and 161. There is not a blade of grass in the place, and I seemed to breathe dust rather than air. At both these places there seemed to be a 'mighty maze', – in which they differ altogether from the Kimberley mines which I will attempt to describe presently. Out of the dry dusty ground, which looked so parched and ugly that one was driven to think that it had never yet rained in those parts, were dug in all directions pits and walls and roadways, from which and by means of which the dry dusty soil is taken out to some place where it is washed and the debris examined. Carts are going hither and thither, each with a couple of horses, and Kafirs above and below, – not very much above or very much below, – are working for 10s. a week and their diet without any feature of interest. What is done at Du Toit's Pan is again done at Bultfontein.

At Du Toit's Pan there are 1441 mining claims which are possessed by 214 claimholders. The area within the reef, – that is within the wall of rocky and earthy matter containing the diamondiferous soil, – is 31 acres. This gives a revenue to the Griqualand Government of something over £2,000 for every three months. In the current year, 1877, – it will amount to nearly £9,000. About 1,700 Kafirs are employed in the mine and on the stuff taken out of it at wages of 10s. a week and their diet, – which, at the exceptionally high price of provisions prevailing when I was in the country, costs about 10s. a week more. The wages paid to white men can hardly be estimated as they are only employed in what I may call superintending work. They may perhaps be given as ranging from £3 to £6 a week. The interesting feature in the labour question is the Kafir. This black man, whose body is only partially and most grotesquely clad, and who is what we mean when we speak of a Savage, earns more than the average rural labourer in England. Over and beyond this board and lodging he carries away with him every Saturday night 10s. a week in hard money, with which he has nothing to do but to amuse himself if it so pleases him.

At Bultfontein there are 1,026 claims belonging to 153 claimholders. The area producing diamonds is 22 acres. The revenue derived is £6,000 a year, more or less. About 1,300 Kafirs are employed under circumstances as given above. The two diggings have been and still are successful, though they have never reached the honour and glory and wealth and grandeur achieved by that most remarkable spot on the earth's surface called the Colesberg Kopje, the New Rush, or the Kimberley mine.

I did not myself make any special visit to the Old De Beer mine. De Beer was the farmer who possessed the lands called

Vooruitzuit of the purchase of which I have already spoken,
and he himself, with his sons, for awhile occupied himself in
the business; – but he soon found it expedient to sell his land, –
the Old De Beer mine being then established. As the sale was
progressing a lady on the top of a little hill called the
Colesberg Kopje poked up a diamond with her parasol. Dr.
Atherstone who had visited the locality had previously said
that if new diamond ground were found it would probably be
on this spot. In September 1872 the territory of Griqualand
West became a British Colony, and at that time miners from
the whole district were congregating themselves at the hill,
and that which was at once called the 'New Rush' was
established. In Australia where gold was found here and there
the miners would hurry off to the spot and the place would be
called this or that 'Rush'.

The New Rush, the Colesberg Kopje, – pronounced
Coppy, – and the Kimberley mine are one and the same place.
It is now within the town of Kimberley, – which has in fact
got itself built around the hill to supply the wants of the
mining population. Kimberley has in this way become the
capital and seat of Government for the Province. As the mine
is one of the most remarkable spots on the face of the earth I
will endeavour to explain it with some minuteness, and I will
annex a plan of it which as I go on I will endeavour also to
explain.

The Colesberg hill is in fact hardly a hill at all, – what little
summit may once have entitled it to the name having been cut
off. On reaching the spot by one of the streets from the square
you see no hill but are called upon to rise over a mound, which
is circular and looks to be no more than the debris of the mine
though it is in fact the remainder of the slight natural ascent. It
is but a few feet high and on getting to the top you look down
into a huge hole. This is the Kimberley mine. You
immediately feel that it is the largest and most complete hole
ever made by human agency.

At Du Toit's Pan and Bultfontein the works are scattered.
Here everything is so gathered together and collected that it is
not at first easy to understand that the hole should contain the
operations of a large number of separate speculators. It is so
completely one that you are driven at first to think that it must

be the property of one firm, – or at any rate be entrusted to the
management of one director. It is very far from being so. In
the pit beneath your feet, hard as it is at first to your
imagination to separate it into various enterprises, the persons
making or marring their fortunes have as little connection
with each other as have the different banking firms in Lombard Street. There too the neighbourhood is very close, and
common precautions have to be taken as to roadway, fires,
and general convenience.

You are told that the pit has a surface area of 9 acres; – but
for your purposes as you will care little for diamondiferous or
non-diamondiferous soil, the aperture really occupies 12 acres.
The slope of the reef around the diamond soil has forced itself
back over an increased surface as the mine has become deeper.
The diamond claims cover 9 acres.

You stand upon the marge and there, suddenly, beneath
your feet lies the entirety of the Kimberley mine, so open, so
manifest, and so uncovered that if your eyes were good
enough you might examine the separate operations of each of
the three or four thousand human beings who are at work
there. It looks to be so steep down that there can be no way to
the bottom other than the aerial contrivances which I will
presently endeavour to explain. It is as though you were
looking into a vast bowl, the sides of which are smooth as
should be the sides of a bowl, while round the bottom are
various marvellous incrustations among which ants are
working with all the usual energy of the ant-tribe. And these
incrustations are not simply at the bottom, but come up the
curves and slopes of the bowl irregularly, – half-way up
perhaps in one place, while on another side they are confined
quite to the lower deep. The pit is 230 feet deep, nearly
circular, though after awhile the eye becomes aware of the fact
that it is oblong. At the top the diameter is about 300 yards of
which 250 cover what is technically called 'blue', – meaning
diamondiferous soil. Near the surface and for some way
down, the sides are light brown, and as blue is the recognized
diamond colour you will at first suppose that no diamonds
were found near the surface; – but the light brown has been in
all respects the same as the blue, the colour of the soil to a
certain depth having been affected by a mixture of iron. Below

this everything is blue, all the constructions in the pit having been made out of some blue matter which at first sight would seem to have been carried down for the purpose. But there are other colours on the wall which give a peculiar pictur-esqueness to the mines. The top edge as you look at it with your back to the setting sun is red with the gravel of the upper reef, while below, in places, the beating of rain and running of water has produced peculiar hues, all of which are a delight to the eye.

As you stand at the edge you will find large high-raised boxes at your right hand and at your left, and you will see all round the margin crowds of such erections, each box being as big as a little house and higher than most of the houses in Kimberley. These are the first recipients for the stuff that is brought up out of the mine. And behind these, so that you will often find that you have walked between them, are the whims by means of which the stuff is raised, each whim being worked by two horses. Originally the operation was done by hand-windlasses which were turned by Kafirs – and the practice is continued at some of the smaller enterprises; – but the horse whims are now so general that there is a world of them round the claim. The stuff is raised on aerial tramways, – and the method of an aerial tramway is as follows. Wires are stretched taught from the wooden boxes slanting down to the claims at the bottom, – never less than four wires for each box, two for the ascending and two for the descending bucket. As one bucket runs down empty on one set of wires, another comes up full on the other set. The ascending bucket is of course full of 'blue'. The buckets were at first simply leathern bags. Now they have increased in size and importance of construction, – to half barrels and so upwards to large iron cylinders which sit easily upon wheels running in the wires as they ascend and descend and bring up their loads, half a cart load at each journey.

As this is going on round the entire circle it follows that there are wires starting everywhere from the rim and converg-ing to a centre at the bottom, on which the buckets are always scudding through the air. They drop down and creep up not altogether noiselessly but with a gentle trembling sound which mixes itself pleasantly with the murmur from the voices below. And the wires seem to be the strings of some wonderful harp, – aerial or perhaps infernal, – from which the beholder expects that a louder twang will soon be heard. The wires are there always of course, but by some lights they are hardly visible. The mine is seen best in the afternoon and the visitor looking at it should stand with his back to the setting sun; – but as he so stands and so looks he will hardly be aware that there is a wire at all if his visit be made, say on a Saturday afternoon, when the works are stopped and the mine is mute.

When the world below is busy there are about 3,500 Kafirs at work, – some small proportion upon the reef which has to be got into order so that it shall neither tumble in, nor impede the work, nor overlay the diamondiferous soil as it still does in some places; but by far the greater number are employed in digging. Their task is to pick up the earth and shovel it into the buckets and iron receptacles. Much of it is loosened for them by blasting which is done after the Kafirs have left the mine at 6 o'clock. You look down and see the swarm of black ants busy at every hole and corner with their picks moving and shovelling the loose blue soil.

But the most peculiar phase of the mine, as you gaze into its one large pit, is the subdivision into claims and portions. Could a person see the sight without having heard any word of explanation it would be impossible, I think, to conceive the meaning of all those straight cut narrow dikes, of those mud walls all at right angles to each other, of those square separate pits, and again of those square upstanding blocks, looking like houses without doors or windows. You can see that nothing on earth was ever less level than the bottom of the bowl, – and that the black ants in traversing it, as they are always doing, go up and down almost at every step, jumping here on to a narrow wall and skipping there across a deep dividing channel as though some diabolically ingenious architect had contrived a house with 500 rooms, not one of which should be on the same floor, and to and from none of which should there be a pair of stairs or a door or a window. In addition to this it must be imagined that the architect had omitted the roof in order that the wires of the harp above described might be brought into every chamber. The house has then been furnished with picks, shovels, planks, and a few barrels, populated with its black legions, and there it is for you to look at.

At first the bottom of the bowl seems small. You know the size of it as you look, – and that it is nine acres, enough to make a moderate field, – but it looks like no more than a bowl. Gradually it becomes enormously large as your eye dwells for a while on the energetic business going on in one part, and then travels away over an infinity of subdivided claims to the work in some other portion. It seems at last to be growing under you and that soon there will be no limit to the variety of partitions on which you have to look. You will of course be anxious to descend and if you be no better than a man there is nothing to prevent you. Should you be a lady I would advise you to stay where you are. The work of going up and down is hard, everything is dirty, and the place below is not nearly so interesting as it is above. One firm at the mine, Messrs. Baring Gould, Atkins, & Co. have gone to the expense of sinking a perpendicular shaft with a tunnel below from the shaft to the mine, – so as to avoid the use of the aerial tramway; and by Mr. Gould's kindness I descended through his shaft. Nevertheless there was some trouble in getting into the mine and when I was there the labour of clambering about from one chamber to another in that marvellously broken house was considerable and was not lessened by the fact that the heat of the sun was about 140. The division of the claims, however, became apparent to me and I could see how one was being worked, and another left without any present digging till the claim-owner's covenience should be suited. But there is a regulation compelling a man to work if the standing of his 'blue' should become either prejudicial or dangerous to his neighbours. There is one shaft, – that belonging to the firm I have mentioned; and one tramway has been cut down by another firm through the reef and circumjacent soild so as to make an inclined plane up and down to the mine.

On looking at the accompanying plan the reader will see that the ground was originally divided into 801 claims with some few double members to claims at the east end of the mine; – but in truth nearly half of those have never been of value, consisting entirely of reef, the diamondiferous matter, the extent of which has now been ascertained, not having travelled so far. There are in truth 408 existing claims. The plan, which shews the locality of each claim as divided whether of worth or of no worth, shows also the rate at which they are all valued for purpose of taxation. To ascertain the rated value the reader must take any one of the sums given in red figures and multiply it by the number of subdivisions in the compartment to which those figures are attached. For instance at the west end is the lowest figure, – £100, and as there are 37 marked claims in this compartment, the rated value of the compartment is £3,700. This is the poorest side of the mine and probably but few of the claims thus marked are worked at all. The richest side of the mine is towards the south, where in one compartment there are 12 claims each rated at £5,500, so that the whole compartment is supposed to be worth £66,000. The selling value is however much higher than at which the claims are rated for the purpose of taxation.

But though there are but 408 claims there are subdivisions in regard to property very much more minute. There are shares held by individuals as small as one-sixteenth of a claim. The total property is in fact divided into 514 portions, the amount of which of course varies extremely. Every master miner pays 10s. a month to the Government for the privilege of working whether he own a claim or only a portion of a claim. In working this the number of men employed differs very much from time to time. When I was there the mine was very full, and there were probably almost 4,000 men in it and as many more employed above on the stuff. When the 'blue' has come up and been deposited in the great wooden boxes at the top it is then lowered by its own weight into carts, and carried off to the 'ground' of the proprietor. Every diamond digger is obliged to have a space of ground somewhere round the town, – as near his whim as he can get it, – to which his stuff is carted and then laid out to crumble and decompose. This may occupy weeks, but the time depends on what may be the fall of rain. If there be no rain, it must be watered – at a very considerable expense. It is then brought to the washing, and is first put into a round puddling trough where it is broken up and converted into mud by stationary rakes which work upon the stuff as the trough goes round. The stones of course fall to the bottom, and as diamonds are the heaviest of stones they

fall with the others. The mud is examined and thrown away –
and then the stones are washed, and rewashed, and sifted, and
examined. The greater number of diamonds are found during
this operation; – but the large gems and those therefore of by
far the greatest value are generally discovered while the stuff is
being knocked about and put into the buckets in the mine.

It need hardly be said that in such an operation as I have
described the greatest care is necessary to prevent stealing and
that no care will prevent it. The Kafirs are the great thieves, –
to such an extent of superexcellence that white superin-
tendence is spoken of as being the only safeguard. The honesty
of the white man may perhaps be indifferent, but such as it is it
has to be used at every point to prevent, as far as it may be
prevented, the systematized stealing in which the Kafirs take
an individual and national pride. The Kafirs are not only most
willing but most astute thieves, feeling a glory in their theft
and thinking that every stone stolen from a white man is a
duty done to their Chief and their tribe. I think it may be taken
as certain that no Kafir would feel the slightest pang of
conscience at stealing a diamond, or that any disgrace would
be held to attach to him among other Kafirs for such a
performance. They come to the Fields instructed by their
Chiefs to steal diamonds and they obey the orders like loyal
subjects. Many of the Kafir Chiefs are said to have large
quantities of diamonds which have been brought to them by
their men returning from the diggings; – but most of those
which are stolen no doubt find their way into the hands of
illicit dealers. I have been told that the thefts perpetrated by the
kafirs amount to 25 per cent. on the total amount found; – but
this I do not believe.

The opportunities for stealing are of hourly occurrence and
are of such a nature as to make prevention impossible. These
men are sharpsighted as birds and know and see a diamond
much quicker than a white man. They will pick up stones with
their toes and secrete them even under the eyes of those who
are watching them. I was told that a man will so hide a
diamond in his mouth that no examination will force him to
disclose it. They are punished when discovered with lashes
and imprisonment, – in accordance with the law on the
matter. No employer is now allowed to flog his man at his

own pleasure. And the white men who buy diamonds from Kafirs are also punished when convicted, by fine and imprisonment for the simple offence of buying from a Kafir; but with flogging also if convicted of having instigated a Kafir to steal. Nevertheless a lucrative business of this nature is carried on, and the Kafirs know well where to dispose of their plunder though of course but for a small proportion of its value.

Ten shillings a week and their food were the regular wages here as elsewhere. This I found to be very fluctuating, but the money paid had rarely gone lower for any considerable number of men than the above-named rate. The lowest amount paid has been 7s. 6d. a week. Sometimes it had been as high as 20s. and even 30s. a week. A good deal of the work is supplied by contract, certain middlemen undertaking to provide men with all expenses paid at £1 a week. When mealies have become dear from drought, – there being no grass for oxen on the route, – no money can be made in this way. Such was the case when I was in Griqualand West. It is stated by Mr. Oats, an engineer, in his evidence given to the Committee on the Griqualand West Annexation Bill, in June 1877, – that the annual amount of wages paid at Kimberley had varied from £600,000 to £1,600,000 a year. Nearly the whole of this had gone into the hands of the Kafirs.

Perhaps the most interesting sight at the mine is the escaping of the men from their labour at six o'clock. Then, at the sound of some welcomed gong, they begin to swarm up the sides close at each other's heels apparently altogether indifferent as to whether there be a path or no. They come as flies come up a wall, only capering as flies never caper, – and shouting as they come. In endless strings, as ants follow each other, they move, passing along ways which seem to offer no hold to a human foot. Then it is that one can best observe their costume in which a jacket is never absent but of which a pair of trowsers rarely forms a portion. A soldier's red jacket or a soldier's blue jacket has more charms than any other vestment. They seem always to be good humoured, always well-behaved, – but then they are always thieves. And yet how grand a thing it is that so large a number of these men should have been brought in so short a space of time to the habit of receiving wages and to the capacity of bargaining as to the wages for which they will work. I shall not, however, think it so grand a thing if any one addresses them as the free and independent electors of Kimberley before they have got trowsers to cover their nakedness.

I must add also that a visitor to Kimberley should if possible take an opportunity of looking down upon the mine by moonlight. It is weird and wonderful sight, and may almost be called sublime in its peculiar strangeness.

CHAPTER IX

KIMBERLEY

Having described the diamond mines in the Kimberley district I must say a word about the town of Kimberley to which the mines have given birth. The total population as given by a census taken in 1877 was 13,590, shewing the town to be the second largest in South Africa. By joining to this Du Toit's Pan and Bultfontein which are in fact suburbs of Kimberley we get a total urban population of about 18,000. Of these nearly 10,000 are coloured, and something over 8,000 are Europeans. Among the Europeans two-fifths are females, and of course there is the ordinary population of children – with the coloured people the females are about 1 to 7. Of the adult male population two-thirds are of coloured races, – Kafirs for the most part, – and one-third is European. At present both the one and the other are a shifting people; – but the Kafirs shift much the quickest. Each man remains generally six or eight months on the Fields and then returns home to his tribe. This mode of life, however, is already somewhat on the decrease, and as the love of making money grows, and as tribal reverence for the Chieftains dies out, the men will learn to remain more constantly at their work. Unless the diamonds come to an end all together, – which one cannot but always feel to be possible, – the place will become a large town with a settled Kafir population which will fall gradually into civilized ways of life. There is no other place in South Africa where this has been done, or for many years can be done to the same extent. I mention this here because it seems to be so essentially necessary to remember that South Africa is a land not of white but of black men, and that the progress to be most desired is that which will quickest induce the Kafir to put off his savagery and live after the manner of his white brothers.

Throughout the whole country which the English and the

Dutch between them have occupied as their own, the Kafirs
are the superiors in numbers in much greater proportion than
that stated above in reference to the town of Kimberley; – but
these numbers are to be found, not in towns, but out in their
own hitherto untouched districts, where they live altogether
after their old ways, where the Kafirs of today are as were the
Kafirs of fifty years ago. And even with those who have come
under our dominion and who live to some degree intermixed
with us, the greater proportion still follow their old customs
of which idleness and dependence on the work of women for
what is absolutely necessary to existence, may be said to be the
most prominent. The work of civilizing as it has been carried
out by simple philanthropy or by religion is terribly slow.
One is tempted sometimes to say that nothing is done by
religion and very little by philanthropy. But love of money
works very fast. In Griqualand West, especially in the
Diamond Fields, and above all at Kimberley, it is not only out
in the wilds, by the river sides, on the veld, and in their own
kraals, that the black men outnumber the white; but in the
streets of the city also and in the work shops of the mine. And
here they are brought together not by the spasmodic energy of
missionaries or by the unalluring attraction of schools but by
the certainty of earning wages. The seeker after diamonds is
determined to have them because the making of his fortune
depends upon them; and the Kafir himself is determined to
come to Kimberley because he has learned the loveliness of
10s. a week paid regularly into his hand every Saturday night.

Who can doubt but that work is the great civilizer of the
world, – work and the growing desire for those good things
which work will only bring? If there be one who does he
should come here to see how those dusky troops of labourers,
who ten years since were living in the wildest state of
unalloyed savagery, whose only occupation was the slaughter
of each other in tribal wars, each of whom was the slave of his
Chief, who were subject to the dominion of most brutalizing
and cruel superstitions, have already put themselves on the
path towards civilization. They are thieves no doubt; – that is
they steal diamonds though not often other things. They are
not Christians. They do not yet care much about breeches.
They do not go to school. But they are orderly. They come to

work at six in the morning and go away at six in the evening. They have an hour in the middle of the day, and know that they have to work during the other hours. They take their meals regularly and, what is the best of all, they are learning to spend their money instead of carrying it back to their Chiefs.

Civilization can not come at once. The coming I fear under any circumstances must be slow. But this is the quickest way towards it that has yet been found. The simple teaching of religion has never brought large numbers of Natives to live in European habits; but I have no doubt that European habits will bring about religion. The black man when he lives with the white man and works under the white man's guidance will learn to believe really what the white man really believes himself. Surely we should not expect him to go faster. But the missionary has endeavoured to gratify his own soul by making here and there a model Christian before the pupil has been able to understand any of the purposes of Christianity. I have not myself seen the model Christian perfected; but when I have looked down into the Kimberley mine and seen three or four thousand of them at work, – although each of them would willingly have stolen a diamond if the occasion came, – I have felt that I was looking at three or four thousand growing Christians.

Because of this I regard Kimberley as one of the most interesting places on the face of the earth. I know no other spot on which the work of civilizing a Savage is being carried on with so signal a success. The Savages whom we have encountered in our great task of populating the world have for the most part eluded our grasp by perishing while we have been considering how we might best deal with them. Here, in South Africa, a healthy nation remains and assures us by its prolific tendency that when protected from self-destruction by our fostering care it will spread and increase beneath our hands. But what was to be done with these people? Having found that they do not mean to die, by what means might we instruct them how to live? Teach them to sing hymns, and all will be well. That is one receipt. Turn them into slaves, and make them work. That is another receipt. Divide the land with them, and let them live after their own fashions; – only subject to some little control from us. That was a third. The hymns have done nothing. The slavery was of course impossible. And that division of land has been, perhaps not equally futile, but insufficient for the growing needs of the people; – insufficient also for our own needs. Though we abuse the Kafir we want his service, and we want more than our share of his land. But that which no effort of intelligence could produce has been brought about by circumstances. The Diamond Fields have been discovered and now there are ten thousand of these people receiving regular wages and quite capable of rushing to a magistrate for protection if they be paid a shilling short on Saturday night.

This the diamonds have done, and it is the great thing which they have done. We have fair reason to believe that other similar industries will arise. There are already copper mines at work in Namaqualand, on the western coast of South Africa, in which the Natives are employed, and lead mines in the Transvaal. There are gold fields in the Transvaal at which little is now being done, because the difficulties of working them are at present overwhelming. But as years roll quickly on these, too, will become hives of coloured labour, and in this way Kimberleys will arise in various parts of the continent.

I cannot say that Kimberley is in other respects an alluring town; – perhaps as little so as any town that I have ever visited. There are places to which men are attracted by the desire of gain which seem to be so repulsive that no gain can compensate the miseries incidental to such an habitation. I have seen more than one such place and have wondered that under any inducement men should submit themselves, their wives and children to such an existence. I remember well my impressions on reaching Charles Dickens' Eden at the junction of the Ohio and Mississipi rivers and my surprise that any human being should have pitched his tent in a place so unwholesome and so hideous. I have found Englishmen collected on the Musquito Coast, a wretched crew; and having been called on by untoward Fate and a cruel Government to remain a week at Suez have been driven to consider whether life could have been possible there for a month. During my sojourn at Kimberley, though I was the recipient of the kindest hospitality and met two or three whom I shall ever remember among the pleasant acquaintances of my life, – yet the place itself was distasteful to me in the extreme. When I was there the heat was very great, the thermometer registering 160 in the sun, and 97 in the shade. I was not absolutely ill, but I was so nearly ill that I was in fear the whole time. Perhaps having been in such personal discomfort, I am not a fair judge of the place. But an atmosphere composed of dust and flies cannot be pleasant, – of dust so thick that the sufferer fears to remove it lest the raising of it may aggravate the evil, and of flies so numerous that one hardly dares to slaughter them by the ordinary means lest their dead bodies should be noisome. When a gust of wind would bring the dust in a cloud hiding everything, a cloud so thick that it would seem that the solid surface of the earth had risen diluted into the air, and when flies had rendered occupation altogether impossible. I would be told, when complaining, that I ought to be there, in December say, or February, – at some other time of the year than that the present, – if I really wanted to see what flies and dust could do. I sometimes thought that the people of Kimberley were proud of their flies and their dust.

And the meat was bad, the butter uneatable, vegetables a rarity, – supplied indeed at the table at which I sat but supplied at a great cost. Milk and potatoes were luxuries so costly that one sinned almost in using them. A man walking about with his pocket full of diamonds would not perhaps care for this; but even at Kimberley there are those who have fixed incomes, – an unfortunate Deputy Governor or the like, – to whom sugar at 2s. 6d. a pound and other equally necessary articles in the same proportion, must detract much from the honour and glory of the position. When I was there 'transport', no doubt, was unusually high. Indeed, as I arrived, there were muttered threats that 'transport' would be discontinued altogether unless rain would come. For the understanding of this it must be known that almost everything consumed at Kimberley has to be carried up from the coast, five hundred miles, by ox-waggons, and that the oxen have to feed themselves on the grasses along the road. When there has been a period of drought there are no grasses, and when there are no grasses the oxen will die instead of making progress. Periods of drought are by no means uncommon in South Africa. When I was at Kimberley there had been a period of drought for many months. There had, indeed, been no rain to speak of for more than a year. As one consequence of this the grocers were charging 2s. 6d. a pound for brown sugar. Even the chance of such a state of things militates very much against the comfort of a residence.

I do not think that there is a tree to be seen within five miles of the town. When I was there I doubt whether there was a blade of grass within twenty miles, unless what might be found on the very marge of the low water of the Vaal river. Everything was brown, as though the dusty dry uncovered ugly earth never knew the blessing of verdure. To ascertain that the roots of grass were remaining one had to search the ground. There is to be a park; and irrigation has been proposed so that the park may become green; – but the park had not as yet progressed beyond the customary brown. In all Kimberley and its surroundings there was nothing pretty to meet the eye; – except, indeed, women's faces which were as bright there as elsewhere. It was a matter of infinite regret to me that faces so bright should be made to look out on a world so ugly.

The town is built of corrugated iron. My general readers will probably not have seen many edifices so constructed. But even in England corrugated iron churches have been erected, when the means necessary for stone buildings have been temporarily wanting; and I think I have seen the studios of photographers made of the same material. It is probably the most hideous that has yet come to man's hands; – but it is the most portable and therefore in many localities the cheapest, – and in some localities the only material possible. It is difficult to conceive the existence of a town in which every plank used has had to be dragged five hundred miles by oxen; but such has been the case at Kimberley. Nor can bricks be made which will stand the weather because bricks require to be burned and cannot well be burned without fuel. Fuel at Kimberley is so expensive a luxury that two thoughts have to be given to the boiling of a kettle. Sun-burned bricks are used and form the walls of which the corrugated iron is the inside casing; but sun-burned bricks will not stand the weather and can only be used when they are cased. Lath and plaster for ceilings there is little or none. The rooms are generally covered with canvas which can be easily carried. But a canvas ceiling does not remain long clean, or even rectilinear. The invincible dust settled upon it and bulges it, and the stain of the dust comes through it. Wooden floors are absolutely necessary for comfort and cleanliness; but at Kimberley it will cost £40 to floor a moderate room. The consequence is that even people who are doing well with their diamonds live in comfortless houses, always meaning to pack up and run after this year, or next year, or perhaps the year after next. But if they have done ill with their diamonds they remain till they may do better; and if they have done well then there falls upon them the Auri sacra fames. When £30,000 have been so easily heaped together why not have £60,000; – and when £60,000 why not £100,000? And when they spend money largely in this state of trial, in a condition which is not intended to be prolonged, – but which is prolonged from year to year by the desire for more? Why try to enjoy life here, this wretched life, when so soon there is a life coming which is to be so infinitely better? Such is often the theory of the enthusiastic Christian, – not however often carried out to its logical conclusions. At such a place as Kimberley the theory becomes more lively; but the good time is postponed till the capacity for enjoying it is too probably lost.

The town of Kimberley is chiefly notable for a large square, – as large perhaps as Russell Square. One or two of the inhabitants asked me whether I was not impressed by the grandeur of its dimensions so as to feel that there was something of sublimity attached to it! 'I though it very ugly at first,' said one lady who had been brought out from England to make her residence among the diamonds; – 'but I have looked at it now till I have to own its magnificence.' I could not but say that corrugated iron would never become magnificent in my eyes. In Kimberley there are two buildings with a storey above the ground, and one of these is in the square. This is its only magnificence. There is no pavement. The roadway is all dust and holes. There is a market place in the midst which certainly is not magnificent. Around are the corrugated iron shops of the ordinary dealers in provisions. An uglier place I do not know how to imagine. When I was called upon to admire it, I was lost in wonder; but acknowledged that it was well that necessity should produce such results.

I think that none of the diamond dealers live in this square. The various diamond shops to which I was taken were near the mine, or in the street leading down from the mine to the square. These were little counting houses in which the dealers would sit, generally two together, loosely handling property worth many thousands of pounds. I was taken to them to see diamonds, and saw diamonds without stint. It seemed that one partner would buy while another would sort and pack. Parcel after parcel was opened for me with almost as little reserve as was exhibited when Lothair asked for pearls. Lothair was an expected purchaser; while the diamond dealer knew that nothing was to be made by me. I could not but think how easy it would be to put just one big one into my pocket. The dealers, probably, were careful that I did nothing of the kind. The stones were packed in paper parcels, each parcel containing perhaps from fifty to two hundred according to their size. Then four or five of these parcels would be fitted into a paper box – which would again be enclosed in a paper envelope. Without other safeguard than this the parcels are registered and sent by post, to London, Paris, or Amsterdam as the case may be. By far the greater number go to London. The mails containing these diamonds then travel for six days and six nights on mail carts to Capetown, – for four-fifths of the way without any guard, and very frequently with no one on the mail cart except the black boy who drives it. The cart travels day and night along desolate roads and is often many miles distant from the nearest habitation. Why the mails are not robbed I cannot tell. The diamond dealers say that the robber could not get away with his plunder, and would find no market for it were he to do so. They, however, secure themselves by some system of insurance. I cannot but think that the insurers, or underwriters, will some day find themselves subjected to a heavy loss. A great robbery might be effected by two persons, and the goods which would be stolen are of all property the most portable. Thieves with a capital, – and thieves in these days do have capital, – might afford to wait, and diamonds in the rough cannot be traced. I should have though that property of such immense value would have paid for an armed escort. The gold in Australia, which is much less portable, is always accompanied by an escort.*

I was soon sick of looking at diamonds though the idea of holding ten or twenty thousand pounds lightly between my fingers did not quite lose its charm. I was however disgusted at the terms of reproach with which most of the diamonds were described by their owners. Many of them were 'off colours,' stones of a yellowish hue and therefore of comparatively little value, or stones with a flaw, stones which would split in the cutting, stones which could not be cut to any advantage. There were very many evil stones to one that was good, so that nature after all did not appear to have been as generous as she might have been. And these dealers when the stones are brought to them for purchase, have no certain standard of value by which to regulate their transactions with their customers. The man behind the counter will take the stones, one by one, examine them, weigh them, and then make his offer for the parcel. Dealing in horses is precarious work, – when there is often little to show whether an animal be worth £50, or £100, or £150. But with diamonds it must be much more so. A dealer offers £500 when the buyer has perhaps expected £2,000! And yet the dealer is probably nearest to the mark. The diamonds at any rate are bought and sold, and are sent away by post at the rate of about £2,000,000 in the year. In 1876 the registered export of diamonds from Kimberley amounted in value to £1,414,590, and reached 773 pounds avoirdupois in weight. But it is computed that not above three quarters of what are sent from the place are recorded in the accounts that are kept. There is no law to make such record necessary. Anyone who has become legally possessed of a diamond may legally take it or sent it away as he pleases.

The diamond dealers whom I saw were the honest men,

---

* Since this was written a mail steamer with a large amount of these diamonds among the mails has gone to the bottom of the sea. The mails, and with the mails, the diamonds have been recovered; but in such a condition that they cannot be recognised and given up to the proper owners. They are lying at the General Post Office, and how to dispose of them nobody knows.

who keep their heads well above water, and live in the odour of diamond sanctity, dealing only with licensed diggers and loving the law. But there are diamond dealers who buy from the Kafirs, – or from intermediate rogues who instigate the Kafirs to steal. These are regarded as the curse of the place, and, as may be understood, their existence is most injurious to the interests of all who traffic honestly in this article. The law is very severe on them, imprisoning them, and subjecting them to lashes if in any case it can be proved that a delinquent has instigated a Kafir to steal. One such dealer I saw in the Kimberley gaol, a good-looking young man who had to pass I think two years in durance among black thieves and white thieves because he had bought dishonestly. I pitied him because he was clean. But I ought to have pitied him the less because having been brought up to be clean he, nevertheless, had become a rogue.

Next to diamond dealing the selling of guns used to be the great trade in Kimberley, the purchasers being Kafirs who thus disposed of their surplus wages. But when I was there the trade seemed to have come to an end, the Kafirs, I trust, having found that they could do better with their money than buy guns, – which they seldom use with much precision when they have them. There was once a whole street devoted to this dealing in guns, but the gun shops had been converted to other purposes when I was there. Great complaint had been made against the Government of Griqualand West for permitting the unreserved sale of guns to the Kafirs, and attempts have been made by the two Republics – of the Transvaal and the Orange Free State – to stop the return of men when so armed. The guns were taken away from those who had not a pass, and such passes were rarely given. Now they may travel through the Transvaal with any number of guns, as the British authorities do not stop them. Why it has come to pass that the purchases are no longer made I do not understand. Whether the trade should or should not have been stopped I am not prepared to say. We have not hesitated to prevent the possession of arms in Ireland when we have though that the peace of the country might be endangered by them. I do not think that the peace of South Africa has been endangered by the guns which the Kafirs have owned, or that the guns in the hands of

Kafirs have been very fatal to us in the still existing disturbance. But yet the Kafirs are very numerous and the white
men are comparatively but a handful! I would have a Kafir as
free to shoot a buck as a white man. And yet I feel that the
Kafir must be kept in subjection. The evil, if it be an evil, has
now been done, for guns are very numerous among the
Kafirs.

There can hardly be a doubt that Kimberley and the
diamond fields have been of great service to the black men
who obtain work. No doubt they are thieves, – as regards the
diamonds, – but their thievery will gradually be got under by
the usual processes. To argue against providing work for a
Kafir because a Kafir may steal is the same as to say that
housemaids should not be taught to write lest they should
learn to forge. That argument has been used, but does not
now require refutation. And there can be as little doubt that
the finding of diamonds has in a commercial point of view
been the salvation of South Africa. The Orange Free State, of
which 'The Fields' at first formed a part, and which is closely
adjacent to them, has been so strengthened by the trade thus
created as to be now capable of a successful and permanent
existence, – a condition of things which I think no observer of
South African affairs would have considered to be possible had
not Kimberley with its eighteen thousand much-consuming
mouths been established on its border. As regards the Cape
Colony generally, if quite the same thing need not be said, it
must be acknowledged that its present comparative success is
due almost entirely to the diamonds, – or rather to the
commercial prosperity caused by the consumption in which
diamond finders and their satellites have been enabled to
indulge. The Custom duties of the Cape Colony in 1869,
before the diamond industry existed, were less than
£300,000.* In 1875 that sum had been very much more than

---

* In 1869 the amount was £295,661. In 1875 it was £735,380. In 1869
the total revenue was £580,026. In 1875 it was £1,602,918; the increase
being nearly to three-fold. The increase in the expenditure was still
greater, – but that only shows that the Colony found itself sufficiently
prosperous to be justified in borrowing money for the making of
railroads. The reader must bear in mind that these Custom Duties

doubled. And it must be remembered that this rapid increase did not come from any great increase in numbers. The diamond-digging brought in a few white men no doubt, but only a few in comparison with the increase in revenue. There are but 8,000 Europeans in the diamond fields altogether. Had they all been new comers this would have been no great increase to a population which now exceeds 700,000 persons. The sudden influx of national wealth has come from the capability for consumption created by the new industry. White men looking for diamonds can drink champagne. Black men looking for diamonds can buy clothes and guns and food. It is not the wealth found which directly enriches the nation, but the trade created by the finding. It was the same with the gold in Australia. Of the national benefit arising from the diamonds there can be no doubt. Whether they have been equally beneficial to those who have searched for them and found them may be a matter of question.

What fortunes have been made in this pursuit no one can tell. If they have been great I have not heard of them. There can be no doubt that many have ruined themselves by fruitless labours, and that others who have suddenly enriched them-selves have been unable to bear their prosperity with equanimity. The effect of a valuable diamond upon a digger who had been working perhaps a month for nothing was in the early days almost maddening. Now, as with gold in Australia, the pursuit has settled itself down to a fixed industry. Companies have been formed. Individuals are not suddenly enriched by the sudden finding of a stone. Dividends are divided monthly and there is something approaching to a fixed rate of finding from this claim or from that, from this side of the mine or from the other. There is less of excitement and consequently less of evil. Men are no longer prone to the gambler's condition of mind which induces an individual to think that he, – he specially, – will win in opposition to all

---

were all received and pocketed by the Cape Colony, though a large proportion of them was levied on goods to be consumed in the Diamond Fields. As I have stated elsewhere, the Cape colony has in this respect been a cormorant, swallowing what did not rightfully belong to her.

established odds and chances, and prompts him to anticipate his winning by lavish expenditure, – to waste it when it does come by such puerile resources as shoeing a horse with gold or drinking champagne out of a bucket. The searching for gold and diamonds has always had this danger attached to it, – that the money when it has come has too frequently not been endeared to the finder by hard continuous work. It has been 'easy come and easy gone.' This to some degree is still the case. There is at Kimberley much more of gambling, much more of champagne, much more of the rowdy exhiliration coming from sudden money, than at older towns of the same or much greater population, or of the same or much greater wealth. But the trade of Kimberley is now a settled industry and as such may be presumed to be beneficent to those who exercise it.

Nevertheless there is a stain sticking to the diamonds, – such a stain as sticks to gold, which tempts one to repeat the poet's caution:-

> Aurum irrepertum, et sic melius situm
> Cum terra celat, spernere fortior,
> Quam cogere humanos in usus.

It would be untrue to say that he who works to ornament the world is necessarily less noble than the other workman who supplies it with what is simply useful. The designer of a room-paper ranks above the man who hangs it, – and the artist whose, picture decorates the wall is much above the designer of the paper. Why therefore should not the man who finds diamonds be above the man who finds bread? And yet I feel sure that he is not. It is not only the thing procured but the manner of procuring it that makes or mars the nobility of the work. If there be an employment in which the labourer has actually to grovel in the earth it is this search for diamonds. There is much of it in gold-seeking, but in the search after diamonds it is all grovelling. Let the man rise as high as he may in the calling, be the head of the biggest firm at Kimberley, still he stands by and sees the grit turned, – still he picks out the diamonds from the other dirt with his own fingers, and carries his produce about with him in his own pocket. If a man be working a coal mine, though he be himself the hardest worked as well as the head workman in the business, he is removed from actual contact with the coal. But here, at Kimberley, sharp prying eyes are wanted, rather than an intelligence fitted for calculations, and patience in manipulating dirt than skill in managing men or figures.

And the feeling engendered, – the constant recollection that a diamond may always be found, – is carried so far that the mind never rests from business. The diamond-seeker cannot get out of his task and take himself calmly to his literature at 4 P.M. or 5 or 6. This feeling runs through even to his wife and children, teaching them that dirt thrice turned may yet be turned a fourth time with some hope of profit. Consequently ladies, and children, do turn dirt instead of making pretty needle-work or wholesome mud pies. When I heard of so much a dozen being given to young bairns for the smallest specks of diamonds, specks which their young eyes might possibly discover, my heart was bitterly grieved. How shall a child shake off a stain which has been so early incurred? And when ladies have told me, as ladies did tell me, – pretty clever well-dressed women, – of hours so passed, of day after day spent in the turning of dust by their own fingers because there might still be diamonds among the dust, I thought that I could almost sooner have seen my own wife or my own girl with a broom at a street crossing.

There is not so much of this now as there was, and as years roll on, – if the diamonds still be to be found, – there will be less and less. If the diamonds still be there in twenty years' time, – as to which I altogether decline to give my opinion, – a railway will have been carried on to Kimberley, and planks will have been carried up, and perhaps bricks from some more favoured locality, and possibly paving stones, so that the town shall be made to look less rowdy and less abominable. And pipes will be laid on from the Vaal river, and there will be water carts. And with the dust the flies will go into abeyance. And trees will have been planted. And fresh butter will be made. And there will be a library and men will have books. And houses will have become pleasant, so that a merchant may love to sit at home in his own verandah, – which he will then afford to have broad and cool and floored. And as the nice things come the nasty habits will sink. The ladies will live far away from the grit, and small diamonds will have become too common to make it worth the parents' while to endanger their children's eyes. Some mode of checking the Kafir thieves will perhaps have been found, – and the industry will have sunk into the usual grooves. Nothing, however, will tend so much to this as the lessening of the value of diamonds. The stone is at present so precious that a man's mind cannot bear to think that one should escape him.

I should be doing injustice to Kimberley and to those who have managed Kimberley if I did not say that very great struggles have been made to provide it with those institutions which are peculiarly needed for the welfare of an assembled population. Churches are provided plentifully, – at one of which, at any rate, sermons are to be heard much in advance of those which I may call the sermon at sermon par. I could have wished however that the clergymen who preached them had not worn a green ribbon. And there are hospitals, which have caused infinite labour and are now successful; – especially one which is nearly self-supporting and is managed exquisitely by one of those ladies who go out into the world to do good wherever good may be done. I felt as I spoke to her that I was speaking to one of the sweet ones of the earth. To bind up a man's wounds, or to search for diamonds among the dirt! There is a wide difference there certainly.

I could have wished that the prison had been better, – that is more prisonly, – with separate rooms for instance for those awaiting trial and those committed. But all this will be done within those twenty next coming years. And I know well how difficult it is to get money to get such things afloat in a young community.

THE ORANGE FREE STATE

CHAPTER X

THE ORANGE FREE STATE – ITS EARLY HISTORY

The history of the origin of the Orange Free State, as a certain district of South Africa is called, is one which when really written will not I think redound to the credit of England. This I say not intending to accuse any British statesman of injustice, – much less of dishonesty. In all that has been done by the Colonial Office in reference to the territory in question the attempt to do right has from first to last been only too anxious and painstaking. But as is generally the case when over anxiety exists in lieu of assured conviction, the right course has not been plainly seen, and the wrong thing has been done and done, perhaps, in a wrong manner.

Our system of government by Cabinets is peculiarly open to such mistakes in reference to Colonial matters. At the Foreign office, as is well known, there is a prescribed course of things and whether Lord Granville be there or Lord Derby the advice given will probably be the same. At the Home office the same course is followed whether the gentleman there be a Liberal or a Conservative, and if one dispenser of the Queen's prerogative be more prone than another to allow criminals to escape, the course of Government is not impeded by his proclivities. But in looking back at the history of the Colonies during the last fifty years we see the idiosyncrasies of the individual ministers who have held the office of Secretary of State rather than a settled course of British action, and we are made to feel how suddenly the policy of one minister may be made to give way to the conscientious convictions of another. Hence there have come changes each of which may be evidence of dogged obstinacy in the mind of some much respected Statesman, but which seem to be proof of vacillation in the nation.

It would be thought that a colonizing nation like Great

Britain, – now the only colonizing nation in existence, – should have a policy of colonization. The Americans of the United States have such a policy, though they do not colonize in our sense. They will not colonize at all beyond their own continent, so that all the citizens of their Republic may be brought into one homogeneous whole. The Spaniards and Dutch who have been great Colonists have a colonial policy, – which has ever consisted in getting what can be got for the mother country. Among ourselves, with all that we have done and all that we are doing, we do not yet know whether it is our intention to limit or to extend our colonial empire; we do not yet know whether we purpose to occupy other lands or to protect in their occupation those who now hold them; we do not yet know whether as a nation we wish our colonial dependants to remain always loyal to the British Crown or whether we desire to see them start for themselves as independant realms. All we do know is that with that general philanthropy and honesty without which a British Cabinet cannot now exist we want to do good and to avoid doing evil. But when we look back, and, taking even three liberal Colonial Secretaries, see the difference of opinion on colonial matters of such men as Lord Glenelg, Lord Grey, and Lord Granville, we have to own that our colonial policy must vacillate.

Are we to extend or are we not to extend our colonial empire? That was a question on which some years ago it did seem that our Statesmen had come to a decision. The task we had taken upon us was thought to be already more than enough for our strength, and we would not stretch our hands any further. If it might be practicable to get rid of some of the least useful of our operations it would be well to do so. That dream of a settled purpose has, however, been very rudely broken. The dreamers have never been able to act upon it as a policy. It will not be necessary to do more than name the Fiji Islands, – not the last but one of the last of our costly acquirements, – to show how unable the Colonial office at home has been to say, 'so far will we go but no further.' Had the Colonial office recognised it as a policy that wherever Englishmen settle themselves in sufficient numbers to make a disturbance if they be not governed, then government must go after them, then the Fiji Islands might have been accepted as a necessity. But there is no such policy even yet; – though the annexation of the Transvaal will go far to convince men that such must be our practice.

It is because of our vacillation in South Africa, – vacillation which has come from the varying convictions of varying Ministers and Governors, – that I say that the history of the Orange Free State will not be creditable to our discernment and statesmanship. Much heavier accusations have been brought against our Colonial office in reference to the same territory by Dutch, American, and by English censors. It has been said that we have been treacherous, tyrannical, and dishonest. To none of these charges do I think that the Colonial office is fairly subject; and though I cannot acquit every Governor of craft, – or perhaps of tyranny, – I think that there has on the whole been an anxious desire on the part of the emissaries from Downing Street to do their duty to their country. But there has been a want of settled purpose as to the nature and extent of the duties which fell upon England when she became mistress of the Dutch settlement at the Cape of Good Hope.

There are some who think that we might have confined ourselves to Table Mountain and Simon's Bay, drawing a rampart across the isthmus which divides the Cape from the mainland, – so as to have kept only a station for the protection of our East India intercourse. But as the Dutch whom we took upon ourselves to govern had already gone far inland when we arrived, that would hardly have been possible, and a restiction so selfish would have been contrary to our instincts. Others would have limited our power at various boundaries, – especially towards the East, where were the Kafir tribes, an evident source of coming trouble, should we meddle with them. The Orange river as a northern boundary did seem to offer a well-defined geographical limit, which would still allow us enormous scope for agricultural and pastoral energy within its southern banks and give sufficient room for every immigrant of whatever nation, and for every Africander who wished to live under British rule, to find a home within its borders.

But, as has been told before, the Dutch fled away across the Orange river as soon as they began to feel the nature of British rule. Then arose the question, which we have never yet been quite able to answer. When they went was it our duty to go after them, – not to hinder them from going but to govern them whither they went? Certainly not; we said, when they went only in such numbers as to cause us no disturbance by their removal. But how was it to be when they threatened, without any consent of ours, to erect a separate nationality on our borders? They tried it first in Natal, threatening us not only with the rivalry of their own proposed Republic, but with the hostile support of Holland. This was not to be allowed and we sent 250 men, very insufficiently, to put down the New Republic. We did, however, put it down at last.

But the Dutch were determined to go out from us. Our ways were not their ways. I am now speaking of a period nearly half a century back and the following quarter of a century. Our philanthropy disgusted them, and was to their minds absolutely illogical, – not to be reconciled to that custon of our nation of landing here and there and taking the land away from the natives. The custom to them was good enough and seemed to be clearly the intention of God Almighty. It was the purpose of Providence that white men should use the land which was only wasted while in the possession of black men; – and, no doubt, the purpose of Providence also that black men should be made to work. But that attempt to strike down the Native with the right hand and to salve the wound with the left was to the Dutchman simply hypocritical. 'Catch the nigger and make him work.' That was the Dutchman's idea. 'Certainly; – if you can agree about wages and other such matters,' said the British Authorities. 'Wages, – with this Savage; with this something more but very little more than a monkey! Feed him, and perhaps baptize him; but at any rate get work out of him,' said the Dutchman. Of course the Dutchman was disgusted. And then the slaves had been manumitted. I will not go into all that again; but I think it must be intelligible that the British philanthropical system of government was an hypocritical abomination to the Dutchman who knew very well that in spite of his philanthropy the Englishman still kept taking the land; – land upon land.

It was natural that the Dutchman should go across the Orange River, and natural too that the English governor should not quite know how to treat him when he had gone. But it would have been well if some certain policy of treatment could have been adopted. Many think that had we not interfered with him in Natal, had we never established what was called an Orange River Sovereignty subject to British rule, a Dutch-speaking nation would have been formed between our Cape Colony and the swarming native tribes, which would have been a protecting barrier for us and have ensured the security of our Colony. I myself do not agree with this. I think that a Dutch Republic if strong enough for this, stretching from the confluence of the Vaal and Orange rivers down to the shores of Natal would have been a neighbour more difficult to deal with than Kafir tribes. My opinion on such a subject goes for very little; – and there would at any rate have been a policy. Or, when we had after much hesitation forbidden the Dutch to form a Republic in Natal and had declared that country to be one among Her Majesty's possessions, we might have clung to the South African theory which was then promulgated. In that case we should have recognized the necessity of treating those wandering warlike patriarchs as British subjects and have acknowledged to ourselves that whither they went and thither we must go after them. This, too, would have been a policy. But this we have not done. At first we went after them. Then we abandoned them. And now that they are altogether out of our hands in the Free State we are hankering after them again. It is impossible not to see that the ideas as to Colonial extension entertained by the late Duke of Newcastle are altogether different from those held by Lord Carnarvon; – and that the Colonial office lacks traditions.

In some respects the history of the Orange Free State has been similar to that of the Transvaal. Its fate has been very different, a difference which has resulted partly from the characters of the men employed, partly from their external circumstances in regard to the native tribes which have been near to them. Mr Boshof and Mr Brand have been very superior as Statesmen to Mr Pretorius and Mr Burgers, and the Basutos under Moshesh their Chief, – though they almost succeeded in destroying the Orange Republic, – were at last less dangerous, at any rate very much less numerous, than Cetywayo and the Zulus.

The Dutch when they first crossed the Orange River asked whether they might go, and were then told that the law offered no impediment. 'I am not aware,' said Lieutenant Governor Stockenstrom in answer to a deputation which appealed to him on the subject, 'of any law which prevents any of His Majesty's subjects from leaving his dominions and settling in another country; and such a law, if it did exist, would be tyrannical and oppressive.' That was in 1835. It was in 1837 that the migration across the river really began, when many of the wanderers first found their way down to Natal. Some however settled directly across the Orange River, where however they soon fell into difficulties requiring government. While there was fighting with hostile tribes far north across the Vaal, and while Dingaan was endeavouring to exterminate the white men in Natal, the farmers across the Orange quarrelled in a milder way with the bastard Hottentots and Griquas whom they found there. But there were many troubles. When the Dutch declared themselves to be supreme, – in reference to the Natives rather than the British, – there came a British judge across the river, who happened then to be on circuit in the neighbourhood, and told them that they were all British subjects. But his assertion was very soon repudiated by the Governor, Sir George Napier, – for at that time the idea was prevalent at the Colonial office that England's hands should be stretched no further. This, however, did not stand long, and the next Governor, Sir Peregrine Maitland, found himself compelled by growing troubles to exercise authority across the rivers. He did not take possession of the country, but established a resident at the little town of Bloemfontein. The resident was to keep the peace between the Dutch and the various tribes; – but had no commission to govern the country. The British had found it impossible to allow the Dutch to drive the Natives from their land, – and equally impossible to allow the Natives to slaughter the Dutch. But yet we were very loth to declare the country British territory.

It was in 1848 that Sir Harry Smith, who was then in Natal, whither he had gone intending if possible to conciliate the Dutch would-be Republicans in that country, at last found himself compelled to claim for the mother country sovereignty over the region between the Orange and the Vaal rivers, and this proclamation he had to support by arms. Pretorius, who had become the leader of the Dutch in Natal, and who on account of personal slights to himself was peculiarly hostile to the English, came over the Drakenburg mountains, and put himself at the head of his countrymen between the rivers. He gathered together an army, – a commando, as it was then called in South African language, – and coming near to Bloemfontein ordered Major Warden, the British Resident, to move himself off into the Cape Colony south of the river with all that he had about him of soldiers and officials. This the Major did, and then Pretorius prepared himself to encounter with his Boers the offended majesty of Great Britain in arms. The reader will perhaps remember that the Dutch had done the same thing in Natal, – and had at first been successful.

Then, on 29th August, 1848, was fought the battle of Boom Plats half-way between the Orange River and Bloemfontein. Sir Harry Smith, the Governor, had come himself with six or seven hundred English soldiers and were joined by a small body of Griquas, – who were as a matter of course hostile to the Dutch. There were collected together about a thousand Dutch farmers all mounted. They were farmers, ready enough to fight, but no trained soldiers. More English were killed and wounded than Dutch. A dozen Dutchmen fell, and about four times that number of English. But the English beat the Dutch. This decided the fate of that territory for a short time, – and it became British under the name of the Orange River Sovereignty. Pretorius with his friends trekked away north, crossed the Vaal River, and there founded the Transvaal Republic, – as has been told elsewhere. A reward of £2,000 was offered for his apprehension; – an offer which might have been spared and which was happily made in vain.

Major Warden was reinstated as governing Resident, and the British power was supposed to be so well consolidated that many colonists who had hitherto remained contented on the south of the river now crossed it to occupy the lands which the followers of Pretorius had been compelled to desert. But the British were not very strong. The Basutos, a tribe of Natives who have now for some years lived in the odour of loyal sanctity and are supposed to be a pattern to all other Natives,

harassed the Europeans continually, War had to be proclaimed
against them. Basuto Land will be found in the map lying to
the north of Kafraria, to the south east of the Orange Free
State, south west of Natal, and north-east of the Cape Colony,
– to which it is bound only by a narrow neck, and of which it
now forms a part. How it became British shall be told
hereafter; – but at the time of which I am now writing, about
1850, it was very Anti-British, and gave poor Major Warden
and the Dutchmen who were living under his rule a great deal
of trouble.

Then, in 1851, the Sovereignty was declared to be to all
intents and purposes a separate Colony, – such as is the
Transvaal at this moment. A Lieutenant Governor was
appointed, who with the assistance of a council was
empowered to make laws, – but with a proviso that such laws
should not be binding upon Natives. To speak sooth British
laws are not absolutely binding upon the Natives in any of the
South African Colonies. In the Cape Colony or in Natal a
Native may buy a wife, – or ten wives. There has always been
the acknowledged impossibility of enforcing Africans to live
at once after European habits. But here, in this new Colony
which we had at last adopted, there was to be something
peculiarly mild in our dealings with the black men. There was
to be interference with acts done within the limits of the
jurisdiction of any native Chief. The Lieutenant Governor or
'Resident was instructed to maintain the government of the
native Chiefs over their people and lands in the utmost
integrity.'* It is odd enough that from this territory, on which
the British Governor or British Colonial Secretary of the day
was so peculiarly anxious to defend the Natives from any
touch of European tyranny, all the native tribes have been
abolished, and here alone in South Africa the European master
is fettered by no native difficulty; – is simply served by native
servants. The native locations were to be peculiarly sacred; –
but every Native has been scared away. The servants and
workmen are foreigners who have come into the land in
search of wages and food. The remarkable settlement at Thaba
'Ncho, of which I shall speak in a following chapter, is no

* Mr. Theal's History of South Africa,' vol. ii. p. 147.

contradiction to this statement, as the territory of the Baralongs of which Thaba 'Ncho is the capital is not a portion of
the Orange Free State.

But with all our philanthropy we could not make things run
smoothly in our new Colony. Moshesh and the Basutos
would have grievances and would fight. The Governor of the
Cape, who should have had no trouble with a little Colony
which had a Governor of its own, and a Council, and
instructions of a peculiarly philanthropic nature in regard to
the Natives, was obliged to fight with these Basutos on behalf
of the little Colony. This cost money, – of which the people in
England heard the facts. It was really too much that after all
that we had done we should be called upon to pay more
money for an uncomfortable internal Province in South Africa
which was not of the slightest use to us, which added no
prestige to our name, and of which we had struggled hard to
avoid the possession. There was nothing attractive about it. It
was neither fertile nor pretty, – nor did it possess a precious
metal of any kind, as far as we knew. It was inhabited by
Dutch who disliked us, – and by a most ungrateful horde of
fighting Natives. Why, – why should we be compelled to go
rushing up to the Equator, crossing river after river, in a
simple endeavour to do good, when the very people whom
we wanted to serve continually quarrelled with us, – and made
us pay through the nose for all their quarrels?

It seems to have been forgotten then, – it seems often to
have been forgotten, – that the good people and the peaceable
people have to pay for the bad people and the quarrelsome
people. There would appear to be a hardship in this; – but if
any one will look into it he will see that after all the good
people and the peaceable have much the best of it, and that the
very money which they are called upon to pay in this way is
not altogether badly invested. They obtain the blessing of
security and the feeling, not injurious to their peace of mind,
of having obtained that security by their own exertions.

But the idea of paying money and getting nothing for it
does create irritation. At home in England the new Colony
was not regarded with favour. In 1853 we had quite enough of
fighting in hand without having to fight the Basutos in
defence of the Dutch, or the Dutch in defence of the Basutos.

The Colonial Secretary of that time was also War minister and may well have had his hands full. It was decided that the Orange Free State should be abandoned. We had claimed the Dutch as our subjects when they attempted to start for themselves in Natal, and had subjugated them by force of arms. Then we had repudiated them in the nearer region across the Orange. Then again we had claimed them and had again subjugated them by force of arms. Now we again repudiated them. In 1854 we executed, and forced them to accept, a convention by which we handed over the Government of the country to them, – to be carried on after their own fashion. But yet it was not to be carried on exactly as they pleased. There was to be no Slavery. They were to be an independent people, living under a Republic; but they were not to be allowed to force labour from the Natives. To see that this stipulation was carried out it would have been necessary for us to maintain magistrates all over the country; – or spies rather than magistrates, as such magistrates could have had no jurisdiction. The Republic, however, assented to a treaty containing this clause in regard to slavery.

In 1854 we got rid of our Orange River Sovereignty, Sir George Clerk having been sent over from England to make the transfer; – and we congratulated ourselves that we had now two independent Republics between us and the swarming hordes of the north. I cannot say how soon there came upon Downing Street a desire to resume the territory, but during the following troubles with the Basutos such a feeling must, one would say, have arisen. When the Diamond Fields were discovered it is manifest that the independence of the Orange Free State was very much in our way. When we were compelled by the run of circumstances to have dealings with native tribes which in 1854 seemed to us to be too remote from our borders to need thought, we must have regretted a certain clause in the convention by which, – we did not indeed bind ourselves to have no dealings with natives north of the Vaal river, but in which we declared that we had no 'wish or intention' to enter into such treaties. No doubt that clause was intended to imply only that we had at that time no hidden notion of interference with the doings of the proposed Republic by arrangements with its native neighbours, – no notion of which it was to be kept in the dark. To think the contrary would be to suppose that the occupants of the Colonial Office at home were ignorant of language and destitute of honesty. But there soon came troubles from the clause which must have caused many regrets in the bosoms of Secretaries and Under Secretaries. Now at any rate we are all sure that Downing Street must repent her liberality, and wish, – ah, so fruitlessly, – that Sir George Clerk had never been sent upon that expedition. With a Permissive South Africa Confederation Bill carried after infinite trouble, and an independent State in the middle of South Africa very little inclined to Confederation, the present holder of the Colonial seals* cannot admire much the peculiar virtue which in 1854 induced his predecessor to surrender the Orange territory to the Dutch in opposition to the wish of all the then inhabitants of the country.

For the surrender was not made to please the people of the country. Down in Natal the Dutch had wanted a Republic. Up in the Sovereignty, as it was then called, they also had wanted a Republic when old Pretorius was at their head. But since that time there had come troubles with the Basutos, – troubles which were by no means ended, – and the Dutch were now willing enough to put up with dependence and British protection. The Dutch have been so cross-grained that the peculiar colonial tribe of the day has never been able to take their side. 'We have come here only because you have undertaken to govern us and protect us', said those of the Dutch who had followed and not preceded us across the Orange. And it was impossible to contradict them. I do not think that anybody could now dispassonately inquire into the circumstances of South Africa without calling in question the wisdom of the Government at home in abandoning the control of the territory north of the Orange River.

But the Republic was established. For some years it had a most troubled life. Mr. Boshof was elected the first President and retained that office till 1859. He seems to have been a man of firmness and wisdom, but to have found his neighbours the Basutos to be almost too much for him. There was war with

* Lord Carnarvon was Colonial Secretary when this was written.

this tribe more or less during his whole time. There was a
branch of the tribe of the Basutos living on a territory in the
Free State, – a people whom I will describe more at length in
a following chapter, – over whom and over whose property
Moshesh the Chief of the Basutos claimed sovereignty; but it
was impossible for the Free State to admit the claim as it
could itself only exist by dictating boundaries and terms to
the Baralongs, – which they were willing enough to receive
as being a protection against their enemies the Basutos.

In 1860 Mr. Pretorius became President of the Free State, –
the son of the man who had been the first President of the
Transvaal, – and the man himself who was President of the
Transvaal before Mr. Burgers. But the difficulties were
altogether beyond his power, and in 1863 he resigned. Then
Mr. Brand was appointed, the gentleman who now holds the
office and who will hold it probably, if he lives, for many
years to come. His present condition, which is one of
complete calm, is very much at variance with the early years
of his Presidency. I should hardly interest my reader if I were
to attempt to involve them in the details of this struggle. It
was a matter of life and death to the young Republic in
which national death seemed always to be more probable
than national life. The State had no army and could depend
only on the efforts of its burghers and volunteers, – men who
were very good for a commando or a spasmodic struggle,
men who were well used to sharp skirmishes in which they
had to contend in the proportion of one to ten against their
black enemies. But this war was maintained for four years,
and the burghers and volunteers who were mostly married
men could not long remain absent from home. And when a
peace was made at the instance of the Governor of the Cape
Colony and boudaries established to which Moshesh agreed,
the sons of Moshesh broke out in another place, and
everything was as bad as before. All the available means of
the Free State were spent. Blue-backs as they were called
were printed, and the bankers issued little scraps of paper, –
'good-fors', as they were called, – representing minute sums
of money. Trade there was none and the farmers had to fight
the Basutos instead of cultivating their land. At that time the
condition of the Free State was very bad indeed. I think I

may say that its preservation was chiefly due to the firmness of Mr. Brand.

At length the Basutos were so crushed that they were driven to escape the wrath of their Dutch enemies by imploring the British to take them in as subjects. In March 1868 this was done, – by no means with the consent of the Free State which felt that it ought to dictate terms and to take whatever territory it might desire from its now conquered enemy and add such territory to its own. This was the more desirable as the land of the Basutos was peculiarly good and fit for cultivation, – whereas that of the Orange Free State was peculiarly bad, hardly admitting cultivation at all without the expensive process of irrigation. The English at last made a boundary line, to which the Free State submitted. By this a considerable portion of the old Basuto land was given up to them. This they have held ever since under the name of the Conquered Territory. Its capital is called Ladybrand, and its possession is the great pride of the Republic. In completing this story I must say that the Republic has been most unexpectedly able to redeem every inch of paper money which it created, and now, less than ten years after a war which quite exhausted and nearly destroyed it, the Orange Free State stands unburdened by a penny of public debt. This condition has not doubt come chiefly from its good luck. Diamonds were found, and the Diamond Fields had to be reached through the Free State. Provisions of all sorts were required at the Diamond Fields, and thus a market was created for everything that could be produced. There came a sudden influx of prosperity which enabled the people to bear taxation, – and in this way the blue-backs were redeemed.

There were other troubles after 1869; – but the little State has floated through them all. Its chief subsequent trouble has been the main cause of its prosperity. The diamonds were found and the Republic claimed the territory on which they were being collected. On that subject I have spoken in a previous chapter, and I need not again refer to the details of the disagreement between Great Britain and the Republic. But it may be as well to point out that had that quarrel ended otherwise than it did, the English of the Diamond Fields would certainly have annexed the Dutch of the Free State, instead of allowing the Dutch of the Free State to annex them; – and then England would have obtained all the country between the Orange and the Vaal instead of only that small but important portion of it in which the diamonds lie. To imagine that Kimberley with all its wealth would have allowed itself to be ruled by a Dutch Volksraad at the little town of Bloemfontein, is to suppose that the tail can permanently wag the dog, instead of the dog wagging the tail. Diamond diggers are by no means people of a kind to submit quietly to such a condition of things. It was bitter enough for the Volksraad to abandon the idea of making laws for so rich and strong a population, – bitter perhaps for Mr. Brand to abandon the idea of governing them. But there can now, I think, be no doubt that it was better for the Free State that Griqualand West and Kimberley should be separated from it, – especially as Mr Brand was sent home to England by his parliament, – where he probably acquired softer feelings than heretofore towards a nationality with which he had been so long contending, and where he was able to smooth everything by inducing the Secretary of State to pay £90,000 by way of compensation to his own Government. I should think that Mr. Brand looking back on his various contentions with the British, on the Basuto wars and the Griqualand boundary lines, must often congratulate himself on the way he has steered his little bark. There can be no doubt that his fellow citizens in the Republic are very proud of his success.

Since Mr. Brand returned from London in 1876 nothing material has happened in the history of the Free State. In regard to all states it is said to be well that nothing material should happen to them. This must be peculiarly so with a Republic so small, and of which the success and the happiness must depend so entirely on its tranquillity. That it should have lived through the Basuto wars is astonishing. That it should not continue to live now that it is protected on all sides from the possibility of wars by the contiguity of British territory would be as astonishing. It seems to be expected by some politicians in England that now, in the days of her prosperity, the Republic will abandon her indpendence and ask to be received once more under the British aegis. I cannot conceive anything to be less probable, nor can I see cause for such a step. But I will refer again to this matter when attempting to described the present condition of the country.

In this little sketch I have endeavoured to portray the Colonial Ministers at home as actuated by every virtue which should glow within the capacious bosom of a British Statesman. I am sure that I have attributed no sinister motive, no evil idea, no blindness to honesty, no aptitude for craft to any Secretary of State. There are I think no less than eleven of them still living, all of whom the British public regards as honourable men who have deserved well of their country. I can remember almost as many more of whom the same may be said, who are now at peace beyond the troubles of the Native Question. I will endeavour to catalogue the higher public virtues by which they have endeared themselves to their country, – only remarking that those virtues have not, each of them, held the same respective places in the bosoms of all of them. A sensitiveness to the greatness and glory of England, – what we may perhaps call the Rule Britannia feeling, – which cannot endure the idea that the British foot should ever go back one inch! Is it not national ardour such as this which recommends our Statesmen to our love? And then there has been that well-weighed economy which has been acquired in the closet and used in the House of Commons, without no minister can really be true to his country. To levy what taxes be needed, but to take care that no more is spent than is needed; – is not that the first duty of a Cabinet Minister? But it has been England's destiny to be the arbiter of the fate of hundreds of millions of dusky human beings, – black, but still brethren, – on distant shores. The Queen has a hundred coloured subjects to one that is white. It has been the peculiar duty of the Colonial Minister to look after and to defend the weakest of these dark-skinned brothers; and this has had to be done in the teeth of much obloquy! Can any virtue rank higher than the performance of so sacred a duty? And then of how much foresight have our ministers the need? How accurately must they read the lessons which history and experience should teach them if Great Britain is to be saved from a repitition of the disgrace which she encountered before the American Colonies declared themselves independent? When we find a man who can look forward and say to himself, – 'while we can hold these people, for their own content, to their own welfare, so long we will keep them; but not a moment longer for any selfish aggrandisement of our own;' – when we find a Statesman rising to that pitch, how fervently should we appreciate the greatness of the man, and how ready should we be to acknowledge that he has caught the real secret of Colonial administration.

These splended qualities have so shone over our Colonial office that the sacred edifice is always bright with them. They scintillate on the brows of every Assistant Secretary, and sit as a coronet on the shining locks of all the clerks. But unfortunately they are always rotatory, so that no one virtue is ever long in the ascendant. Rule Britannia! and the Dutch Member of Parliament has to walk out of his Volksaal and touch his hat to an English Governor. Downing Street and the Treasury have agreed to retrench! Then the Dutch Member of Parliament walks back again. We will at any rate protect the Native! Then the Boer's wife hides the little whip with which she is accustomed to maintain discipline over her apprenticed nigger children. Let those people go forth and govern themselves! Then the little whip comes out again. Among all these British virtues what is a bewildered Dutch Colonist to do? If one virtue would remain always in the ascendant, – though I might differ or another, – there would be an intelligible policy. If they could be made to balance each other, – as private virtues do in private bosoms when the owners of those bosoms are possessed of judgment, – then the policy would assuredly be good. But while one virtue is ever in the ascendant, but never long there, the Dutch Colonist, and the English, are naturally bewildered by the rotation.

CHAPTER XI

THE ORANGE FREE STATE – PRESENT CONDITION

Sir George Grey, who was at that time Governor of the Cape of Good Hope writing to Lord John Russell on 17th November 1855, – Lord John having then been Secretary of State for the Colonies, – expresses himself in the following glowing terms as to the region of which I am now writing. 'The territory of the Orange Free State forms one of the finest pastoral countries I have ever seen. There is no district of country in Australia which I have visited which throughout so great an extent of territory affords so uniformly good a pastoral country.' A short time previous to this, Sir George Clerk, when he was about to deliver the State up to the Government of the Dutch, declared, – or at any rate is popularly reported to have declared, – that the land was a 'howling wilderness.' I think that the one colonial authority was quite as far astray as the other. Sir George Grey had ever a way with him of contending for his point either by strong language or by strong action. He was at one time Governor of South Australia, but perhaps never travelled as far north as the Salt Bush country of that Colony. The Colony in his time was in its infancy and was not known as far north as the pastoral district in question. I do not know whether Sir George ever visited the Riverina in New South Wales, or the Darling Downs in Queensland. Had he done so, – and had he then become as well acquainted with the pastoral properties of land as he has since become, – he would hardly with all his energy have ventured upon such an assertion. It will be only necessary for any investigator to look at the prices of Australian and South African wool to enable him to form an opinion on the subject. The average price in London of medium Australian wool in 1877 was 1s. 6d. a pound. In both countries it is common to hear that the land should be stocked at about the rate of 3 sheep to the acre; but in Australia patches of land which will bear heavier stocking occur much more numerously than in South Africa. The Orange Free State has not yet arrived at the ponderous glory of full statistics so that I cannot give the amount of wool produced, nor can I divi le her wool from that of the Cape Colony, through which it is sent to England without special record. But I feel sure that no one who knows the two countries will venture to compare the flocks of the Free State with those of either of the four great Australian Colonies, or with the flocks of New Zealand.

But if Sir George Grey spoke too loudly in one direction Sir George Clerk spoke very much too loudly in the other. He was probably struck by the desolate and unalluring appearance of the lands to the north of the Orange. They are not picturesque. They are not well-timbered. They are not even well-watered. If Sir George Clerk saw them in a drought, as I did, he certainly did not look upon a lovely country. But it is a country in which men may earn easy bread by pastoral or agricultural pursuits; in which with a certain amount of care, – which has to show itself mainly in irrigation, – the choicest fruits of the earth can be plenteously produced; in which the earth never refuses her increase if she be asked for it with many tears. A howling wilderness certainly it is not. But Sir George Clerk when he described the country was anxious to excuse the conduct of Great Britain in getting rid of it, while Sir George Grey was probably desirous of showing how wrong Great Britain had been on the occasion.

I do not know that I ever travelled across a less attractive country than the Orange Free State, or one in which there is less to gratify the visitor who goes to see things and not to see men and women. And the men and women are far between; for over an area presumed to include 70,000 square miles, a solid block of territory about 300 miles long by 120 miles broad, there are probably not more than 30,000 white people, and half that number of coloured people. The numbers I know are computed to be greater by the officials of the Free State itself, – but no census has been taken, and with customary patriotism they are perhaps disposed to over-estimate their own strength. They, however, do not give much above half an inhabitant to every square mile. It must be remembered that in the Free State the land is all occupied; – but that it is occupied at the rate I have described. I altogether deny that the Free State is a howling wilderness, but I do not recommend English autumn tourists to devote their holidays to visiting the land, unless they have become very tired indeed of their usual resorts.

The farmer in the Orange Free Sate is generally a Dutch Boer, – but by no means always so. During my very short visit I came across various Englishmen who were holding or who had held land there, – Africanders perhaps, persons who had been born from British parents in the Cape Colony, – but altogether British as distinguished from Dutch. In the towns the shopkeepers are I think as generally English as the farmers are Dutch in the country. We hear of the Republic as an essentially Dutch country; – but I think that if a man about to live there had to choose the possession of but one of the two languages, English would be more serviceable to him of the two. In another twenty years it certainly will be so.

I travelled from the Diamond Fields to Bloemfontein and thence through Smithfield to the Orange River at Aliwal North. I also made a short excursion from Bloemfontein. In this way I did not see the best district of the country which is that which was taken from the Basutos, – where the town of Ladybrand now is, – which is good agricultural land, capable of being sown and reaped without artificial irrigation. The normal Dutch farmer of the Republic, such as I saw him, depends chiefly upon his flocks which are very small as compared with those in Australia, – three or four thousand sheep being a respectable pastoral undertaking for one man. He deals in agriculture also, not largely, but much more generally than his Australian brother. In Australia the squatter usually despises agriculture, looking upon it as the fitting employment for a little free-selector, – who is but a mean fellow in his estimation. He grows no more than he will use about his place for his own cattle. The flour to be consumed by himself and his men he buys. And as his horses are not often corn-fed a very few acres of ploughed land suffices for his purpose. The Dutch patriarch makes his own bread from the wheat he had himself produced. The bread is not white, but it is so sweet that I am inclined to say I have never eaten better. And he sells his produce, – anything which he can grow and does not eat himself. The Australian woolgrower sells nothing but wool. The Dutch Boer will send peas twenty miles to market, and will sell a bundle of forage, – hay made out of unripened oats or barley, – to any one who will call at his place and ask for it.

A strong Boer will probably have thirty, forty or perhaps fifty acres of cultivated land round his house, – including his garden. And he will assuredly have a dam for holding and husbanding his rain water. He would almost better be without a house than without a dam. Some spot is chosen as near to his homestead as may be, – towards which there is something, be it ever so slight, of a fall of ground. Here a curved wall or stoned bank is made underlying the fall of ground, and above it the earth is hollowed out, – as is done with a haha fence, only here it is on larger and broader dimensions, – and into this artificial pond when it is so made the rain water is led by slight watercourses along the ground above. From the dam, by other watercourses, the contents are led hither and thither on to the land and garden as required, – or into the house. It is the Boer's great object thus to save enough water to last him through any period of drought that may come; – an object which he generally attains as far as his sheep, and cattle, and himself are concerned; – but in which he occasionally fails in reference to his ground. I saw more than one dam nearly dry as I passed through the country, and heard it asserted more than once that half a day's rain would be worth a hundred pounds to the speaker.

The Boer's house consists of a large middle chamber in which the family live and eat and work, – but do not cook. There is not usually even a fireplace in the room. It is very seldom floored. I do not know that I ever saw a Boer's house floored in the Free State. As the planks would have had to be brought up four hundred miles by oxen, this is not wonderful. The Boer is contented with the natural hard earth as it has been made for him. The furniture of his room is good enough for all domestic purposes. There are probably two spacious tables, and settees along the walls of which the seats are made of ox-riems, and open cupboards in the corners filled not sparingly with crockery. And there is always a pile of books in a corner of the room, – among which there is never one not of a religious tendency. There is a large Dutch Bible, and generally half a dozen Dutch hymn-books, with a smaller Bible to two, and not improbably an English prayer-book and English hymn-book if any of the younger people are affecting the English language. The younger members of the family generally are learning English and seem to be very much better off in regard to education than are their relations in the Transvaal.

Opening out of the living room there are generally bedrooms to the right and left, – probably two at one end and one at the other, – of which the best will be surrendered to the use of any respectable stranger who may want such accommodation. It matters not who may be the normal occupant of the room. He or she, – or more probably they, – make way for the stranger, thinking no more of surrendering a bedroom than we do of giving up a chair. The bedroom is probably close and disagreeable, lacking fresh air, with dark suspicious corners of which the stranger would not on any account unravel the mysteries. Behind the centre chamber there is a kitchen to which the stranger does not probably penetrate. I have however been within the kitchen of a Dutch Boeress and have found that as I was to eat what came out of it, I had better not have penetrated so far. It will be understood that a Dutch Boer's house never has an upper storey.

The young men are large strapping youths, and well made though awkward in their gait. The girls can hardly be said to be good-looking though there is often a healthy bloom about them. One would be inclined to say that they marry and have children too young were it not that they have so many children, and afterwards become such stout old matrons. Surely no people ever attended less to the fripperies and frivolities of dress. The old men wear strong loose brown clothes well bestained with work. The old women do the same. And so do the young men, and so do the young women. There seems to be extant among them no taste whatever for smartness. None at any rate is exhibited about their own homesteads. There are always coloured people about, living in adjacent huts, – very probably within the precincts of the same courtyard. For with the white children there are always to be seen black children playing. Nor does

there seem to be any feeling of repugnance at such intercourse
on the part of any one concerned. As such children grow up
no doubt they are required to work, but I have never seen
among the Dutch any instance of personal cruelty to a
coloured person; – nor during my travels in South Africa, did
any story of such cruelty reach my ear. The Dutchman would
I think fain have the black man for his slave, – and, could he
have his way in this, would not probably be over tender. But
the feeling that the black man is not to be personally ill-used
has I think made its way so far, that at any rate in the Orange
Free State such ill-usage is uncommon.

In regard to the question of work, I found that in the Free
State as in all the other provinces and districts of the country
so much of the work as is done for wages is invariably done by
coloured people. On a farm I have seen four young men
working together, – as far as I could see on equal terms, – and
two have been white and two black; but the white lads were
the Boer's sons, while the others were his paid servants.
Looking out of a window in a quiet dreary little town in the
Free State I saw opposite to me two men engaged on the
plastering of a wall. One was a Kafir and the other probably
was a west coast Negro. Two or three passed by with loads on
their shoulders. They were Bechuanas or Bastard Hottentots.
I strolled out of the village to a country house where a Fingo
was gardener and a Bushman was working under him. Out in
the street the two men who had driven the coach were loading
round it. They were Cape Boys as they are called, – a coloured
people who came from St. Helena and have white blood in
their veins. I had dined lately and had been waited upon by a
Coolie. Away in the square I could see bales of wool being
handled by three Basutos. A couple of Korannas were pre-
tending to drive oxen through the street but were apparently
going where the oxen led them. Then came another Hottentot
with a yoke and a pair of buckets on his shoulder. I had little
else to do and watched the while that I was there; – but I did
not see a single white man at work. I heard their voices, –
some Dutch, though chiefly English; but the voices were
voices of masters and not of men. Then I walked round the
place with the object of seeing, and nowhere could I find a
white man working as a labourer. And yet the Orange Free

State is supposed to be the one South African territory from which the black man has been expelled. The independent black man who owned the land has been expelled, – but the working black man has taken his place, allured by wages and diet.

The Dutch Boer does not love to pay wages, – does not love to spend money in any way, – not believing in a return which is to come, or possibly may come, from an outlay of capital in that direction. He prefers to keep what he has and to do what can be done by family labour. He will, however, generally have a couple of black men about his place, whose services he secures at the lowest possible rate. Every shilling so paid is grudged. He has in his heart an idea that a nigger ought to be made to work without wages.

In the Free State as in the Transvaal I found every Boer with whom I came in contact, and every member of a Boer's family, to be courteous and kind. I never entered a house at which my hand was not grasped at going in and coming out. This may be a bore, when there are a dozen in family all shaking hands on both occasions; but it is conclusive evidence that the Boer is not a churl. He admits freedoms which in more civilized countries would be at once resented. If you are hungry or thirsty you say so, and hurry on the dinner or the cup of tea. You require to be called at four in the morning and suggest that there shall be hot coffee at that hour. And he is equally familiar. He asks your age, and is very anxious to know how many children you have and what is their condition in the world. He generally boasts that he has more than you have, – and, if you yourself be so far advanced in age, that he has had grandchildren at a younger age than you. 'You won't have a baby born to you when you are 67 years old,' and old Boer said to me exulting. When I expressed a hope that I might be saved from such a fate, he chuckled and shook his head, clearly expressing an opinion that I would fain have a dozen children if Juno and the other celestials concerned would only be so good to me. His young wife sat by and laughed as it was all explained to her by the daughter of a former marriage who understood English. This was customary Boer pleasantness intended by the host for the delectation of his guest.

I was never more convinced of anything than that those people, the Dutch Boers of the Free State, are contented with their present condition and do not desire to place themselves again under the dominion of England. The question is one of considerable importance at the present moment as the permissive bill for the suggested Confederation of the South African districts has become law, and as that Confederation can hardly take place unless the Free State will accept it. The Free State is an isolated district in South Africa, now surrounded on all sides by British territory, by no means rich, not populous, in which the Dutch and English languages prevail perhaps equally, and also Dutch and English habits of life. It would appear therefore at first sight to be natural that the large English Colonies should swallow up and assimilate the little Dutch Republic. But a close view of the place and of the people, – and of the circumstances as they now exist and would exist under Dutch rule, – have tended to convince me that such a result is improbable for at any rate some years to come.

In the Orange Free State the Volksraad or Parliament is plenipotentiary, – more so if it be possible than our Parliament is with us because there is but one Chamber and because the President has no veto upon any decision to which that Chamber may come. The Volksraad is elected almost exclusively by the rural interest. There are 54 members, who are returned, one for each chief town in a district, and one for each Field-Cornetcy, – the Field-Cornetcies being the divisions into which the rural districts are divided for police and military purposes. Of these towns, such as they are, there are 13, and from them, if from any part of the State, would come a desire for English rule. But they, with the exception of the capital, can hardly be said to be more than rural villages. It is in the towns that the English language is taught and spoken, – that English tradesmen live, and that English modes of life prevail. The visitor to Bloemfontein, the capital, will no doubt feel that Bloemfontein is more English than Dutch. But Bloemfontein returns but one member to the Volksraad. From the rural districts there are 41 members, all of whom are either Boers or have been returned by Boers. Were the question extended to the division even of the 13 town members I do not

doubt but that the present state of things would be maintained, – so general is the feeling in favour of the independence
of the Republic. But seeing that the question rests in truth
with the country members, that the country is essentially a
farmer's country, a country which for all purposes is in the
hands of the Dutch Boers, it seems to be to be quite out of the
question that the change should be voted by the legislature of
the country.

An Englishman, or an Africander with an English name and
an English tongue, is under the constitution as capable of
being elected as a Dutchman. A very large proportion of the
wealth of the country is in English hands. The large
shopkeepers are generally English; and I think that I am right
in saying that the Banks are supported by English, or at any
rate, by Colonial capital. And yet, looking through the names
of the present Volksraad, I find but two that are English, – and
the owner of one of them I believe to be a Dutchman. How
can it be possible that such a House should vote away its own
independence? It is so impossible that there can be no other
way of even bringing the question before the House than that
of calling upon it for a unanimous assertion of its will in
answer to the demand, or request, or suggestions now made
by Great Britain.

Nor can I conceive any reason why the Volksraad should
consent to the proposed change. To a nationality labouring
under debt, oppressed by external enemies, or unable to
make the property of its citizens secure because of external
disorders, the idea of annexing itself to a strong power
might be acceptable. To have its debts paid, its frontiers
defended, and its rebels controlled might be compensation
for the loss of that self-rule which is as pleasant to
communities as it is to individuals. Such I believe is felt to be
the case by the most Dutch of the Dutch Boers in the
Transvaal. But the Orange Free State does not owe a penny.
Some years since it had been so impoverished by Basuto
wars that it was reduced to the enforced use of paper money
which sank to half its nominal value. Had England then
talked of annexation the Boers might have listened to her
offer. But the enormous trade produced by the sudden influx
of population into the Diamond Fields created a wealth

which has cured this evil. The bluebacks, – as the Orange Free State banknotes were called, – have been redeemed at par, and the Revenue of the country is amply sufficient for its modest wants. Enemies it has none, and from its position can have none, – unless it be England. Its own internal affairs are so quiet and easily regulated that it is hardly necessary to lock a door. No annexation could make a Boer more secure in the possession of his own land and his own chattels than he is at present.

It may of course be alleged that if the State were to join her lot with that of the Cape Colony or of a wide South African Confederation, she would increase her own wealth by sharing that of the larger nationality of which she would become a part, – and that the increase of national wealth would increase the means of the individuals forming the nation. This, however, is an argument which, even though it were believed, would have but little effect on the minds of a class of men who are peculiarly fond of self-government but are by no means desirous of a luxurious mode of life. It is often said that the Boer is fond of money. He is certainly averse to spending it and will grasp at it when it comes absolutely in his way; but he is the last man in the world to trust to its coming to him from a speculative measure of which he sees the certain immediate evil much more clearly than the possible future advantage.

There is one source of public wealth from which the Orange Free State is at present debarred by the peculiarity of its position, and of which it would enjoy its share were it annexed to the Cape Colony or joined in some federation with it. But I hope that no British or Colonial Statesman has trusted to force the Republic to sacrifice herself for the sake of obtaining justice in this respect. If, as I think, wrong is being done to the Orange Free State in this matter that wrong should be remedied for the sake of justice, and not maintained as a weapon to enforce the self-annihilation of a weak neighbour. On whatever produce from the world at large the Free State consumes, the Free State receives no Custom duties. The duties paid are levied by the Cape Colony, and are spent by it as a portion of its own revenues. The Free State has no seaboard and therefore no port.* Her sugar, and tea, and whisky come to her through Capetown, or Fort Elizabeth, or East London, and there the Custom duties are collected, – and retained. I need hardly point out to English readers that the Custom duties of a country form probably the greatest and perhaps the least objectionable portion of its revenue. It will be admitted, at any rate, that to such extent as a country chooses to subject its people to an increased price of goods by the addition of Custom duties to the cost of production, to that extent the revenue of the consuming country should be enriched. If I, an individual in England, have to pay a shilling on the bottle of French wine which I drink, as an Englishman I am entitled to my share of the public advantage coming from that shilling. But the Republican of the Orange Free State pays the shilling while the Colonist of the Cape has the spending of it. I hope, I say, that we on the south side of the Orange River do not cling to this prey with any notion that by doing so we can keep a whip hand over our little neighbour the Republic.

Two allegations are made in defence of the course pursued. It is said that the goods are brought to the ports of the Colony by Colonial merchants and are resold by them to the traders of the Orange Free State, so as to make it impossible for the Colony to know what is consumed within her own borders and what beyond. Goods could not therefore be passed through in bond even if the Cape Government would permit it. They go in broken parcels, and any duties collected must therefore be collected at the ports whence the goods are distributed. But this little difficulty has been got over in the intercourse between Victoria and New South Wales. A considerable portion of the latter Colony is supplied with its seaborne goods from Melbourne, which is the Capital and seaport of Victoria. Victoria collects the duties on those goods, and, having computed their annual amount, pays a certain lump sum to New South Wales in lieu of the actual

---

* Nevertheless there is a beautifully self-asserting clause in a treaty made in 1876 between the Orange Free State and Portugal, which provides – 'That ships sailing under the flag of the Orange Free State shall in every respect enjoy the same treatment and shall not be liable to higher duties than Portuguese vessels.'

duties collected. Why should not the Cape Colony settle with the Orange Republic in the same way?

The other reason put forward for withholding the amount strikes me as being – almost mean. I have heard it put forward only in conversation, and I am bringing no charge against any Statesman in the Cape Colony by saying this. I trust that the argument has had no weight with any Statesman at the Cape. The Cape Colony makes the roads over which the goods are carried up to the Free State. She does do so, – and the railroads. But she collects toll on the former, and charges for carriage on the latter. And she enjoys all the money made by the continued traffic through her territory. And she levies the port duties, which no one begrudges her. I felt it to be a new thing to be informed that a country was so impoverished by being made the vehicle for traffic from the sea to the interior that it found itself compelled to reimburse itself by filching Custom Duties.* England might just as well claim the customs of the Cape Colony because she protects the seas over which the goods are carried.

But the Orange Free State can carry on her little business even without the aid of Custom Duties, and will certainly not be driven back into the arms of the mother who once repudiated her by the want of them. She can pay her modest way; and while she can do so the Boer of the Volksraad will certainly not be induced to give up the natural delight which he takes in ruling his own country. The Free State might send perhaps six members to the central Congress of a South African Federation, where they would called upon to hear debates, which they would be unable to share or even to understand because spoken in a foreign language. They would be far from their farms and compelled to live in a manner altogether uncomfortable to them. Is it probable that for this privilege they will rob themselves of the honour and joy they now have in their own Parliament? In his own Parliament the Boer is close, phlegmatic, by no means eloquent, but very firm. The two parliamentary ideas most prominent in his

* What I have said here as to duties levied say at Fort Elizabeth on goods for the Orange Free State applies equally to goods for the Transvaal landed in Natal at Durban.

mind are that he will vote away neither his independence nor his money. It is very hard to get from him a sanction for any increased expenditure. It would I think be impossible to get from him sanction for a measure which would put all control over expenditure out of his own hands. 'We will guard as our choicest privilege that independence which Her Majesty some years since was pleased to bestow upon us.' It is thus that the Boer declares himself, – somewhat sarcastically, – when he is asked whether he does not wish to avail himself of the benefit of British citizenship.

Somewhat sarcastically; – for all he is well aware that when England repudiated him, – declaring that she would have nothing to do with him across the Orange River, she did so with contempt and almost with aversion. And he is as well aware that England now wants to get him back again. The double consciousness is of a nature likely to beget sarcasm. 'You though nothing of me when I came here a poor wanderer, daring all dangers in order that I might escape from your weaknesses, your absurdities, your mock philanthropies, – when I shook off from the sole of my foot the dust of a country in which the black Savage was preferred to the white Colonist; but now, – now that I have established myself successfully, – you would fain have me back again so that your broad borders may be extended, and your widened circle made complete. But, by the Providence of God, after many difficulties we are well as we are; – and therefore we are able to decline your offers.' That is the gist of what the Boer is saying when he tells us of the independence bestowed upon him by Her Majesty.

Thinking as I do that Great Britain was wrong when she repudiated the Orange Free State in 1854, believing that there was then a lack of patience at the Colonial Office and that we should have been better advised had we borne longer with the ways of the Dutch, I must still acknowledge here that they were a provoking people, and one hard to manage. Omitting small details and some few individual instances of misrule, I feel that when the Dutch complained of us they complained of what was good in our ways and not of what was evil. It was with this conviction that we repudiated both the Transvaal and the other younger but more stable Republic. Good excuses can be made for what we did, – not the worst of which is the fact that a people whom we desired to rule themselves, have ruled themselves well. But we did repudiate them, and I do not know with what face we can ask them to return to us. If the offer came from them of course we could assent; but that offer will hardly be made.

We could certainly annex the Republic by force, – as we have done the Transvaal. If we were to send a High Commissioner to Bloemfontein with thirty policemen and an order that the country should be given up to us, I do not know that President Brand and the Volksraad could do better than comply, – with such loudest remonstrance as they might make. 'The Republic cannot fight Great Britain,' President Brand might say, as President Burgers said when he apologized for the easy surrender of his Republic. But there are things which a nation cannot do and hold up its head, and this would be one of them. There could be no excuse for such spoliation. It is not easy to justify what we have done in the Transvaal. If there be any laws of right and wrong by which nations should govern themselves in their dealings with other nations it is hard to find the law in conformity with which that act was done. But for that act expediency can be pleaded. We have taken the Transvaal not that we might strengthen our own hands, not that we might round our own borders, not that we might thus be enabled to carry out the policy of our own Cabinet, – but because by doing so we have enabled Englishmen, Dutchmen, and natives to live one with another in comfort. There does seem to have been at any rate expedience to justify us in the Transvaal. But no such plea can be put forward in reference to the Free State. There a quiet people are being governed after their own fashion. There a modest people are contented with the fruition of their own moderate wealth. There a secure and well ordered people are able to live without fear. I cannot see any reason for annexing them; – or any other excuse beyond that spirit of spoliation which has so often armed the strong against the weak, but which England among the strong nations have surely repudiated.

The Legislature of the Orange Republic consists, as I have said, of a single House called the Volksraad, which is elected for four years, of which one half goes out at the end of every two years, so that the change is not made all at once as with us, half the House being dissolved at the end of one period of two years, and half at the end of another. The members are paid 20s. a day while the House is sitting. The House elects its own Speaker, at the right hand of whom the President has a chair. This he may occupy or not as he pleases; but when he is not there it is expected that his place shall be filled by the Government Secretary. The President can speak when he likes but cannot vote. The House can, if it please, desire him to withdraw, but, I was informed, had never yet exercised its privilege in this respect.

The President is elected for a term of five years and may, under the present Constitution, be re-elected for any number of terms. The present President has now nearly served his third term, and will no doubt be re-elected next year. But there is a bill now before the Volksraad by which the renewal of the President's term is to be confined to a single reappoint-ment. One re-election only will be allowed. This change has received all the sanction which one Session can give it. The period of the term is also to be curtailed from five to four years. It is necessary however that such a change in the Constitution shall be passed by the House in three consecutive Sessions, and on each occasion by a three-fourth majority. It is understood also that the bill if passed will not debar the existing President from one re-election after the change. President Brand therefore will be enabled to serve for five terms, and should he live to do so will thus have been the Head of the Executive of the Free State for a period of twenty-four years, – which is much longer than the average reign of hereditary monarchs. His last term will in this case have been shortened one year by the new law. It would be I think impossible to overrate the value of his services to the country which adopted him. He was a member of Assembly in the Cape Colony when he was elected, of which House his father was then Speaker. A better choice could hardly have been made. It is to his patience, his good sense, his exact appreciation of both the highness and the lowness of the place which he has been called on to occupy, that the Republic has owed its security. I have expressed an opinion as to the qualifications of President Burgers for a similar position. It is because President Brand has been exactly the reverse of President Burgers, that he is now trusted by the Volksraad and loved by the people. It would be hard to find a case in which a man has shown himself better able to suit himself to peculiar duties than has been done by the President of this little Republic.

The right of voting in the Free State belongs to the burghers, and the burghers are as follows;—

1. All white male persons born in the State.
2. All white male persons who have resided one year in the State, and are registered owners of property to the value of £150.
3. All white male persons who have lived for three consecutive years in the State.

Those however who are included in the 2nd and 3rd clauses will not be recognized as burghers unless they produce to the State President a certificate of good conduct from the authorities of their last place of abode and a written promise of allegiance to the State.

Burghers who have attained the age of 16, and all who at a later age shall have acquired citizenship are bound to enrol themselves under their respective field-cornets and to be liable for burgher duty, – which means fighting, – till they be 60 years old.

Burghers of 18 are entitled to vote for Field Cornets and Field Commandants. To vote for a member of the Volksraad or for the President a burgher must be 21, must have been born in the State, – when no property qualification is necessary, – or must be the registered owner of property to the value of £150, or be the lessor of a property worth £36 per annum; or have a yearly income of £200, or possess moveable property worth £300.

From this it will be seen that the parliamentary system of the Republic is protected from a supposed evil by a measure of precaution which would be altogether inadmissable in any Constitution requiring the sanction of the British Crown. No coloured person can vote for a Member of Parliament.

However expedient it may be thought by Englishmen to exclude Kafirs or Zulus from voting till such changes shall have been made in their habits as to make them fit for the privilege, the restrictions made for that purpose must with us be common both to the coloured and to the white population. We all feel that no class legislation as to the privilege of voting should be adopted and that in giving or withholding qualification no allusion should be made to race or colour. But the Dutch of the Free State have no such scruple. They at once proclaim that this privilege shall be confined to those in whose veins European blood runs pure. I will here say nothing as to the comparative merits of British latitude or of Dutch restraint, but I will ask my readers to consider whether it be probable that a people who have not scrupled to make for themselves such a law of exclusion will willingly join themselves to a nationality which is absolutely and vehemently opposed to any exclusion based on colour.

In the Free State the executive power is in the hands of the President in which he is assisted by a Council of five, of whom two are official. There is now a bench of three judges who go circuit, and there is a magistrate or Landroost sitting in each of the thirteen districts and deciding both civil and criminal cases to a certain extent. The religion and education of the State will both require a few words from me, but they will come better when I am speaking of Bloemfontein, the capital.

The Revenue of the country is something over £100,000 a year, and the expenditure has for many years been kept within the Revenue. It has been very fluctuating, having sunk below £60,000 in 1859 when the war with the Basutos had crippled all the industries of the country and had forced the burghers to spend their time in fighting instead of cultivating their lands and looking after their sheep. There is nothing, however, that the Boer hates so much as debt, and the Boer of the Volksraad has been very careful to free his country from that incubus.

Land in the Orange Free State is very cheap, an evil condition of things which has been produced by the large grants of land which were made to the original claimants. The average value throughout the State may now be fixed at about 5s. an acre. It is said that in the whole State there are between six and seven thousand farms.

CHAPTER XII

BLOEMFONTEIN

Bloemfontein, the capital of the Orange Republic, is a pleasant little town in the very centre of the country which we speak of as South Africa, about a hundred miles north of the Orange River, four hundred north of Fort Elizabeth whence it draws the chief part of its supplies, and six hundred and eighty north west of Capetown. It is something above a hundred miles from Kimberley which is its nearest neighbour of any importance in point of size. It is about the same distance from Durban, the seaport of Natal, as it is from Fort Elizabeth; – and again about the same distance from Pretoria the capital of the Transvaal. It may therefore be said to be a remote town offering but little temptations to its inhabitants to gad about to other markets. The smaller towns within the borders of the Republic are but villages containing at most not more than a few hundred inhabitants. I am told that Bloemfontein has three thousand; but no census has as yet been taken, and I do not know whether the number stated is intended to include or exclude the coloured population, – who as a rule do not live in Bloemfontein but at a neighbouring hamlet, devoted to the use of the natives, called Wray Hook. I found Bloemfontein a pleasant place when I was there, but one requiring much labour and trouble both in reaching and leaving. For a hundred miles on one side and a hundred on the other I saw hardly a blade of grass or a tree. It stands isolated in the plain, – without any suburb except the native location which I have named, – with as clearly defined a boundary on each side as might be a town built with a pack of cards, or one of those fortified citadels with barred gates and portcullises which we used to see in picture books. After travelling through a country ugly, dusty and treeless for many weary hours the traveller at last reaches Bloemfontein and finds himself at rest from his joltings, with his bones not quite dislocated, in the quiet little Dutch capital, wondering at the fate which has led him to a spot on the world's surface, so far away, apparently so purposeless, and so unlike the cities which he has known.

I heard of no special industries at Bloemfontein. As far as I am aware nothing special is there manufactured. It is needful that a country should have a Capital, and therefore the Orange Free State has Bloemfontein. I was told that some original Boer named Bloem first settled there by the side of the stream in which water runs when there has been rain, and that hence has come the name. But the little town has thriven with a success peculiarly its own. Though it would seem to have no raison d'etre just there where it stands, – though it has been encouraged and fostered by no peculiar fertility, adorned with no scenic beauty, enriched by no special gifts or water or of metals, even though the population has not grown beyond that of the suburb of some European town, still it carries its metropolitan honours with a good air, and shocks no one by meanness, dirt, or poverty. It certainly is not very grand, but it is grand enough. If there be no luxury, everything is decent. The members of the Volksraad are not carried about in gorgeous equipages, but when they have walked slowly to their Chamber they behave themselves there with decorum. There is nothing pretentious in Bloemfontein, – nothing to raise a laugh at the idea that a town with so small a population should call itself a capital.

It is a town, white and red, built with plastered walls or of brick, – with a large oblong square in the centre; with four main streets running parallel to each other and with perhaps double that number of cross streets. The houses are generally but one storey high, though this is not so invariably the case as at Kimberley. I do not remember, however, that I was ever required to go up-stairs, – except at the schools. The supply of water is I am assured never-failing, though in dry weather it has to be drawn from tanks. A long drought had prevailed when I reached the place, and the bed of the riverlet had been dry for many days; but the supply of water seemed to be sufficient. Fuel is very scarce and consequently dear. This is of the less importance as but little is wanted except for the purpose of cooking.

At one extreme end of the town are the public buildings in which the Volksraad is held and the judges sit. Here also are the offices of the President and the Secretary. Indeed all public business is here carried on. The edifice has but the ground floor with a clock tower rising from the centre. It is long and roomy and to my eye handsome in its white neatness. I have heard it laughed at and described as being like a railway station. It seems to be exactly that which such a Capital and such a Republic would require. The Volksraad was not sitting when I was there and I therefore could only see the beautiful arm-chairs which have lately been imported at a considerable expense for the use of the Members; – £13 10s. a chair I think I was told! It is impossible to conceive that gentlemen who have been accommodated with such chairs should wilfully abandon any of the dignity attached to them. For a central parliament the chairs may be fitting, but would be altogether out of place in a small provincial congress. Except the churches and the schools there are not any public buildings of much note in Bloemfontein, – unless the comfortable residence of the President may be so called. This belongs to the State but is not attached to the House of Parliament.

My residence when I was at Bloemfontein was at the Free State Hotel, and I do not know that I was ever put up much better. Two circumstances militated against my own particular comfort, but they were circumstances which might probably recommend the house to the world at large. I was forced to take my meals in public at stated hours; – and I had a great deal too much put before me to eat. I am bound, however, to say that all I had given to me was good, though at that time it must have been very difficult to supply such luxuries. The butter had to be bought at 5s. 6d. a pound, but was as plentiful as though the price had been only a shilling, – and it was good which I had not found to be the case elsewhere in South Africa. What was paid for the peas and beans and cauliflowers I don't know; but I did know that the earth around was dry and parched and barren everywhere, – so that I was almost ashamed to eat them. These details may be of interest to some readers of my pages, as the place of which I am speaking is becoming at present the sanitorium to which many an English consumptive patient is sent. Such persons, at any rate when first reaching Bloemfontein, are obliged to find a home in an hotel, and will certainly find one well provided at the Free State. It commended itself to me especially because I found no difficulty in that very serious and often troublesome matter of a morning club.

Bloemfontein is becoming another Madeira, another Algiers, another Egypt in regard to English sufferers with weak chests and imperfect lungs. It seems to the ignorant as though the doctos were ever seeking in increased distance that relief for their patients which they cannot find in increased skill. But a dry climate is now supposed to be necessary and one that shall be temperate without great heat. This certainly will be found at Bloemfontein, and perhaps more equably so through the entire year than at any other known place. The objection to it is the expense arising from the distance and the great fatigue to patients from the long overland journey. Taking the easiest mode of reaching the capital of the Free State the traveller must be kept going six weary days in a Cobb's coach, being an average of about thirteen hours a day upon the road. This is gradually and very slowly becoming lightened by the opening of bits of the railway from Fort Elizabeth; but it will be some years probably before the coaching work can be done in less than five days. The road is very rough through the Catberg and Stromberg mountains, – so that he who has made the journey is apt to think that he has done something considerable. All this is so much against an invalid that I doubt whether they who are feeble should be sent here. There can I imagine be no doubt that the air of the place when reached is in the highest degree fit for weak lungs.

There is at present a difficulty felt by those who arrive suddenly at Bloemfontein in finding the accomodation they desire. The hotel, as I have said above, is very good; but an hotel must of its nature be expensive and can hardly afford the quiet which is necessary for an invalid. Nor during my sojourn there did I once see a lady sitting at table. There is no reason why she should not do so, but the practice did not seem as yet to have become common. I am led by this to imagine that a house comfortably kept for the use of patients would well repay a medical speculator at Bloemfontein. It should not be called a sanitorium, and should if possible have the name of the doctor's wife on the brass plate on the door rather than that of the doctor. And the kitchen should be made to do more than the dispensary, – which should be kept a little out of sight. And there should be fiddles and novels and plenty of ribbons. If possible three or four particularly healthy guests should be obtained to diminish the aspect of sickness which might otherwise make the place gloomy. It this could be done, and the coach journey somewhat lightened, then I think that the dry air of Bloemfontein might be made very useful to English sufferers.

In reference to the fatigue, tedium, and expense of the coach journey, – a seat to Bloemfontein from the Fort Elizabeth railway costs £18, and half a crown a pound extra is charged for all luggage beyond a small bag, – it may be as well to say that in the treaty by which £90,000 have been given by Great Britain to the Free State to cover any damage she may have received as to the Diamond Fields, it is agreed that an extra sum of £15,000 shall be paid to the Free State if she shall have commenced a railway with the view of meeting the Colonial railway within a certain period. As no Dutchman will throw over a pecuniary advantage if it can be honestly obtained, a great effort will no doubt be made to secure this sum. It may be difficult to decide, when the time comes, what constitutes the commencement of a railway. It appears impossible that any portion of a line shall be opened in the Free State till the entire line shall have been completed from the sea to the borders of the State, as everything necessary for the construction of a line, including wooden sleepers, must be conveyed overland. As the bulk so to be conveyed will necessarily be enormous it can only be carried up by the rail as the rail itself progresses. And there must be difficulty even in surveying the proposed line till it be known actually at what point the colonial line will pass the Orange River or which of the colonial lines will first reach it. Nevertheless I feel assured that the Dutchman will get his £15,000. When an Englishman has once talked of paying and a Dutchman has been encouraged to think of receiving, the money will probably pass hands.

A railway completed to Bloemfontein would double the value of all property there and would very soon double the population of the town. Everything there used from a deal plank or a bar of iron down to a pair of socks or a pound of sugar, has now to be dragged four hundred miles by oxen at an average rate of £15 a ton. It is not only the sick and weakly who are prevented from seeking the succour of its climate by the hardness of the journey, but everything which the sick and weakly can require is doubled in price. If I might venture to give a little advice to the Volksraad I would counsel them to open the purse strings of the nation, even though the purse should be filled with borrowed money, so that there should be no delay on their part in joining themselves to the rest of the world. They should make their claim to the £15,000 clear and undoubted.

At present there is no telegraph to Bloemfontein, though the line of wires belonging to the Cape Colony passes through a portion of the State on its way to Kimberley, – so that there is a telegraph station at Fauresmith, a town belonging to the Republic. An extension to the capital is much wanted in order to bring it within the pale of modern civilization.

The schools at Bloemfontein are excellent, and are peculiarly interesting as showing the great steps by which the English language is elbowing out the Dutch. This is so marked that though I see no necessity for a political Confederation in South Africa I think I do see that there will soon be a unity of language. I visited all the schools that are supported or assisted by Government, as I did also those which have been set on foot by English enterprise. In the former almost as fully as in the latter English seemed to be the medium of communication between scholar and teacher. In all the public schools the Head Teacher was either English or Scotch. The inspector of schools for the Republic is a Scotch gentleman, Mr. Brebner, who is giving himself heart and soul to the subject he has in hand and is prospering admirably. Even in the infant school I found that English was the language of the great majority of the children. In the upper schools, both of the boys and girls, I went through the whole establishment, visiting the bedrooms of pupils. As I did so I took the opportunity of looking at the private books of the boys and girls. The books which I took off the shelves were all without exception English. When I mentioned this to one of the teachers who was with me in the compartment used by a lad who had well provided himself with a little library, he made a search to show me that I was wrong, and convicted me by finding, – a Dutch dictionary. I pointed out that the dictionary joined to the fact that the other books were English would seem to indicate that the boy was learning Dutch rather than reading it. I have no hesitation in saying that in these Dutch schools, – for Dutch they are as being supported in a Dutch Republic by grants of Dutch money voted by an exclusively Dutch Volksraad, – English is the more important language of the two and the one the best understood.

I say this rather in a desire to tell the truth than in a spirit of boasting. I do not know why I should wish that the use of my own tongue should supersede that of the native language in a foreign country. And the fact as I state it will go far with some thinkers to prove the arguments to have been ill-founded with which I have endeavoured to show that the Republic will retain her independence. Such persons will say that this preference for the English language will surely induce a preference for English Government. To such persons I would reply first that the English language was spoken in the United States when they revolted. And I would then explain that the schools of which I am speaking are all in the capital, which is undoubtedly an English town rather than Dutch. In the country, from whence come the Members of the Volksraad, the schools are probably much more Dutch, though by no means so Dutch as are the Members themselves. The same difference prevails in all things in which the urban feeling or the rural feeling is exhibited. Nothing can be more Dutch than the Volksraad. Many members, I was assured, cannot speak a word of English. The debates are all in Dutch. But the President was chosen from a British community, having been a member of the Cape House of Assembly, and the Government Secretary was imported from the same Colony, – and the Chief Justice. As I have said above the Inspector of Schools is a Scotchman. The Boers of the Orange Free State have been too wise to look among themselves for occupants for these offices. But they believe themselves to be perfectly capable of serving their country as legislators. Nothing can be better than these public schools in Bloemfontein, giving another evidence of the great difference which existed in the internal arrange-

ments of the two Republics. Large grants of public money
have been made for the support of the Free State schools. In
1875 £18,000 was voted for this purpose, and in 1876 £10,000.
Money is also set aside for a permanent education fund which
is to be continued till the amount in hand is £176,800. This it is
thought will produce an income sufficient for the required
purpose.

There are two thoroughly good English schools for pupils
of the better, or at any rate, richer class, as to which it has to be
said that they are set on foot and carried on by ladies and
gentlemen devoted to High Church doctrines. I could not
speak of these schools fairly without saying so. Having so
liberated my conscience I may declare that their pupils are by
no means drawn specially from that class and that as far as I
could learn nothing is inculcated to which any Protestant
parent would object. When I was at Bloemfontein the President had a daughter at the girls' school and the President is a
Member of the Dutch Reformed Church. The Government
Secretary had four daughters at the same school. There was at
least one Roman Catholic educated there. It is in fact a
thoroughly good school and as such of infinite value in that far
distant place. The cost of board and education is £60 for each
girl, which with extra charges for music and other incidental
expenses becomes £80 in most cases. I thought this to be
somewhat high, but it must be remembered that the 400 miles
and the bullock wagons affect even the price of schools. The
boys' school did not seem to have been so prosperous, the
number educated being much less than at the other. The
expense is about the same and the advantages given quite as
great. At both establishments day scholars are taken as well as
boarders. The result is that Bloemfontein in respect to climate
and education offers peculiar advantages to its residents. It is
not necessary to send a child away either for English air or for
English teaching.

In church matters Bloemfontein has a footing which is
peculiarly its own. The Dutch Reformed Church is the
Church of the people. There are 18, – only 18, – congregations
in the State, of which 16 receive Government support. The
worshippers of the Free State must, it is feared, be called upon
to travel long distances to their churches. As a rule those living

in remote places, have themselves taken by their ox-wagons into the nearest town once in three months for the Nichtmaal, – that is for the celebration of the Lord's Supper; and on these occasions the journey there and back, together with a little holiday-making in the town, takes a week or ten days. In this there is nothing singular, as it is the custom of the Dutch in South Africa, – but the Anglican Church in Bloemfontein is peculiar. There is a Bishop of Bloemfontein, an English Bishop, consecrated I think with the assistance of an English Archbiship, appointed at any rate with the general sanction and approval of the English Church. The arrangement has no doubt been beneficial and is regarded without disfavour by the ruling powers of the State in which it has been made; – but there is something singular in the position which we as a people have assumed. We first repudiate the country and then we take upon ourselves to appoint a high church dignitary whom we send out from England with a large accompaniment of minor ecclesiastics. In the United States they have bishops of the Protestant Episcopal Church as well as of the Roman Catholic. But they are not Bishops of the Church of England. Here, in Bloemfontein, the Church is English, and prays for the Queen before the President, – for which latter it sometimes does pray and sometimes does not. I attended the Cathedral service twice and such was my experience.

This is strange to an Englishman who visits the Republic prepared to find it a nationality of itself, – what in common language we may call a foreign country. There are English bishops also among savage nations, – a bishop for instance of Central Africa who lives at present at Zanzibar. But in the Free State we are among a civilized people who are able to manage their own affairs. I am very far from finding fault. The Church of Bloemfontein has worked very well and done much good. But in acknowledging this I think we ought to acknowledge also that very much is due to the forbearance of the Boers.

The Bishop of Bloemfontein with his numerous staff gives to the town a special ecclesiastical hue. It is quite true that his presence adds to the importance of the place, and that their influence is exercised all for good. The clergymen as a set are peculiarly clerical. Were I to call them High Church it might be supposed that I were accusing them of a passion for ribbons. I did see a ribbon or two but not vehemently pronounced. There is a Home too, to which the girls' school is attached, – which has attracted various young ladies who have come as assistants to the good work. The Bishop too has attracted various young men in orders. There has I think been some gentle feeling of disappointment in serious clerical minds at Bloemfontein created by the natural conclusion brought about by this state of things. All the clerical young men, who were perhaps intended to be celebate, had when I was at Bloemfontein become engaged to all the clerical young ladies, – from whom also something of the same negative virtue may have been expected. There has, I think, been something of a shock! I was happy enough to meet some of the gentlemen and some of the ladies, and am not at all surprised at the happy result which has attended their joint expatriation.

The stranger looking at Bloemfontein, and forgetting for a while that it is the capital of a country or the seat of a Bishop, will behold a pretty quiet smiling village with willow trees all through it, lying in the plain, – with distinct boundaries, most pleasing to the eye. Though it lies in a plain still there are hills close to it, – a little hill on the east on which there is an old fort and a few worn-out guns which were brought there when the English occupied the country, and a higher one to the west which I used to mount when the sun was setting, because from the top I could look down upon the place and see the whole of it. The hill is rocky and somewhat steep and, with a mile of intervening ground, takes half an hour in the ascent. The view from it on an evening is peculiarly pleasing. The town is so quiet and seems to be so happy and contented, removed so far away from strife and want and disorder, that the beholder as he looks down upon it is tempted to think that the peace of such an abode is better than the excitement of a Paris, a London, or a New York. I will not say that the peace and quiet can be discerned from the hill top, but he who sits there, knowing that the peace and quiet are lying beneath him, will think that he sees them.

Nor will I say that Bloemfontein is itself peculiarly beautiful. It has not rapid rivers running through it as has the capital of the Tyrol, no picturesqueness of hills to make it lovely as has Edinburgh, no glory of buildings such as belongs to

Florence. It is not quaint as Nuremberg, romantic as Prague, or even embowered in foliage as are some of the Dutch villages in the western province of the Cape Colony. But it has a completeness and neatness which makes it very pleasant to the eye. One knows that no one is over-hungry there, or over-worked. The work indeed is very light. Friday is a half holiday for everybody. The banks close at one o'clock on Saturday. Three o'clock ends the day for all important business. I doubt whether any shop is open after six. At eight all the servants, – who of course are coloured people, – are at home at their own huts in Wray Hook. No coloured person is allowed to walk about Bloemfontein after eight. This, it may be said, is oppressive to them. But if they are expelled from the streets, so also are they relieved from their work. At Wray Hook they can walk about as much as they please, – or go to bed.

There is much in all this which is old-fashioned, – contrary to our ideas of civilization, contrary to our ideas of liberty. It would also be contrary to our ideas of comfort to have no one to wait upon us after eight o'clock. But there is a contentment and general prosperity about Bloemfontein which is apt to make a dweller in busy cities think that though it might not quite suit himself, it would be very good for everybody else. And then there comes upon him a question of conscience as he asks himself whether it ought not to be very good for him also.

NATIVE TERRITORIES

CHAPTER XIII

THABA 'NCHO

The name written above is to be pronounced Tabaancho and belongs to one of the most interesting places in South Africa. Thaba 'Ncho is a native town in which live about 6,000 persons of the Baralong tribe under a Chief of their own and in accordance with their own laws. There is nothing like this elsewhere on the continent of South Africa, or, as I believe, approaching it. Elsewhere it is not the custom of the South African Natives to live in towns. They congregate in kraals, more or less large, – which kraals are villages surrounded generally by a fence, and containing from three or four huts up to perhaps a couple of hundred. Each hut has been found to contain an average of something less than four persons. But Thaba 'Ncho is a town, not fenced in, with irregular streets, composed indeed of huts, but constructed with some idea of municipal regularity. There has been no counting of these people, but from what information I could get I think I am safe in saying that as many as 6,000 of them live at Thaba 'Ncho. There are not above half-a-dozen European towns in South Africa which have a greater number of inhabitants, and in the vicinity of Thaba 'Ncho there are other Baralong towns or villages, – within the distance of a few miles, – containing from five hundred to a thousand inhabitants each. They possess altogether a territory extending about 35 miles across each way, and within this area fifteen thousand Natives are located, living altogether after their own fashion and governed in accordance with their own native laws.

Their position is the more remarkable because their territory is absolutely surrounded by that of the Orange Free State, – as the territory of the Orange Free State is surrounded by the territories of Great Britain. The Republic which we know as the Free State is as it were an island within the ocean of the

British Colonies, and the land of the Baralongs is again an island circled by the smaller sea of the Republic. And this is still more remarkable from the fact that whereas the Natives have been encouraged on all sides to make locations on British territory they have been altogether banished as a land-holding independent people from the Free State. Throughout the British Colonies of South Africa the number of the Natives exceeds that of the Europeans by about eight to one. In the Republic the Europeans exceed the Natives by two to one. And the coloured people who remain there, – or who have emigrated thither, which has been more generally the case, – are the servants employed in the towns and by the farmers. And yet, in spite of this, a separate nation of 15,000 persons live quietly and, I must say, upon the whole prosperously within the Free State borders, altogether hemmed in, but in no way oppressed.

It would take long to explain how a branch of the great tribe of the Bechuanas got itself settled on this land, – on this land, and probably on much more; – how they quarrelled with their cousins the Basutos, who had also branched off from the Bechuanas; and how in the wars between the Free State and the Basutos, the Baralongs, having sided with the Dutch, have been allowed to remain. It is a confused story and would be interesting to no English reader. But it may be interesting to know that there they are, established in their country by treaty, with no fear on their part that they will be swallowed up, and with no immediate intention on the part of the circumambient Dutchmen of swallowing them.

I went to visit the Chief, accompanied by Mr. Höhne the Government Secretary from Bloemfontein, and was very courteously received. I stayed during my sojourn at the house of Mr. Daniel the Wesleyan Minister where I was very comfortably entertained, finding him in a pretty cottage surrounded by flowers, and with just such a spare bedroom as we read of in descriptions of old English farmhouses. There was but one spare bedroom; but, luckily for us, there were two Wesleyan Ministers. And as the other Wesleyan Minister also had a spare bedroom the Government Secretary went there. In other respects we divided our visit, dining at the one house and breakfasting at the other. There is also a clergyman of the Church of England at Thaba 'Ncho; but he is a bachelor and we preferred the domestic comforts of a family. Mr. Daniel does, I think, entertain all the visitors who go to Thaba 'Ncho, as no hotel has as yet been opened in the city of the Baralongs.

Maroco is the Chief at present supreme among the Baralongs, an old man, very infirm by reason of weakness in his feet, who has not probably many more years of royalty before him. What few Europeans are living in the place have their houses low on the plain, while the huts of the Natives have been constructed on a hill. The word Thaba means hill in Maralong language, – in which language also the singular Maralong becomes Baralong in the plural. The King Maroco is therefore 'the Maralong' par excellence; – whereas he is the King of the Baralongs. The Europeans living there, – in addition to the Ministers, – are three or four shopkeepers who supply those wants of the Natives with which an approach to civilization has blessed them. We walked up the hill with Mr. Daniel and had not been long among the huts when we were accosted by one Sapena and his friends. Now there is a difficulty with these people as to the next heir to the throne, – which difficulty will I fear be hard of solving when old King Maroco dies. His son by his great wife married in due order a quantity of wives among whom one was chosen as the 'great wife' as was proper. In a chapter further on a word or two will be found as to this practice. But the son who was the undoubted heir died before his great wife had had a child. She then went away, back to the Bechuanas from whom she had come, and among whom she was a very royal Princess, and there married Prince Sapena. This marriage was blessed with a son. But by Bechuana law, by Baralong law also, – and I believe by Jewish law if that were anything to the purpose, – the son of the wife of the heir becomes the heir even though he be born from another father. These people are very particular in all matters of inheritance, and therefore, when it began to be thought that Maroco was growing old and near his time, they sent an embassy to the Bechuanas for the boy. He had arrived just before my visit and was then absent on a little return journey with the suite of Bechuanas who had brought him. By way of final compliment he had gone back with them a few miles so that I did not see him. But his father Sapena had been living for some time with the Baralongs, having had some difficulties among the Bechuanas with the Royal Princess his wife, and, being a man of power and prudence, had become half regent under the infirm old Chief. There are fears that when Maroco dies there may be a contest as to the throne between Sapena and his own son. Should the contest amount to a war the Free State will probably find it expedient to settle the question by annexing the country.

Sapena is a well built man, six feet high, broad in the shoulders, and with the gait of a European. He was dressed like a European, with a watch and chain at his waistcoat, a round flat topped hat, and cord trousers, and was quite clean. Looking at him as he walks no one would believe him to be other than a white man. He looks to be about thirty, though he must be much older. He was accompanied by three or four young men who were all of the blood royal, and who were by no means like to him either in dress or manner. He was very quiet, answering our questions in few words, but was extremely courteous. He took us first into a large hut belonging to one of the family, which was so scrupously clean as to make me think for a moment that it was kept as a show hut; but those which we afterwards visited, though not perhaps equal to the first in neatness, were too nearly so to have made much precaution necessary. The hut was round as are all the huts, but had a door which required no stopping. A great portion of the centre – though not quite the centre – was occupied by a large immoveable round bin in which the corn for the use of the family is stored. There was a chair, and a bed, and two or three settees. If I remember right, too, there was a gun standing against the wall. The place certainly looked as though nobody was living in it. Sapena afterwards took us to his own hut which was also very spacious, and here we were seated on chairs and had Kafir beer brought to us in large slop-bowls. The Kafir beer is made of Kafir corn, and is light and sour. The Natives when they sit down to drink swallow enormous quantities of it. A very little sufficed with me, as its sourness seemed to be its most remarkable quality. There were many Natives with us but none of them drank when we did. We sat for ten minutes in Sapena's house, and then were taken on to that of the King. I should say however that in the middle of Sapena's hut there stood a large iron double bedstead with mattress which I was sure had come from Mr. Heal's establishment in Tottenham Court Road.

Round all these huts, – those that is belonging to the royal family and those no doubt of other magnates, – there is a spacious courtyard enclosed by a circular fence of bamboo canes, stuck into the ground perpendicularly, standing close to each other and bound together. The way into the courtyard is open, but the circle is brought round so as to overlap the entrance and prevent the passer-by from looking in. It is not, I imagine, open to every one to run into his neighbour's courtyard – especially into those belonging to royalty. As we were going to the King's Palace the King himself met us on the road surrounded by two or three of his councillors. One old councillor stuck close to him always, and was, I was told, never absent from his side. They had been children together and Maroco cannot endure to be without him. We had our interview out in the street, with a small crowd of Baralongs around us. The Chief was not attired at all like his son's wife's husband. He had an old skin or korass around him, in which he continually shrugged himself as we see a beggar doing in the cold, with a pair of very old trousers and a most iniquitous slouch hat upon his head. There was nothing to mark the King about his outward man; – and, as he was dressed, so was his councillor. But it is among the 'young bloods' of a people that finery is always first to be found.

Maroco shook hands with each of us twice before he began to talk, as did all his cortege. Then he told us of his bodily ailments, – how his feet were so bad that he could hardly walk, and how he never got any comfort anywhere because of his infirmity. And yet he was standing all the time. He sent word to President Brand that he would have been in to see him long ago, – only that his feet were so bad! This was probably true as Maroco, when he goes into Bloemfontein, always expects to have his food and drink found for him while there, and to have a handsome present to carry back with him. He grunted and groaned, poor old King, and then told Sapena to take us to his hut, shaking hands with us all twice again. We went to his hut, and there sitting in the spacious courty we found his great wife. She was a woman about forty years of age, but still remarkably handsome, with brilliant quick eyes, of an olive rather than black colour. She wore a fur hat or cap, – somewhat like a pork-pie hat, – which became her wonderfully; and though she was squatting on the ground with her knees high and her back against the fence, – not of all attitudes the most dignified, – still there was much of dignity about her. She shook hands with us, still seated, and then bade one of the girls take us into the hut. There was nothing in this especial, except that a portion of it was screened off by furs, behind which we did not of course penetrate. All these huts are very roomy and perfectly light. They are lofty, so that a man cannot touch the roof in the centre, and clean. Into the ordinary Kafir hut the visitor has to creep, – and when there he creeps out at once because of the heat, the smell, and the smoke. These were of course royal huts, but the huts of all the Baralongs are better than those of the Kafirs.

The King or Chief administers justice sitting outside in his Court with his Councillors round him; and whatever he pronounces, with their assistance, – that is law. His word without theirs would be law too, – but would be law probably at the expense of his throne or life if often so pronounced. There are Statutes which are well understood, and a Chief who persistently ignored the Statutes would not long be Chief. For all offences except one the punishment is a fine, – so many cattle. This if not paid by the criminal must be paid by the criminal's family. It may be understood therefore how disagreeable it must be to be nearly connected by blood with a gay Lothario or a remorseless Iago. The result is that Lotharios and Iagos are apt to come to sudden death within the bosoms of their own families. Poisoning among the Baralongs is common, but no other kind of violence. The one crime beyond a fine, – which has to be expiated by death from the hand of an executioner, – is rebellion against the Chief. For any mutiny Death is the doom. At the time of my visit Sapena was exercising the chief authority because of Maroco's infirmity. Everything was done in Maroco's name, though Sapena did it. As to both, – the old man and the young, – I was assured that they were daily drunk. Maroco is certainly killing himself by drink. Sapena did not look like a drunkard.

President Brand assured me that in nothing that they do are these people interfered with by the Free State or its laws. If there be thieving over the border of the Free State the Landroost endeavours to settle it with the Chief who is by no means averse to summary extradition. But there is not much of such theft, the Baralongs knowing that their independence depends on their good behaviour. 'But a bloody Chief,' – I asked the President, – 'such as Cetywayo is represented to be among the Zulus! If he were to murder his people right and left would that be allowed by your Government?' He replied that as the Baralongs were not given to violent murder, there would never probably be a case requiring decision on this point. In my own mind I have no doubt but that if they did misbehave themselves badly they would be at once annexed.

Maroco and all his family, and indeed the great body of the people, are heathen. There is a sprinkling of Christianity, sufficient probably to justify the two churches, but I doubt whether Thaba 'Ncho is peculiarly affected by missionary zeal. There are schools there, and, as it happened, I did hear some open air singing, – in the open air because the chapel was under repair. But I was not specially invited 'to hear the children sing a hymn,' as was generally the case where the missionary spirit was strong. At Thaba 'Ncho the medical skill of the pastor seemed to be valued quite as much as his theological power. There was no other doctor, and as Mr. Daniel attended them without fee it is not surprising that much of his time was occupied in this manner.

I have mentioned the extent of the land belonging to the people. On the produce of this land they live apparently without want. They cultivate much of it, growing mealies, or maze, and Kafir corn. They also have flocks of cattle and sheep, – and earn some money by the sale of wool. But it seems to me that so large a number of people, living on such an extent of land, which of course is not closely cultivated, may be subject at any time to famine. If so they could apply only to the Free State for assistance, and such assistance, if given to any extent, would probably lead to annexation. The distribution of the land is altogether in the hands of the Chief who apportions it as he pleases, but never, it seems, withdraws that which has been given, without great cause. It is given out to sub-tribes and again redistributed among the people.

That it cannot as yet have been found to be scanty I gather from the fact that on the road between Thaba 'Ncho and Bloemfontein I found an intelligent Scotch Africander settled on a farm within the territory of the Baralongs. Here he had built for himself a comfortable house, had made an extensive garden, – with much labour in regard to irrigation, – and had flocks and herds and corn. I questioned him as to his holding of the land and he told me that it had been given to him without rent or payment of any kind by Maroco, because he was a friend of the tribe. But he perfectly understood that he held it only during Maroco's pleasure, which could not be valid for a day after Maroco's death. Nevertheless he was going on with his irrigation and spoke of still extended operations. When I hinted that Maroco was mortal, he admitted the precarious nature of his tenure, but seemed to think that the Baralongs would never disturb him. No doubt he well understood his position and was aware that possession is nine points of the law among the Baralongs as it is among the English or Scotch. Even should the territory be annexed, as must ultimately be its fate, his possession will probably be strengthened by a freehold grant.

CHAPTER XIV

KRELI AND HIS KAFIRS

At the time in which I am writing this chapter Kreli and his sons suppose themselves to be at war with the Queen of England. The Governor of the Cape Colony, who has been so far troubled in his serenity as to have felt it expedient to live away from his house for the last three or four months near to the scene of action, supposes probably that he has been called upon to put down a most unpleasant Kafir disturbance. He will hardly dignify the affair with the name of a war. When in Ireland the Fenians were put down by the police without direct military interference we felt that there had been a disagreeable row, – but certainly not a civil war, because the soldiers had not been employed. And yet we should hardly have been comfortable while the row was going on had we not known that there were soldiers at hand in Ireland. For some months it was much the same with Kreli and his rebellious Kafirs. In South Africa there was comfort in feeling that there were one or two regiments near the Kei River, – at head quarters, with a General and Commissaries and Colonels at King Williamstown, where the Governor is also stationed, and that there were soldiers also at East London, on the coast, ready for an emergency should the emergency come. But the fighting up to that time had been done by policemen and volunteers, – and it was hoped that it might be so to the end. Towards the close of November 1877 the end was thought to have almost come; though there were even then those who believed that when we had subdued the Galekas who are Kreli's peculiar people, the Gaikas would rise against us. They are Sandilli's people and live on this, or the western, side of the Kei territory, round about King Williamstown in what we call British Kafraria. Many hundreds of them are working for wages within the boundaries of what was formerly their own territory. I cannot but think that had the Gaikas intended to take part with their Transkeian brethren they would not have waited till Kreli and his Galekas has been so nearly beaten. But now we know that an ending to this trouble so happy as that which was at first anticipated has not been quite accomplished. British troops have entered the territory on the other side of the Kei, and are at present probably engaged in putting down some remnant of the Galekas.

There is nothing more puzzling in South Africa than the genealogy and nomenclature of the Kafir tribes, and nothing, perhaps, less interesting to English readers. In the first place the authorities differ much as to what is a Kafir. In a book now before me on Kafir Laws and Customs, written by various hands and published in 1858 by Colonel Maclean who was Governor of British Kafraria, we are told that 'The general designation of Kafraria has been given to the whole territory extending from the Great Fish River to Delagoa Bay.' This would include Natal and all Zululand. But if there be one native doctrine more stoutly enunciated in and about Natal than another, it is that the Zulus and Kafirs are a different people. The same passage, however, goes on to say that, properly speaking, the territory only should be included which is occupied by the Amaxosa and Abatembu tribes, the Amampondo and the Amazulu being – different. An English reader must be requested to reject as surplusage for his purpose the two first syllables in all these native names when they take the shape of Ama or Aba or Amam. They are decorous, classical, and correct as from Kafir scholars, but are simply troublesome among the simple people who only want to know a little. The Amam Pondos, so called from one Pondo a former chief, are familiarly called Pondos. The Aba Tembus, – from Tembu a chief thirteen or fourteen chiefs back from the present head of the tribe, – are Tembus. They have been also nick-named Tambookies, an appellation which they themselves do not acknowledge, but which has become common in all Kafir dissertations. The Amaxosas, who among the Kafirs are certainly the great people of all, in the same way are Xosas, from Xosa a chief eleven chiefs back from Kreli. But these Xosas, having been divided, have taken other names, – among which the two principal are the Galekas of which Kreli is king, from Galeka Kreli's great-grandfather; and the Gaikas, of which Sandilli is chief, – from Gaika, Sandilli's father. But the student may encounter further difficulty here as he will find this latter name learnedly written as Ngqika, and not uncommonly spelt as Ghika. The spelling I have adopted is perhaps a little more classical than the latter and certainly less pernicious than the former.

But though, as above stated, one of the authors of the book from which I have quoted has eliminated the Pondos as well as the Zulus from the Kafirs, thus leaving the descendants of Xosa and of Tembu to claim the name between them, I find in the same book a genealogical table, compiled by another author who includes the Pondos among the Kafirs, and derives the Galekas, Ghikas, Pondos, and Tembus from one common ancestor whom he calls Zwidi, who was fifteen chiefs back from Kreli, and whom we may be justified in regarding as the very Adam of the Kafir race since we have no information of any Kafir before him.

The Galekas, the Pondos, and Tembus will be found in the map in their proper places on the eastern side of the Kei River; and, as being on the eastern side of the Kei River, they were not British subjects when this chapter was written. When the reader shall have this book in his hand they may probably have been annexed. The Gaikas, I am afraid he will not find on the map. As they have been British subjects for the last twenty-five years the spaces in the map of the country in which they live have been wanted for such European names as Frankfort and King Williamstown. Those however whom I have named are the real Kafirs, – living near the Kei whether on one side of the river or the other. The sharp-eyed investigating reader will also find a people called Bomvana, on the sea coast, north of the Galekas. They are a sub-tribe, under Kreli, who have a sub-chief, one Moni, and Moni and the Bomvanas seem to have been troubled in their mind, not wishing to wage war against the Queen of England, and yet fearing to disobey the behests of their Great Chief Kreli.

It will thus be seen that the Kafirs do not occupy very much land in South Africa, though their name has become better known than that of any South African tribe, – and though every black Native is in familiar language called a Kafir. The reason has been that the two tribes, the Gaikas and the Galekas, have given us infinitely more trouble than any other. Sandilli with his Gaikas have long been subjected, though they have never been regarded as quiet subjects, such as are the Basutos and the Fingos. There has ever been a dread, as there was notably in 1876, that they would rise and rebel. The alarmists since this present affair of Kreli commenced have never ceased to declare that the Gaikas would surely be up in arms against us. But, as a tribe, they have not done so yet, – partly perhaps because their Chief Sandilli is usually drunk. The Galekas, however, have never been made subject to us.

But the Galekas and Kreli were conquered in the last Kafir war, and the tribe had been more than decimated by the madness of the people who in 1857 had destroyed their own cattle and their own corn in obedience to a wonderful proph-ecy. I have told the story before in one of the early chapters of my first volume. Kreli has then been driven with his people across the river Bashee to the North, – where those Bomvanas now are; and his own territory had remained for a period vacant. Then arose a question as to what should be done with the land, and Sir Philip Wodehouse, who was then Governor of the Cape Colony, proposed that it should be given out in farms to Europeans. But at that moment economy and protec-tion for the Natives were the two virtues shining most brightly at the Colonial Office, and, as such occupation was thought to require the presence of troops for its security, the Secretary of the day ordered that Kreli should be allowed to return. Kreli was badly off for land and for means of living across the Bashee, and was very urgent in requesting permission to come back. If he might come back and reign in a portion of his old land he would be a good neighbour. He was allowed to come back; – and as a Savage has not kept his word badly till this unfortunate affair occurred.

Among the printed papers which I have at hand as to this rebellion one of the last is the following government notice;—

'KING WILLIAMSTOWN, CAPE OF GOOD HOPE.
'13th November, 1877.

'Applications will be received by the Honourable the Commissioner of Crown Lands and Public Works for grants of Land in the Westernmost portion of Galekaland, formerly known as Kreli's country, between the Cogha and Kei Rivers, from those willing to settle in that country. The condition of the grants, – which will be limited in size to 300 acres, – include immediate settlement and bona fide occupation, and may be ascertained——&c. &c.'

Thus, in 1877, we are again attempting to do that which was recommended twenty years before. On this occasion I presume that no sanction from the Colonial Office at home was needed, as at the date of the notice such sanction could hardly have been received. This is a matter which I do not profess to understand, but the present Governor of the Cape Colony, – who in this war acts as High Commissioner and in that capacity is not responsible to his Ministers, – is certainly not the man to take such a step without proper authority. I hope we are not counting our chickens before they are hatched. I feel little doubt myself but that the hatching will at last be complete.

Though the disturbance has hardly been a war, – if a war, it would have to be reckoned as the sixth Kafir war, – it may be well to say a few words as to its commencement. To do so it will be necessary to bring another tribe under the reader's notice. These are the Fingos, who among South African natives are the special friends of the Britisher, – having precedence in this respect even of the Basutos. They appear to have been originally, – as originally, at least, as we can trace them back, – inhabitants of some portion of the country now called Natal, and to have been driven by Chaka, the great King of the Zulus, down among the Galekas. Here they were absolutely enslaved, and in the time of Hintsa, the father of Kreli, were called the Kafirs' dogs. Their original name I do not know, but Fingo means a dog. After one of the Kafir wars, in 1834, they were taken out from among the Galekas by British authority, relieved from the condition of slavery, and settled on locations which were given to them. They were first placed near the coast between the Great Fish River and the Keiskamma; but many were subsequently moved up to a district which they still occupy, across the Kei, and close to their old masters the Galekas, – but on land which was under

British government and which became part of British Kafraria. Here they have been as good as their old masters, – and as being special occupants of British favour perhaps something better. They have been a money-making people, possessing oxen and waggons, and going much ahead of other Kafirs in the way of trade. And as they grew in prosperity, so probably they grew in pride. They were still Fingos; – but not a Fingo was any longer a Galeka's dog, – which was a state of things not agreeable to the Galekas. This too must have been the more intolerable as the area given up to the Fingos in this locality comprised about 2,000 square miles, while that left to the Galekas was no more than 1,600. The Galekas living on this curtailed territory were about 66,000 souls, whereas only 50,000 Fingos drew their easier bread from the larger region.

In August last the row began by a quarrel between the Galekas and the Fingos. There was a beer-drinking together on the occasion of a Fingo wedding to which certain Galekas had been invited. The guests misbehaved themselves, and the Fingos drove them away. Upon that a body of armed Galekas returned, and a tribal war was started. But the Fingos as being British subjects were not empowered to conduct a war on their own account. It was necessary that we should fight for them or that there should be no fighting. The Galekas were armed, – as they might choose to arm themselves, or might be able; while the Fingos could only possess such arms as we permitted them to use. It thus became necessary that we should defend them.

When it came to this pass Kreli, the old Chief, is supposed to have been urgent against any further fighting. Throughout his long life whatever of misfortune he had suffered, had come from fighting with the English, whatever of peace he had enjoyed had come from the good will of the English. Nor do I think that the Galekas as a body were anxious for a war with the English though they may have been ready enough to bully the Fingos. They too had much to lose and nothing to gain. Ambition probably sat lightly with them, and even hatred for the Fingos by that time must nearly have worn itself out among the people. But the Chief had sons, and there were other Princes of the blood royal. With such as they ambition and revenge linger longer than with the mass. Quicquid delirunt reges plectuntur Achivi. The Kafirs had to fight because royal blood boiled high. The old King in his declining years was too weak to restrain his own sons, – as have been other old Kings. Arms having been taken up against the Fingos were maintained against the protectors of the Fingos. It might be that after all the long prophesied day had now come for driving the white men out of South Africa. Instad of that the day has probably at last come for subjugating the hitherto unsubjugated Kafirs.

I have before me all the details of the 'war' as it has been carried on, showing how in the first battle our one gun came to grief after having been fired seven times, and how the Fingos ran away because the gun had come to grief; – how in consequence of this five of our mounted policemen and one officer were killed by the Galekas; how in the next engagement the Fingos behaved much better, – so much better as to have been thanked for their gallantry; and how from that time to this we have driven poor old Kreli about, taking from him his cattle and his country, – determined if possible to catch him but not having caught him as yet. Colonial history will no doubt some day tell all this at length; but in a work so light as mine my readers perhaps would not thank me for more detailed circumstances.

On the 5th of October, when the affair was becoming serious, the Governor of the Cape, who is also high Commissioner for the management of the natives, issued a proclamation in which he sets forth Kreli's weakness or fault. 'Kreli,' he says, 'either had not the will or the power to make his people keep the peace,' and again – 'The Chief Kreli having distinctly expressed his inability to punish his people, or to prevent such outrages for the future, Commandant Griffith has been directed to advance into Kreli's country, to put down by force, if necessary, all attempts to resist the authority of the British Government or to molest its subjects, and to exact full reparation for the injuries inflicted on British subjects by Kreli's people.'

Read by the assistance of South African commentaries this means that Kreli's country is to be annexed, and for such reading the later proclamation as to 300-acre farms adds an assured light. That it will be much better so, no one doubts.

Let the reader look at the map and he cannot doubt. Can it be well that a corner, one little corner should be kept for independent Kafirs, – not that Kafirs unable to live with the British might run into it as do the American Indians into the Indian Territory or the Maories of New Zealand into the King-County there; – but that a single tribe may entertain dreams of independence and dreams of hostility? Whether we have done well or ill by occupying South Africa, I will not now stop to ask. But if ill, we can hardly salve our consciences by that little corner. And yet that little corner has always been the supposed focus of rebellion from which the sacred colonist has feared that war would come upon him. Of what real service can it be to leave to the unchecked dominion of Kafir habits a tract of 1,600 square miles when we have absorbed from the Natives a territory larger than all British India. We have taken to ourselves in South Africa within this century an extent of land which in area is the largest of all Her Majesty's dominions, and have been wont to tell ourselves that as regards the Natives it is all right because we have left them their own lands in Kafraria Proper. Let the Briton who consoles himself with this thought, – and who would still so console himself, – look at the strip on the map along the coast, an inch long perhaps and an inch deep; and then let him measure across the continent from the mouth of the Orange River to the mouth of the Tugela. It makes a Briton feel like the American who would not swear to the two hundredth duck.

We have not caught Kreli yet. When we have, if we should catch him, I do not in the least know what we shall do with him. There is a report which I do not believe that the Governor has threatened him with Robben Island. Robben Island is a forlorn isle lying off Capetown which has been utilized for malefactors and lunatics. Langalibalele has a comfortable farm house on the Cape Flats where he has a bottle of wine and a bottle of beer allowed him a day, – and where he lives like a second Napoleon at a second St. Helena. I trust that nothing of the kind will be done with Kreli. There is an absurdity about it which is irritating. It is as though we were playing at Indian princes among the African black races. The man himself has not risen in life beyond the taste for squatting in his hut with a dozen black wives around him and a red blanket over his shoulders. Then we put him into a house where he squats on a chair instead, and give him wine and beer and good clothes. When we take the children of such a one and do something in the way of educating them, then the expenditure of money is justified. Many Kafirs, – many thousand Kafirs have risen above squatting in huts and red blankets; but they are the men who have learned to work, as at the Kimberley mine, and not the Chiefs. The only excuse for such treatment as that which Langalibalele receives, which Kreli if caught would probably receive, is that no one knows what else to propose. I am almost inclined to think it better that Kreli should not be caught. Prisoners of that nature are troublesome. What a blessing it was to France when Marshal Bazaine escaped.

I was told before leaving the Cape that the trouble would probably not cost above £50,000. So cheap a disturbance certainly should not be called a war. The cattle taken would probably be worth the money; – and then the 300-acre farms, if they are ever allotted, will it is presumed be of some value. But now I fear that £50,000 will not pay half the bill. There is no luxury on earth more expensive than the British soldier.

It is well that we should annex Kreli's country; – but there is something for the lovers of the picturesque to regret in that the Kafir should no longer have a spot on which he can live quite in accordance with his own habits, in which there shall be no one to bid him cover his nakedness. Though by degrees the really independent part of Kafraria Proper has dwindled down to so small dimensions, there has always been the feeling that the unharrassed unharnessed Kafir had still his own native wilds in which to disport himself as he pleased, in which the Chief might rule over his subjects, and in which the subjects might venerate their Chiefs without the necessity of obeying any white man. On behalf of such lovers of the picturesque it should be explained that in making the Kafirs subject to Great Britain, Great Britain interferes but very little with their habits of life. There is hardly any interference unless as an introduction of wages among them may affect them. The Gaika who has been subjugated has been allowed to marry as many wives as he could get as freely as the hitherto unsubjugated Galeka.

Unless he come into the European towns breeches have not
been imposed upon him, and indeed not then with any
rigorous hand. The subject Kafirs are indeed made to pay hut
tax, – 10s. a hut in the Cape Colony and 14s. in Natal; but this
is collected with such ease as to justify me in saying that they
are a people not impatient of taxation. The popular idea seems
to be that the 10s. demanded has to be got as soon as possible
from some European source, – by a week's work, by the sale
of a few fowls, or perhaps in some less authorized manner. A
sheep or two taken out of the nearest white man's flock will
thoroughly indemnify the native for his tax.

But their habits of life remain the same, unless they be
openly renounced and changed by the adoption of
Christianity; or until work performed in the service of the
white man gradually induces the workman to imitate his
employer. I think that the latter cause is by far the more
operative of the two. But even that must be slow, as a
population to be counted by millions cannot be taught to
work all at once.

A short catalogue of some of the most noticeable of the
Kafir habits may be interesting. I have taken my account of
them from the papers published under Colonel Maclean's
name. As polygamy is known to be the habit of Kafirs, usages
as to Kafir marriages come first in interest. A Kafir buys his
wife, giving a certain number of cattle for her as may be
agreed upon between him and the lady's father. These cattle
go to the father, or guardian, who has the privilege of selling
the young lady. A man therefore to have many wives must
have many cattle, – or in other words much wealth, the riches
of a Kafir being always vested in herds of oxen. Should a man
have to repudiate his wife, and should he show that he does so
on good ground, he can recover the cattle he has paid for her.
Should a man die without children by a wife, the cattle given
for her may be recovered by his heirs. But should a woman
leave her husband before she has had a child, he may keep the
cattle. Should only one child have been born when the
husband dies, and the woman be still young and marriageable,
a part of the cattle can be recovered. I have known it to be
stated, – in the House of Commons and elsewhere, – that
wives are bought and sold among the Kafirs. Such an assertion

gives a wrong idea of the custom. Wives are bought, but are never sold. The girl is sold, that she may become a wife; but the husband cannot sell her. The custom as it exists is sufficiently repulsive. As the women are made to work, – made to do all the hard work where European habits have not been partially introduced, – a wife of course is valuable as a servant. To call them slaves is to give a false representation of their position. A wife in England has to obey her husband, but she is not his slave. The Kafir wife though she may hoe the land while the husband only fights or searches for game, does not hold a mean position in her husband's hut. But the old are more wealthy than the young, and therefore the old and rich buy up the wives, leaving no wives for the young men, – with results which may easily be understood. The practice is abominable, – but we shall not alter it by conceiving or spreading false accounts of it. In regard to work it should be understood that the men even in their own locations are learning to become labourers and to spare the women. The earth used to be turned only by the hoe, and the hoe was used by the women. Ploughs are now quite common among the Kafirs, and the ploughing is done by men.

There is no system of divorce; but a man may repudiate his wife with or without reason, giving back the cattle or a part of them. A wife often leaves her husband, through ill-usage or from jealousy, – in which case the cattle remain with the husband and, if not as yet paid in full, can be recovered. According to law not only the cattle agreed upon but the progeny of the cattle can be recovered; – but it seldom happens that more than the original number are obtained. When there is a separation the children belong to the father.

When a man has many wives he elects one as his 'great wife', – who may not improbably be the youngest and last married. The selection is generally made in accordance with the rank of the woman. Her eldest son is the heir. Then he makes a second choice of a 'right hand wife', – whose eldest son is again the heir of some portion of the property which during the father's life has been set apart for the right hand house. If he be rich he may provide for other children, but the customs of his tribe do not expect him to do so. If he die without having made such selections, his brothers or other relatives do it for him.

A husband may beat his wife, – but not to death. If he do that he is punished for murder, – by a fine. If he knock out her eye, or even her tooth, he is fined by the Chief. The same law prevails between parents and children as long as the child remains domiciled in the parents' family. A father is responsible for all that his child does, and must pay the fines inflicted for the child's misdeeds; – unless he has procured the outlawing of his child, which he can do if the child has implicated him in many crimes and caused him to pay many fines. Near relations of criminals must pay, when the criminals are unable to do so.

Kafir lands are not sold or permanently alienated. Any man may occupy unoccupied land and no one but the Chief can disturb him. Should he quit the land he has occupied, and another come upon it, he can recover the use of the land he has once cultivated.

Murder is punished by a fine, – which seems to be of the same amount whatever be the circumstances of the murder. The law makes no difference between premeditated and unpremeditated murder, – the injury done being considered rather than the criminality of the doer. A husband would be fined for murder if he killed an adulteress, let the proof have been ever so plain. Even for accidental homicide a Chief will occasionally fine the perpetrator, – though in such a case the law does not hold him to be guilty. For adultery there is a fine of cattle, great or small in accordance with the rank of the injured husband. Rape is fined, the cattle going to the husband, if the woman be married. If a girl be seduced, the seducer is fined, – perhaps three head of cattle. The young man probably has not got three head of cattle. Then his older friends pay for him. Among Kafir customs there are some which might find approbation with a portion of our European communities. It cannot, at any rate, be said that the Kafirs have a bloody code.

All theft is punished by a fine of cattle, the fine being moderated if the property stolen be recovered. But the fine is great or small according to the rank of the injured person. If a Chief have been robbed general confiscation of everything is the usual result of detection. The fine is paid to the injured person. A Chief cannot be prosecuted for theft by one of his own tribe. The children of Chiefs are permitted to steal from people of their own tribe, and no action can be brought against them. Should one be taken in the fact of so stealing and be whipped, or beaten, all the property of the whipper or beater may be confiscated by the Chief. There was a tribe some years ago in which there were so many royal offshoots, that not a garden, not a goat was safe. A general appeal was made to the paramount Chief and he decided that the privilege should in future be confined to his own immediate family.

For wilful injury a man has to pay the full amount of damage; but for accidental injury he pays nothing. This seems to be unlike the general Kafir theory of law. There is no fine for trespass; the idea being that as all lands are necessarily and equally open, the absence of any recovery on account of damage is equal to all. When fencing has become common this idea will probably vanish. If cattle that are trespassing be driven off and injured in the driving, fines can be recovered to the amount of damage done.

When illness comes a doctor is to be employed. Should death ensue without a doctor a fine is imposed, – which goes to the Chief.

There are many religious rites and ceremonies and many laws as to cleanness and uncleanness; but it would hardly interest the reader were I to describe them at length. At the age of puberty, or what is so considered among the Kafirs, both boys and girls go through certain rites by which they are supposed to be introduced to manhood and womanhood. There is much in these ceremonies which is disgusting and immoral, and it has been the anxious endeavours of missionaries to cause their cessation. But such cessation can only come by the gradual adoption of European manners. Where the Kafirs have lived in close connexion with the Europeans many of these customs have already been either mitigated or abandoned.

When a child dies but little notice is taken of the circumstance. Among adults, the dying man or woman, when known to be dying, is taken away to die in a ditch. So at least the Rev. Dr. Dugmore says in one of the papers from which I am quoting. When death has occurred the family become unclean and unable to mix in society for a certain period. It used to be the custom to cast the dead body forth to be devoured by beasts, the privilege of burial being only accorded to the Chiefs. But now all are buried under the ground, a hole being dug not far from the hut. The funeral of a Chief is attended with many ceremonies, his arms and ornaments being buried with him. Friends are appointed to watch by the grave, – for longer or lesser periods according to the rank of the deceased. If he have been a great Chief, the period is sometimes a year, during which the watchers may do nothing but watch. These watchers, however, become sacred when the watch is done. Cattle are folded upon the grave which may never after be slaughtered; – nor can anything be done with their increase till the last of the original cattle have died. The grave of the Chief becomes a sanctuary at which an offender may take refuge. The death of a Chief is made known to all other Chiefs around, – who shave their heads and abstain for a time from the use of milk. From all which it may be seen that a Kafir Chief is considered to be a very big person.

Justice is administered by the Chief assisted by Councillors. The Chief, however, is not absolutely bound by the advice of his Councillors. He is compelled to some adhesion to justice or to the national laws by the knowledge that his tribe will dwindle and depart from him if he gives unbearable offence. Cases of gross injustice do occur; – but on the whole the Kafir Chiefs have endeavoured to rule in accordance with Kafir customs. A certain amount of arbitrary caprice the people have been willing to endure; – but they have not been as long-suffering as the Zulus under Dingaan, – nor as the Romans under Nero. Disobedience to a Chief is punished by a fine; – but the crime has been unpopular in the tribes, and though doubtless committed daily under the rose is one of which a Kafir does not wish to have been thought guilty. The very essence of Kafir customs and Kafir life is reverence for the Chief.

I cannot close this short catalogue of Kafir customs without alluding to witch-doctors and rain-makers. Witch-doctoring is employed on two occasions – 1st, when a true but of course mistaken desire exists in a kraal or family village to find out who is tormenting the community by making some member or members of it ill, – and, 2nd, when some Chief has a desire

to get rid of a political enemy, or more probably to obtain the
cattle of a wealthy subject. In either case a priest is called in
who with many absurd ceremonies goes about the work of
selecting or 'smelling out' a victim, whom of course he has in
truth selected before the ceremonies are commenced. In the
former case, after much howling and beating of drums, he
names the unfortunate one, who is immediately pounced upon
and tormented almost to death; and at last forced, in his own
defence, to own to some kind of witchcraft. His cattle are
seized which go to the Chief – and then after a while he is
purified and put upon his legs again, impoverished indeed,
and perhaps crippled, but a free man in regard to the Devil
which is supposed to have been driven out of him. In the
second case the treatment is the same; – only that the man
whose wealth is desired, or whose political conduct has been
objectionable, does not often recover.

The rain-maker is used only in time of drought, when the
Chief sends to him desiring that he will make rain, and
presenting him with a head of cattle to assist him in the
operation. The profession is a dangerous one, as the Chief is
wont to sacrifice the rain-maker himself if the rain is
postponed too long. It is the rain-maker's trade to produce
acceptable excuses till the rain shall come in its natural course.
It is not expected till the bones of the ox shall have been
burned after sacrifice, – which may be about the third day.
Then it may be asserted that the beast was not good enough,
or unfortunately of an acceptable colour; and there is some
delay while a second beast comes. Then it is alleged that there
is manifestly a witch interfering, and the witch-doctoring
process takes place. It is bad luck indeed if rain do not come by
this time; – but, should it not come soon after the witchdoctor's victim has gone through his torments, then the
rain-maker is supposed to be an impostor, and he is at once
drowned by order of the Chief. Mr. Warner, from whose
notes this account is taken, says that the professional rain-
maker was not often a long lived man.

I did not myself visit the Transkeian territory, but in passing
from East London to Durban the small steamer which carried
me ran so near the land that I was enabled to see the coast
scenery as well as though I were in a rowing boat just off the

shore. We could see the Kafirs bathing and the cattle of the Kafirs roaming upon the hills. It is by far the prettiest bit of coast belonging to South Africa. The gates of St. John, as the rocks forming the mouth of the river are called, are peculiarly lovely. When I was there the rebellion had not been commenced, but even then I thought it a pity that English vessels should not be able to run in among that lovely paradise of hills and rocks and waters.

I insert here a table of the population of the Transkeian tribes, giving the estimated numbers of the people and the supposed number of fighting men which each tribe contains. They are all now regarded as Kafirs except the inhabitants of Adam Kok's Land and the district called the Gatberg, who are people that have migrated from the west.

ESTIMATED POPULATION OF THE TRANSKEIAN TERRITORIES

	Total Population	Fighting Men
Fingos	45,000	7,000
Idutywa Reserve	17,000	3,000
Emigrant Tembus	40,000	7,000
Tembus (Tembuland Proper)	60,000	10,000
Gatberg { Bastards, 1,000 / Basutos, 5,000 }	6,000	1,000
Griqualand East, or Adam Kok's Land { including the Bacas }	40,000	7,000
Galekas (Kreli)	66,000	11,000
Bomvanas (Moni)	15,000	2,000
Pondomisi	12,000	2,000
Pondos	200,000	30,000
Total Transkei	501,000	80,000

The number of fighting men has been arrived at by taking one-sixth of the total population.

The number here will be seen to amount to 500,000, whereas the Galekas of whom alone we are speaking when we talk of the hostile Kafirs across the Kei are not in this return given as being more than 66,000. It must always be remembered that there has been no census taken of these tribes and that many of these numbers are estimated by little more than

guess work. The Fingos and the mixed inhabitants of the
district called the Idutywa Reserve are already British subjects.
The Tembus are not so nominally; but are for the most part
obedient to British magistrates who live among them. The
inhabitants of the Gatberg are natives who live there because
the place is vacant for them, – also with a British magistrate.
They certainly cannot be regarded as an independent tribe.
The Griquas of Adam Kok's Land are bastard Hottentots who
have been moved west from one locality to another, and now
inhabit a country which used to be called No Man's Land and
which was probably cleared of its old inhabitants by Chaka,
the great Zulu king. They are British subjects. Of the Galekas
and Bomvanas I have said enough. The Pondomisi are a small
tribe of independent Kafirs among whom a British magistrate
lives. Then we come to the Pondos, the most numerous tribe
of all, – so much so that the reader will be inclined to say that,
while the Pondos remain independent, Kafraria cannot
become English. But the Pondos are a very much less
notorious people than the Galekas, – and constitute a tribe
who will probably be willing to annex themselves when the
Bomvanas and Galekas are annexed. Their present condition is
rather remarkable. The person most dominant among them is
one Mrs. Jenkins, the widow of a missionary, who is said to
rule them easily, pleasantly, and prudently. Mrs. Jenkins,
however, cannot live for ever. But it is thought that the
Pondos will of their own accord become British subjects even
during the reign of Mrs. Jenkins. The mouth of the St. John's
River is in the country of the Pondos, and it would be greatly
to the benefit of South Eastern Africa generally that a harbour
for the purposes of commerce should be opened on that
portion of the coast.

CHAPTER XV

THE BASUTOS

Of the Basutors I have said something in my attempt to tell the story of the Orange Free State; but the tribe still occupy so large a space in South Africa and has made itself so conspicuous in South African affairs as to require some further short mention for the elucidation of South African history. They are a people who have been moved, up and down, about South Africa and have thus travelled much, who have come to be located on the land they now hold partly as refugees and partly as conquerors, who thirty years ago had a great Chief called Moshesh of whom some have asserted that he was a Christian, and others that he was a determined Savage, who are still to be found in various parts of South Africa, and who perhaps possess in their headquarters of Basuto Land the very best agricultural soil on the continent. There are at present supposed to be about 127,000 of them settled on this land, among whom there would be according to the general computation about 21,000 fighting warriors. The fighting men are estimated to be a sixth of the whole tribe, – so that every adult male not incapacitated by age or misfortune is counted as a fighting man. To imagine, however, that if the Basutos were to go to war they could bring an army of 20,000 men into the field, would be to pay an unmerited compliment to their power of combination, to their commissariat supplies, and to their general patriotism. But as in late years they have bought a great many ploughs, as they are great growers of corn, and as they have become lovers of trade, lovers of money, growers of wool, and friends of the English, – as they are loyal English subjects, – we will not be indignant with them on account of any falling off in their military capacity.

The Basutos are not Kafirs or Zulus. They are a branch of the Bechuanas a large tribe or rather race of Natives whose own territory lies west of the Transvaal, and between that and the great Kalahari Desert. I have already spoken of the Baralongs of Thaba 'Ncho as having come out from among the same race. Were I to say much of the Bechuanas I should find myself wandering again all over South Africa. I will therefore not pursue them furter, merely remarking that they too are become irrepressible, and that before long we shall find ourselves compelled to annex one branch of them after another in connection with Griqualand West and the Diamond Fields.

The first record, in date, which I have read of the Basutos is in a simple volume written by a Missionary, the Rev. E. Cassalis, who was one of a party of French Protestants sent out nearly 50 years ago from Paris to the Cape with the double object of comforting the descendants of the French emigrants and of converting the Natives. It was the fate of M. Cassalis, – who though he writes in English I presume to have been a Frenchman, – to establish a mission at a place called Moriah in Basutoland in 1833, and to write a book about Basuto Manners. He does not really tell us very much about the people, as, with laudable enthusiasm, he is more intent on the ways of Providence than on the details of history. If hardships and misfortunes come he recognises them as precious balms. If they are warded off he sees the special mercy of the Lord to him and his flock. The hyaenas were allowed to take his sheep, but an 'inexorable lion,' who made the 'desert echo with the majestic sounds of his voice,' was not permitted by Providence to touch himself. Something, however, is to be gleaned from his tale. The people among whom he had come were harassed terribly by enemies. They were continually attacked by Moselekatze, the Chief of the Matabeles, whom M. Cassalis calls Zulus;* – and also by roaming bands of the Korannas, a tribe of Bedouin South African Savages, only one degree, if one degree, better than the Bushmen. With these Moshesh was always fighting, entrenching himself when hard pressed on a high rock called Thaba Bosio or Thaba Bosigo,

* Moselekatze himself was no doubt a Zulu; but the Matabeles whom he ruled were probably a people over whom he had become master when he ran away from Zululand.

from whence he would hurl down stones upon his assailants
very much to their dismay. The Basutos seem to have been a
brave people, but reduced by their enemies to very hard
straits, so that they were driven by want, in those comparatively modern days, – for we are speaking of a period within
the lifetime of the father of the existing Chief of the tribe, – to
have resort to cannibalism for support.

It has been asserted, with general truth, that cannibalism has
not been a vice of South African Natives. It was not found
among the Hottentots, nor even among the Bushmen except
with rare instances, nor among the Kafirs or Zulus. There is
no reason to believe that the Basutos brought the practice with
them from among their ancestors the Bechuanas. But there is
ample evidence that they practised it during the time of their
wars with the Matabeles and Korannas, and reason to suppose
that it has been carried on in a hidden, shame-faced way, in
opposition to the endeavours of their Chiefs, down to within a
very modern date. M. Cassalis tells us the stories of cannibalism which he had heard from Natives on his arrival in the
country, and, giving 1820 as a date, says that Moshesh put an
end to these horrors. He acknowledges in a note that he has
been accused of inventing these details for the sake 'of giving a
dramatic interest to our recital,' – and goes on to declare that
when he was in the country, 'there were thirty or forty
villages the entire population of which is composed of those
who were formerly cannibals and who make no secret of their
past life.' Had I read all this without light from subsequent
record, I should have felt that M. Cassalis was a writer far too
simple and too honest to have invented anything for the sake
of 'dramatic interest;' – but that he was a man who might have
been hoaxed even by thirty or forty villages. Having been
taught to believe that Cannibalism had not prevailed in South
Africa, I think I might have doubted the unaided testimony of
the French missionary. But there is a testimony very much
subsequent which I cannot doubt.

In November 1869 there appeared a paper in 'Once a Week'
called 'Ethnological Curiosities from South Africa.' From
whom it was supplied to that periodical neither do I know, –
nor does the gentleman by whom the body of the paper was
written. The assumed name of 'Leyland' is there given to that

gentleman, without any authority for the change, and it is told that he had contributed that narrative to the Ethnological Society and had called it a visit to the Cannibal Caves. This is true; but the name of the gentleman was Mr. Bowker who was the first Government Agent in Basutoland. He was not at all sorry to see his paper reappearing in so respectable a periodical, but has never known how it reached 'Once a Week,' or why he was called Mr. Leyland. This is not of much general interest; but he goes on to describe how he, and a party with him, were taken by guides up the side of a mountain, and by a difficult pathway into a cave. The date is not given, but the visit occurred in 1868. The cavern is then described as being black with the smoke of fires, and the floor as being strewn with the bones of human beings – chiefly those of women and children 'The marrow bones were split into small pieces, the rounded joints alone being left unbroken. Only a few of these bones were charred by fire, showing that the prevailing taste had been for boiled rather than for roast meat.' Again he says, 'I saw while at the cavern unmistakeable evidence that the custom has not been altogether abandoned, for among the numerous bones were a few that appeared very recent. They were apparently those of a tall bony individual with a skull hard as bronze. In the joints of these bones the marrow and fatty substances were still evident, showing but too plainly that many months had not elapsed since he met his fate.' This was as late as 1868.

Again. 'There are still a good many old Cannibals in existence. On the day that we visited the cavern I was introduced to one of them, who is now living not very far from his former dwelling-place. He is a man of about sixty, and, not to speak from prejudice, one of the most God-lost looking ruffians that I ever beheld in my life. In former days when he was a young man dwelling in the cavern, he captured during one of his hunting expeditions three young women. From these he selected the best-looking as a partner for life. The other two went to stock his larder.'

This comes from a gentleman who saw the ghastly remains, who well knows the people of whom he is speaking, and who from his official position has had better means of knowing than any other Europeans. They come, too, from a gentleman

who is still alive to answer for his story should a doubt be
thrown upon it. His idea is that a certain number of the
Basutos had been driven into the terrible custom by famine
caused by continued wars, and had afterwards carried it on
from addiction to the taste which had been thus generated. M.
Cassalis, who was right enough in saying that Basutos were
Cannibals, was wrong only in supposing that his disciple
Moshesh had been able to suppress the abomination. There is,
however, reason to believe that it has now been suppressed.

The noble simplicity of individual missionaries as to the
success of their own efforts is often charming and painful at
the same time; – charming as showing their complete enthusiasm, and painful when contrasted with the results. M.
Cassalis tells us how Moshesh used to dine with him in the
middle of the day, on Sunday, because, having come down
from his mountain to morning service, he could not go up the
hill for dinner, and so be back again in time for afternoon
prayers. Moshesh used to have his dinner inside the missionary's house, and the rest of the congregation from the
mountain would remain outside, around, not wasting their
time, but diligently learning to read. And yet I fear that there
are not many Christians now on the mountain, which is still
well known as Thaba Bosigo.

But Moshesh though he was not a Christian was a great
Chief, and gradually under him the Basutos became a great
tribe. Probably their success arose from the fact that the land
on which they lived was fertile. The same cause has probably
led to their subsequent misfortunes, – the fertility of the land
having offered temptation to others. Their mountains and
valleys became populated, and, – as the mountains and valleys
of a still uncivilized race, – very rich. But there arose questions
of boundaries, which so often became questions of robbery. I
have already told how Maroco the Chief of the Baralongs at
Thaba 'Ncho held that the land he occupied was his by right of
purchase, and now Moshesh had declared that he had never
sold an inch of his land. Moshesh was very fond of allegory in
his arguments. The Baralongs were certainly living on land
that had belonged to the Basutos; but Moshesh declared that,
'he had lent them the cow to milk; they could use her; but he
could not sell the cow.' For the full understanding of this it

must be known that no Kafir, no Zulu, no Basuto can bear the
idea of selling his cattle. And then the Boers of the Free State
who had settled upon Basutoland, would have it that they
owned the land. There came days of terrible fighting between
the Basutos and the Boers, – and of renewed fighting between
the Basutos and other tribes. One can imagine that they
should again have been driven by famine to that cannibalism
of which Mr. Bowker saw the recent marks. They were at a
very low ebb at Thaba Bosigo, being at last almost eaten up by
President Brand, and the Boers. Then they asked for British
intervention, and at last, in 1868, Sir Philip Wodehouse issued
a proclamation in which he declared them to be British
subjects. A line of boundary was established between them
and the Orange Republic, giving the Orange Republic the
'Conquered Territory' which they still call by that objectionable name, but leaving to the Basutos the possession of a rich
district which seems to be sufficient for their wants. The
Orange Republic, or Free State, did not at all like what was
done by the British. Their politicians still insisted that Great
Britain was precluded by treaty from concerning itself with
any native tribe north of the Orange River. It tried to make the
most of its position, – naturally enough. Perhaps it did make
the most of its position, for it now holds the peaceable
possession of a great portion of the land of its late enemies, and
no longer has a single hostile nation on its borders. We may
say that the possibility of a hostile nation has passed away.
Nothing can be more secure than the condition of the Orange
Republic since Great Britain has secured her borders. There
was a convention at Aliwal North, and the boundary line was
permanently settled on March 12, 1869.

Since that time the Basutos have been a peculiarly flourishing people, living under the chieftainship of a junior
Moshesh, but undoubted subjects of the Queen of England.
Their territory is a part of the Cape Colony, which they help
to support by the taxes they pay. Their hut tax, at the rate of
10s. a hut amounts to £4,000 a year. Why it should not come
to more I do not understand, as, according to the usual
calculation of four to a hut, there should be about 32,000 huts
among them, which would give £16,000. They also contribute
£2,000 a year in other taxes. In the year ended 30 June, 1876,

they were governed, instructed, and generally provided for at the rate of £7,644 15s. 1d. As their revenue is hardly £5,000, this would shew a serious deficiency, – but they who do the finance work for Basutoland have a very large balance in hand, amounting, after the making up of all deficiencies at the date above named, to £22,577 4s. These figures are taken from the last published financial Report of the Cape of Good Hope. I need not tell an experienced reader that no book or document is produced so unintelligible to an unitiated reader as an official financial report. Why should Basutoland with a revenue of £5,000 a year have a Treasury Balance of £22,577 4s.? Every clerk concerned in the getting up of that report no doubt knows all about it. It is not perhaps intended that any one else should understand it. I have said above that the Basutos are governed and instructed. Alas, no! Under the general head of expenditure, education is a conspicuous detail; but it is followed by no figures. It seems to be admitted that something should be expended for the teaching of the Basutos; but that the duty so acknowledged is not performed.

CHAPTER XVI

NAMAQUALAND

A glance at the map of South Africa will show two regions on the Western side of the Continent to which the name of Namaqualand is given, north and south of the Orange River. The former is Great Namaqualand and cannot as yet be said to form a part of the British Empire. But as it at present belongs to nobody, and is tenanted, – as far as it is tenanted at all, – by a very sparse sprinkling of Hottentots, Bushmen, and Korannas, and as it is undoubtedly metalliferous, it is probable that it will be annexed sooner or later.* Copper has been found north of the Orange River and that copper will not long be left undisturbed. North of Great Namaqualand is Damaraland, whence too have come tokens of copper and whisperings of gold. Even to these hard hot unfertile sandy regions Dutch farmers have trekked in order that they might live solitary, unseen, and independent. We need not, however, follow them at present to a country which is almost rainless and almost uninhabited, and for which we are not as yet responsible. Little Namaqualand, south of the Orange River, is one of the electoral divisions of the Cape Colony, and to that I will confine the few remarks which I will make as to this uncomfortable district.

It is for its copper and for its copper alone that Little Namaqualand is of any real value. On looking at the printed reports of the Commissioner and Magistrate for the division, made in 1874, 1875, and 1876, I find nothing but misfortune mentioned, – except in regard to the copper mines. '1874,'

---

* The Legislature of the Cape of Good Hope has already taken steps towards the annexation of this territory by sending a Commissioner north of the Orange River, both to Great Namaqualand and Damaraland to ascertain the wish of the natives.

says the report for that year, 'has been a very bad year.' 'There has, so to say, been no corn in the land.' 'One person after thrashing out his corn obtained three pannicans.' Poor farmers! 'Living is very expensive, and were it not for the tram line,' – a railroad made by the Copper Company nearly to Springbok Fontein, which is the seat of government and the magistrate's residence, – 'we would have been on the verge of starvation.' Poor magistrate! Then the report goes on. 'The Ookiep mine is steadily progressing.' 'The yield of ore during the year has been 10,000 tons.' It is pretty nearly as bad in 1875. 'The rain came late in the year, and the yield in corn was very small.' 'It is almost impossible to describe the poverty in which the poorer classes exist in a severe drought.' And a severe drought is the normal condition of the country in which the fall of rain and dew together does not exceed five inches in the year. But the copper enterprise was flourishing. 'The Ookiep mine,' says the same report, 'has been steadily progressing, its yield being now 1,000 tons per month.' In 1876 rural matters were not much better. 'The water supply all over the country has much decreased, and the farmers have been put to great straits in consequence.' But there is comfort in the copper. 'The Ookiep mine still continues in the same flourishing condition.' What most raises our surprise in this is thaat there should be farmers at all in such a country as Namaqualand.

The following is Mr. Theal's description of the district. 'A long narrow belt, twenty thousand square miles in extent, it presents to the eye nothing but a dismal succession of hill and gorge and sandy plain, all bare and desolate.' 'A land of drought and famine, of blinding glare and fiery blast, – such is the country of the Little Namaquas. From time immemorial it has been the home of a few wretched Hottentots who were almost safe in such a desert from even European intruders. Half a dozen missionaries and two or three score of farmers were the sole representatives of civilization among these wandering Savages. One individual to about three square miles was all that the land was capable of supporting.'

But there is copper in the regions near the coast and consequently Little Namaqualand is becoming an important and a rich district. Before the Dutch came the Hottentots had found copper here and had used it for their ornaments. In 1683, when the Dutch government was still young and the Dutch territory still small, an expedition was sent by the Dutch Governor in search of copper to the very region in which the Cape Copper Company is now carrying on its works. But the coast was severe and the land hard to travellers, and it was found difficult to get the ore down to the sea. The Dutch therefore abandoned the undertaking and the copper was left at rest for a century and a half. The first renewed attempt was made in 1835, and that was unsuccessful. It was not till 1852 that the works were commenced which led to the present flourishing condition of the South African copper mines.

For some few years after this there seems to have been a copper mania in South Africa, – as there was a railway mania in England, and a gold mania in Australia, and a diamond mania in Griqualand West. People with a little money rushed to the country and lost that little. And those who had none rushed also to the copper mines and failed to enrich themselves as they had expected. In 1863 Messrs. Phillips and King, who had commenced their work in 1852, established the company which is still known as the Cape Copper Mining Company, – and that company has been thoroughly successful altogether, through the Ookiep mine to which the magistrate in all the reports from which I have quoted has referred as the centre and source of Namaqualand prosperity.

About four hundred miles north-west of the Cape and forty-five miles south of the Orange River there is a little harbour called Port Nolloth in Robben Bay. The neighbour-hood is described as being destitute of all good things. The country in this neighbourhood is sandy and barren, and without water. We are told that water may be obtained by digging in the sand, but that when obtained it is brackish. But here is the outlet for South African copper, and therefore the little port is becoming a place of importance. Sailing vessels come from Swansea for the ore, and about once a fortnight a little steamer comes here from Capetown bringing necessaries of life to its inhabitants and such comforts as money can give in a place so desolate and hideous.

From hence there is a railway running 60 miles up to the foot of the mountains constructed by the Copper Mining Company for the use of their men and for bringing down the ore to the coast. This railway goes to Great Ookiep mine, which is distant but a few miles from the miserable little town called Springbok Fontein, which is the capital of the district. The Ookiep mine is thus described in the Gazeteer attached to Messrs. Silver's South African Guide Book. It is 'one of the most important copper mines in existence, its annual production of very rich ore being nearly 7,000 tons;' – since that was written the amount has been considerably increased; – 'and the deeper the shafts are sunk the more extensive appears the area of ore producing ground. The mine is now sunk to a depth of 80 fathoms, but exhibits no sign of decreasing production.' 'These Ookiep ores are found in Europe to be easier smelted than the ores of any other mines whatever, and the deposit of copper ore in the locality seems quite unlimited.'

There have been various other mines tried in the vicinity, and there can be no doubt from the indications of copper which are found all around that the working of copper in the district will before long be carried very much further than at present. But up to this time the Ookiep mine is the only one that has paid its expenses and given a considerable profit. During the copper fury various attempts were made all of which failed. The existing Company, which has been as a whole exceedingly prosperous, has made many trials at other spots none of which according to their own report have been altogether unsuccessful. I quote the following extracts from the report made by its own officers and published by the Company in 1877. 'The operations at Spectakel Mine have been attended with almost unvarying ill fortune.' 'It is thought that the Kilduncan centre has had fair trial and as the ground looks unpromising the miners have been withdrawn.' 'Although yielding quantities of low class ore the workings at Narrap have not so far proved remunerative.' 'The levels at Karolusberg have also failed to reveal anything valuable.' 'A good deal of preparatory work has been done at this place,' – Nabapeep. 'This may be regarded as the most promising trial mine belonging to the Company.' These are all the adventures yet made except that of the Ookiep mine, but that alone has been so lucky that the yield in 1876 amounted to '10,765 tons of 21 cwt., nett dry weight, averaging 28½ per cent.' This perhaps, to the unitiated mind may give but a hazy idea of the real result of the speculation. But when we are told that only £7 a share has been paid up, and that £4 per annum profit has been paid on each share, in spite of the failure of other adventures, then the success of the great Ookiep mine looms clear to the most uninstructed understanding.

There can be no doubt but that Namaqualand will prove to be one of the great copper producing countries of the earth; and as little, I fear, that it is in all other respects one of the most unfortunate and undesirable. I have spoken to some whose duties have required them to visit Springbok Fontein or to frequent Port Nolloth, and they have all spoken of their past experiences without expressing any wish to revisit those places. Missionaries have gone to this land as elsewhere, striving to carry Christianity among, perhaps, as low a form of humanity as there is on the earth, – with the exception of the quickly departing Australian aboriginal. They have probably done something, if only a little, both towards raising the intellect and relieving the wants of those among whom they have placed themselves. But the Bushmen and the Korannas are races very hopeless. Men who have been called upon by Nature to live in so barren a region, – a country almost destitute of water and therefore almost destitute of grass, can hardly be expected to raise themselves above the lowest habits and the lowest tastes incident to man. If anything can give them a chance of rising in the world it will be such enterprise as that of the Cape Mining Company, and such success as that of the Ookiep mine.

CHAPTER XVII

CONCLUSION

I have now finished my task and am writing my last chapter as I make my way home across the Bay of Biscay. It has been laborious enough but has been made very pleasant by the unvarying kindness of every one with whom I have come in contact. My thanks are specially due to those who have travelled with me or allowed me to travel with them. I have had the good fortune never to have been alone on the road, – and thus that which would otherwise have been inexpressibly tedious has been made pleasant. I must take this last opportunity of repeating here, what I have said more than once before, that my thanks in this respect are due to the Dutch as warmly as to the English. I am disposed to think that a wrong impression as to the so-called Dutch Boer of South Africa has become common at home. It has been imagined by some people, – I must acknowledge to have received such an impression myself, – that the Boer was a European who had retrograded from civilization, and had become savage, barbarous, and unkindly. There can be no greater mistake. The courtesies of life are as dear to him as to any European. The circumstances of his secluded life have made him unprogressive. It may, however, be that the same circumstances have maintained with him that hospitality for strangers and easy unobtrusive familiarity of manners, which the contests and rapidity of modern life have banished from us in Europe. The Dutch Boer, with all his roughness, is a gentleman in his manners from his head to his heels.

When a man has travelled through a country under beneficent auspices, and has had everything shown to him and explained to him with frank courtesy, he seems to be almost guilty of a breach of hospitality if, on his coming away, he speaks otherwise than in glowing terms of the country where

232

he has been so received. I know that I have left behind me friends in South Africa who, when they shall have read my book or shall hear how I have spoken of their Institutions, will be ill satisfied with me. I specially fear this in regard to the Cape Colony where I can go on all fours neither with the party in power who think that parliamentary forms of Government must be serviceable for South Africa, because they have been proved to be so for Canada, Australia, and New Zealand; nor with those opposed to them who would fain keep the native races in subjection by military power. I would make the Kafir in all respects equal to the white man; – but I would give him no voting power till he is equal to the white man in education as in other things.

It will be brought against me as an accusation that I have made my enquiries and have written my book in a hurry. It has been done hurriedly. Day by day as I have travelled about the continent in the direction indicated in its pages I have written my book. The things which I have seen have been described within a few hours of my seeing them. The words that I have heard have been made available for what they were worth, – as far as it was within my power to do so, – before they were forgotten. A book so written must often be inaccurate; but it may possibly have something in it of freshness to atone for its inaccuracies. In writing such a book a man has for a time to fill himself exclusively with his subject, – to make every thought that he has South African for the time, to give all his energy to the work in hand, to talk about it, fight about it, think about it, write about it, and dream about it. This I have endeavoured to do, and here is the result. To spend five years in studying a country and then to come home and devote five more to writing a book about it, is altogether out of my way. The man who can do it will achieve much more than I shall. But had I ever attempted it in writing other books I should have failed worse than I have done. Had I thought of it in regard to South Africa my book would never have been written at all.

I fancy that I owe an apology to some whom I have answered rather shortly when they have scolded me for not making a longer stay in their own peculiar spots. 'You have come to write a book about South Africa and you have no right to go away without devoting a day to my ——' sugar plantation, or distillery, or whatever the interesting enterprise may have been. 'You have only been three days in our town and I don't think you are doing us justice.' It has been hard to answer these accusations with a full explanation of all the facts, – including the special fact, – unimportant to all but one or two, that South Africa with all its charms is not so comfortable at my present age as the arm-chair in my own book room. But in truth the man who has an interesting enterprise of his own or who patriotically thinks that his own town only wants to be known to be recognized as a Paradise among municipalities would, if their power were as great as their zeal, render such a task as that I have undertaken altogether impossible. The consciousness of their own merit robs them of all sense of proportion. Such a one will acknowledge that South Africa is large; – but South Africa will not be as large to him as his own mill or his own Chamber of Commerce, and he will not believe that eyes seeing other than his eyes can be worthy of any credit. I know that I did not go to see this gentleman's orchard as I half promised, or the other gentleman's collection of photographs, and I here beg their pardons and pray them to remember how many things I had to see and how many miles I had to travel.

That I have visited all European South Africa I cannot boast. The country is very large. We may say so large as to be at present limitless. We do not as yet at all know our own boundaries. But I visited the seat of Government in each district, and, beyond the Capitals, saw enough of the life and ways of each of them to justify me, I hope, in speaking of their condition and their prospects. I have also endeavoured to explain roughly the way in which each of these districts became what it now is. In doing this I have taken my facts partly from those who have gone before me in writing the history of South Africa, – whose names I have mentioned in my introductory chapter, – partly from official records, and partly from the words of those who witnessed and perhaps bore a share in the changes as they were made. The first thing an Englishman has to understand in the story of South Africa is the fact that the great and almost unnatural extension of our colonization, – unnatural when the small number of English emigrants who have gone there is considered, – has been produced by the continued desire of the Dutch farmers to take themselves out of the reach of English laws, and English feelings. The abolition of slavery was the great cause of this, – though not the only cause; and the abolition of slavery in British dominions is now only forty years old. Since that time Natal, the Transvaal, the Orange Free state, and Griqualand West have sprung into existence, and they were all, in the first instance, peopled by sturdy Dutchmen running away from the to them disgusting savour of Exeter Hall. They would encounter anything, go anywhere, rather than submit to British philanthropy. Then we have run after them with our philanthropy in our hands, – with such results as I have endeavoured to depict in these pages.

This is the first thing that we shall have to understand, – but as the mind comes to dwell on the subject it will not be the chief thing. It must be the first naturally. To an Englishman the Cape of Good Hope, and Natal, and now the Transvaal are British Colonies, – with a British history, short or long. The way in which we became possessed of these and the manner in which they have been ruled; the trouble or the glory which have come to us from them; the success of them or the failure in affording homes for our ever increasing population; – these are the questions which must affect us first. But when we learn that in those South African Colonies though we may not have succeeded in making homes for many English, – not even comparatively for many Europeans, – we have become the arbiters of the homes, the masters of the destinies, of millions of black men; when we recognize the fact that here we have imposed upon us the duty of civilizing, of training to the yoke of labour and releasing from the yoke of slavery a strong, vital, increasing and intelligent population; when this becomes plain to us, as I think it must become plain, – then we shall know that the chief thing to be regarded is our duty to the nations over which we have made ourselves the masters.

South Africa is a country of black men, – and not of white men. It has been so; it is so; and it will continue to be so. In this respect it is altogether unlike Australia, unlike the Canadas, and unlike New Zealand. And, as it is unlike them, so should it be to us a matter of much purer gratification than are those successful Colonies. There we have gone with our ploughs and with our brandy, with all the good and with all the evil which our civilization has produced, and throughout the lands the native races have perished by their contact with us. They have withered by commune with us as the weaker weedy grasses of Nature's first planting wither and die wherever come the hardier plants, which science added to nature has produced. I am not among those who say that this has been caused by our cruelty. It has often been that we have struggled our very best to make our landing on a shore an unmixed blessing to those to whom we have come. In New Zealand we strove hard for this; – but in New Zealand the middle of the next century will probably hear of the existence of some solitary last Maori. It may be that this was necessary. All the evidence we have seems to show that it was so. But it is hardly the less sad because it was necessary. In Australia we have been successful. We are clothed with its wools. Our coffers are filled with its gold. Our brothers and our children are living there in bounteous plenty. But during the century that we have been there we have caused the entire population of a whole continent to perish. It is impossible to think of such prosperity without a dash of suffering, without a pang of remorse.

In South Africa it is not so. The tribes which before our coming were wont to destroy themselves in civil wars have doubled their population since we have turned their assagais to ploughshares. Thousands, ten thousands of them, are working for wages. Even beyond the realms which we call our own we have stopped the cruelties of the Chiefs and the no less fatal superstitions of the priests. The Kafir and the Zulu are free men, and understand altogether the privileges of their freedom. In one town of 18,000 inhabitants, 10,000 of them are now receiving 10s. a week each man, in addition to their diet. Here at any rate we have not come as a blighting poison to the races whom we have found in the country of our adoption. This I think ought to endear South Africa to us.

But it must at the same time tell us that South Africa is a black country and not a white one; – that the important person in South Africa is the Kafir and the Zulu, the Bechuana and the Hottentot; – not the Dutchman or the Englishman. On the

subject of population I have already shown that the information at my command is a little confused. Such confusion
cannot be avoided when only estimates are made. But if I take
credit for 340,000 white people in South Africa, I certainly
claim as many as the country holds; – and I am probably
within the mark if I say that our direct influence extends over
3,000,000 of Natives. What is the number of British subjects
cannot even be estimated, because we do not know our
Transvaal limits. There are also whole tribes to the North-
West, in Bechuanaland, Damaraland, and Namaqualand
anxious to be annexed but not yet annexed. To all those we
owe the duty of protection, and all of them before long will be
British subjects. As in India or Ceylon, where the people are a
coloured people, Asiatic and not European, it is our first duty
to govern them so that they may prosper, to defend them
from ill-usage, to teach them what we know ourselves, to
make them free, so in South Africa it is our chief duty to do
the same thing for the Natives there. The white man is the
master, and the master can generally protect himself. He can
avail himself of the laws, and will always have so many points
in his favour that a paternal government need not be much
harassed on his account. Compared with the Native he is
numerically but one to ten. But in strength, influence, and
capacity he has ten to one the best of it.

What is our duty to the Kafir or Zulu? There are so many
views of our duty! One believes that we have done the
important thing if we teach him to sing hymns. Another
would give him back, – say a tenth of the land that has been
taken away from him, and then leave him. A third, the most
confident of them all, thinks that everything hangs on 'a rod of
iron', – between which and slavery the distance is very
narrow. The rod of iron generally means compelled work, the
amount of wages to be settled by the judgment of the master.
A fourth would give him a franchise and let him vote for a
Member of Parliament, – which of course includes the privilege of becoming a Member of Parliament, and of becoming
Prime Minister if he can get enough of his own class to back
him.

I am afraid that I cannot agree altogether with any of these
four. The hymns, which as I speak of them include all

religious teaching, have as yet gone but a very little way.
Something has been done, – that something having shewn
itself rather in a little book-learning than in amelioration of
conduct as the result of comprehended Christianity. But the
work will progress. In its way it is good, though the good
done is so little commensurate with the missionary labour
given and the missionary money spent!

The land scheme, – the giving up of locations to the people,
– is good also to some extent if it be unmixed with such
missionary attempts as some which I have attempted to
describe as existing in the western province of the Cape
Colony. There is a certain justice in it, and it enables the
people to fall gradually into the way of working for wages. It
has on the other hand the counterbalancing tendency of
teaching the people to think that they can live idle on their
own land, – as used to be the case with the Irishmen who held
a couple of acres of ground.

'The iron rod' is to me abominable. It means always some
other treatment for the coloured man than that which is given
to the white man. There can be no good done till the two
stand before the law exactly on the same ground. The
'iron-rodder' desires to get work our of the black man; – and
so do I, and so does every friend of the black man. 'Make him
work,' says the iron-rodder. 'There he is, idle, fat as a pig on
stolen mutton, and doing nothing; with thews and sinews by
which I could be made so comfortable, if only I could use
them.' 'But how are you entitled to his work?' is the answer
readiest at hand. 'Because he steals my cattle,' says the
iron-rodder, generally with a very limited amount of truth
and less of logic. Because his cattle have been stolen once or
twice he would subject the whole race to slavery, – unconscious that the slave's work, if he could get it, would in the
long run be very much less profitable to him than the free
labour by which, in spite of all his assertions to the contrary,
he does till his land, and herd his cattle, and shear his sheep and
garner his wealth.

Then comes the question of the franchise. He who would
give the black man a vote is generally the black man's most
advanced friend, the direct enemy of the iron-rodder, and is to
be found in London rather than in South Africa. To such a one

I would say certainly let the black man have the franchise on the same terms as the white man. In broadening or curtailing the privilege of voting there should be no expressed reference to colour. The word should not appear in any Act of any Parliament by which the franchise is regulated. If it be so expressed there cannot be that quality before the law without which we cannot divest ourselves of the sin of selfish ascendancy. But the franchise may be so regulated that the black man cannot enjoy it till he has qualified himself, – as the white man at any rate ought to qualify himself. Exclusion of this nature was intended when the existing law of the Cape Colony was passed. A man cannot vote till he has become a fixed resident, and shall be earning 10s. a week wages and his diet. When this scale was fixed it was imagined that it would exclude all but a very small number of Kafirs. But a few years has so improved the condition of the Kafirs that many thousands are now earning the wages necessary for a qualification. 'Then by all means let them vote,' will say the friend of the Negro in Exeter Hall or the House of Commons, – perhaps without giving quite time enough to calculating the result. Does this friend of the Negro in his heart think that the black man is fit to assume political ascendancy over the white; – or that the white man would remain in South Africa and endure it? The white man would not remain, and if the white man were gone, the black man would return to his savagery. Very much has been done, – quite as much probably as we have a right to expect from the time which has been employed. But the black man is not yet civilized in South Africa and, with a few exceptions, is not fit for political power. The safeguard against the possible evil of which I have spoken is the idea that the Kafir is not as yet awake to the meaning of political power and therefore will not exercise the privilege of voting when it is given to him. It may be so at present, but I do not relish the political security which is to come, not from the absence of danger but from the assumed ignorance of those who might be dangerous. An understanding of the nature of the privilege will come before fitness for its exercise; – and then there may be danger. Thus we are driven back to the great question whether a country is fit for parliamentary institutions in which the body of the population is unfit for the privilege of voting.

Our duty to the Kafir of course is to civilize him, – so to treat him that as years roll on he will manifestly be the better for our coming to his land. I do not think that missionaries will do this, or fractions of land, – little Kafrarias, as it may be, separated off for their uses. The present position of Kreli and his Galekas who were to have dwelt in peace on their own territory across the Kei, is proof of this. The iron rod certainly will not do it. Nor will the franchise. But equality of law, equality of treatment, will do it; – and, I am glad to say, has already gone far towards doing it. The Kafir can make his own contract for his own labour the same as a white man; – can leave his job of work or take it as independently as the white workman; – but not more so. Encouraged by this treatment he is travelling hither and thither in quest of work, and is quickly learning that order and those wants which together make the only sure road to civilization.

The stranger in South Africa will constantly be told that the coloured man will not work, and that this is the one insuperable cause by which the progress of the country is impeded. It will be the first word whispered into his ear when he arrives, and the last assurance hurled after him as he leaves the coast. And yet during his whole sojourn in the country he will see all the work of the world around him done by the hands of coloured people. It will be so in Capetown far away from the Kafirs. It will be so on the homesteads of the Dutch in the western province. It will be so in the thriving commercial towns of the eastern province. From one end of Natal to the other he will find that all the work is done by Zulus. It will be the same in the Transvaal and the same even in the Orange Free State. Even there whenever work is done for wages it is done by coloured hands. When he gets to the Diamond Fields, he will find the mines swarming with black labour. And yet he will be told that the 'nigger' will not work!

The meaning of the assertion is this; – that the 'nigger' cannot be made to work whether he will or no. He will work for a day or two, perhaps a week or two, at a rate of wages sufficient to supply his wants for double the time, and will then decline, with a smile, to work any longer just then, – let the employer's need be what it may. Now the employer has old European ideas in his head, even though he may have been born in the Colony. The poor rural labourer in England must work. He cannot live for four days on the wages of two. If he were to decline there would be the poor house, the Guardians, and all the horrors of Bumbledom before him. He therefore must work. And that 'must,' which is known to exist as to the labouring Englishman and labouring Frenchman, creates a feeling that a similar necessity should coerce the Kafir. Doubtless it will come to be so. It is one of the penalties of civilization, – a penalty, or, shall we say, a blessing. But, till it does come, it cannot be assumed, – without a retrogression to slavery. Men in South Africa, the employers of much labour and the would-be employers of more, talk of the English vagrancy laws, – alleging that these Kafirs are vagrants, and should be treated as vagrants would be treated in England; – as though the law in England compelled any man to work who had means of living without work. The law in England will not make the Duke of —— work; nor will it make Hodge work if Hodge has 2s. a day of his own to live on and behaves himself.

This cry as to labour and the want of labour, is in truth a question of wages. A farmer in England will too often feel that the little profit of his farm is being carried away by that extra 2s. a week which the state of the labour market compels him to pay to his workmen. The rise of wages among the coloured people in South Africa has been much quicker than it ever was in England. In parts of Natal a Zulu may still be hired for his diet of Indian corn and 7s. a month. In Kafraria, about King Williamstown, men were earning 2s. 6d. a day when I was there. I have seen coloured labourers earning 4s. 6d. a day for the simple duty of washing wool. All this has to equalize itself, and while it is doing so, of course there is difficulty. The white man thinks that the solution of the difficulty should be left to him. It is disparaging to his pride that the black man should be so far master of the situation as to be able to fix his own wages.

In the meantime, however, the matter is fixed. The work is done by black men. They plough, they reap; they herd and shear the sheep; they drive the oxen; they load the waggons; they carry the bricks; they draw the water; they hew the wood; they brush the clothes; they clean the boots; they run the posts; they make the roads; they wait at table; they cook the food; they wash the wool; they press the grapes; they kill the beef and mutton; they dig the gardens; they plaster the walls; they feed the horses; – and they find the diamonds. A South African farmer and a South African wool grower and a South African shopkeeper will all boast that South Africa is a productive country. If it be so she is productive altogether by the means of black labour.

Another allegation very common in the mouth of the 'iron-rodders' is that the Kafir – steals. 'A nasty beastly thief that will never leave your cattle alone.' The eastern province Cape Colony farmer seems to think that he of all men ought to be made exempt by some special law from the predatory iniquities of his neighbours. I fear the Kafir does occasionally steal sheep and cattle. Up in the Diamond Fields he steals diamonds, – the diamonds, that is, which he himself finds. The accusations which I have heard against Kafirs, as to stealing, begin and end here. It is certainly the case that a man used to the ways of the country will leave his money and his jewelry about among Kafirs, with a perfect sense of security, who will lock up everything with the greatest care when some loafing European is seen about. I remember well how I was warned to be careful about my bag at the little Inn in Natal, because a few British soldiers had quartered themselves for the night in front of the house. The Innkeeper was an Englishman, and probably knew what he was talking about.

The Kafirs ought not to steal cattle. So much may be admitted. And if everything was as it ought to be there would be no thieves in London. But perhaps of all dishonest raids the most natural is that made by a Savage on beasts which are running on the hills which used to belong to his fathers. Wealth to him is represented by cattle, and the wealth of his tribe all came from its land. To drive cattle has to his mind none of the meanness of stealing. How long is it since the same feeling prevailed among Englishmen and Scotchmen living on the borders? It is much the same in regard to diamonds. They are found in the ground, and why should not the treasures of the ground be as free to the Kafir as to his employer? I am using the Kafir's argument; – not my own. I know, as does my reader, and as do the angry white men in South Africa, that the Kafir has contracted for wages to give up what he finds to his employer. I know that the employer has paid for a license to use the bit of land, and that the Kafir has not. I know that a proper understanding as to meum and tuum would prevent the Kafir from secreting the little stone between his toes. But there is much of this which the Kafir cannot yet have learned. Taking the honesty and dishonesty of the Kafir together, we shall find that it is the former which is remarkable.

The great question of the day in England as to the countries which I have just visited is that of Confederation. The Permissive Bill which was passed last Session, – 1877, – entitles me to say that it is the opinion of the Government at home that such Confederation should be consummated in South Africa within the next three or four years. Then there arise two questions, – whether it is practicable, and if practicable whether it is expedient. I myself with such weak voice as I possess have advocated Australian Confederation. I have greatly rejoiced at Canadian Confederation. My sympathies were in favour of West Indian Confederation. I left England hoping that I might advocate South African Confederation. But, alas, I have come to think it inexpedient, – and, if expedient, still impracticable. A Confederation of States implies some identity of interests. In any coming together of Colonies under one flag, one Colony must have an ascendancy. Population will give this, and wealth, – and the position of the chosen capital. It clearly was so in Canada. In South Africa that preponderance would certainly be with the Cape Colony. I cannot conceive any capital to be possible other than Capetown. Then arises the question whether the other provinces of South Africa can improve their condition by identifying themselves with the Cape Colony. They who know Natal will I think agree with me that Natal will never consent to send ten legislators to a Congress at Capetown where they would be wholly inefficient to prevent the carrying of measures agreeable to the Constitution of the Cape Colony but averse to its own theory of Government. I have described the franchise of the Cape Colony. I am well aware that Confederation would not compel one State to adopt the same franchise as another. But Natal will never willingly put herself into the same boat with a Colony in which the negro vote may in a few years become predominant over the white. In Natal there are 320,000 coloured people to 20,000 white. She might still exclude the coloured man from her own hustings as she does now; but she will hardly allow her own poor ten members of a common Congress to be annihilated by the votes of members who may not probably be returned by coloured persons, and who may not impossibly be coloured persons themselves.

With the Transvaal the Government at home may do as it pleases. At the present moment it is altogether at the disposal of the Crown. If the Cape Colony would consent to take it the Transvaal can be annexed tomorrow without any ceremony of Confederation. The Cape Colony would in the first place probably desire to be secured from any repayment of the debts of the late Republic. This would not be Confederation, though in this way the Cape Colony, which will soon have swallowed up Griqualand West, would be enabled to walk round the Free State. But the Boers of the Transvaal would, if consulted, be as little inclined to submit themselves to the coloured political influence of the Cape as would the people of Natal. What should they do in a Parliament of which they do not understand the language? Therefore I think Confederation to be inexpedient.

But though the Cape Colony were to walk round the Free State so as to join the Transvaal, – though it were even to walk on and reach the Eastern Sea by including Natal, – still it would only have gone round the Free State and not have absorbed it. I understand that Confederation without the Free State would not be thought sufficiently complete to answer the purpose of the Colonial Office at home. And as I think that the Free State will not confederate, for reasons which I have given when writing about the Free State, I think that Confederation is impracticable.

It is again the great question of coloured races, – the question which must dominate all other questions in South Africa. Confederation of adjacent Colonies may be very good for white men who can rule themselves, and yet not suit the condition of territories in which coloured men have to be ruled under circumstances which may be essentially different in different States.

Looking back at our dominion over South Africa which has now lasted for nearly three quarters of a century I think that we have cause for national pride. We have on the whole been honest and humane, and the errors into which we have fallen have not been greater than the extreme difficulty of the situation has made, if not necessary, at any rate natural. When we examine the operations of different Governors as they have succeeded each other, and read the varying instructions with which those Governors have been primed from the Colonial Office, it is impossible not to see that the peculiar bias of one Secretary of State succeeding to that of another has produced vacillations. There has been a want of what I have once before ventured to call 'official tradition.' The intention of Great Britain as to her Colonies as expressed by Parliament has not been made sufficiently plain for the guidance of the Colonial Office. This showed itself perhaps more signally than elsewhere in Lord Glenelg's condemnation of Sir Benjamin D'Urban at the close of the third Kafir war in 1835, when he enunciated a policy which was not compatible with the maintenance of British authority in South Africa, – which had to be speedily revoked, – but which could not be revoked till every Kafir had been taught that England, across the seas, was afraid of him. Again I think that by vacillating policy we foolishly forced upon the Dutch the necessity of creating Republics, first across the Vaal and then between the Vaal and the Orange, when, but a short time before, we had refused them permission to do the same thing in Natal. I myself think that there should have been no Republic; – that in the Transvaal, and in the Orange State, as in Natal, we should have recognized the necessity of providing Government for our migrating subjects.

But in all this there has been no lust of power, no dishonesty. There has been little, if anything, of mean parsimony. In that matter of the Diamond Fields as to which the accusations against the Colonial Office have been the heaviest, I feel assured not only of the justice but of the wisdom of what was done. Had we not assumed the duty of government at Kimberley, Kimberley would have been ungovernable.

But the question which is of all the one of moment is the condition of the coloured races. Just now there is still

continued among a small fraction of them a disturbance which
the opponents of the present Government in the Cape Colony
delight to call a War. In spite of this, throughout the length
and breadth of South Africa, – even in what is still called
Kreli's country, – the coloured man has been benefitted by our
coming. He has a better hut, better food, better clothing,
better education, more liberty, less to fear and more to get,
than he had when we came among him, or that he would have
enjoyed had we not come. If this be so, we ought to be
contented with what our Government has done.